The Seductions of Emily Dickinson

THE SEDUCTIONS OF EMILY DICKINSON

Robert McClure Smith

The University of Alabama Press

Tuscaloosa and London

Library of Congress Cataloging-in-Publication Data

Smith, Robert McClure.
The seductions of Emily Dickinson / Robert McClure Smith.
p.   cm.
Includes bibliographical references and index.
ISBN 0-8173-0806-7 (alk. paper)
1. Dickinson, Emily, 1830-1886—Technique.   2. Poetics.   3. Women
and literature—United States—History—19th century.   I. Title.
PS1541.Z5S674   1996
811'.4—dc20   95-12591

British Library Cataloguing-in-Publication Data available

For Barbara

Contents

Acknowledgments   *ix*

Introduction: The Bee and the Flower   *1*

1

The Milieu of Seduction   *19*

2

Seduction and the Male Reader   *56*

3

The Poetics of Seduction   *81*

4

The Word Made Flesh   *108*

5

Reading Seductions (1)   *134*

6

Reading Seductions (2)   *163*

Coda: The Flower and the Bee   *195*

Notes   *197*
Selected Bibliography   *211*
Index   *219*

Acknowledgments

IN WRITING THIS book, I have been helped in essential ways by a number of teachers, colleagues, and friends. Discussions with Kathy Conway, Robert Keefe, Valerie Martin, Tracy Morong, Judith Plotz, Nancy Reisman, Ken Simpson, and Kathleen Swaim helped refine its argument. Special thanks to Deborah Carlin, Martin Orzeck, and Robert Weisbuch, who judiciously critiqued sections of the manuscript, and to Nicole Mitchell, who was most supportive of the project. I was also extremely fortunate to receive extensive critical advice from two of the finest readers of Dickinson's poetry: Cristanne Miller made a number of valuable suggestions for improving the manuscript in the final stages of its preparation; and David Porter taught me how to read the poet, encouraged this book from its inception, and remained supportive of and good-humored about its wayward and parricidal tendencies. My debt to him is immense. I would also like to thank The Columbian College and Graduate School of Arts and Sciences and the English Department of The George Washington University for their generous financial support. Finally, to Barbara Tannert, I am grateful beyond words for time, help, support, criticism, and, most of all, patience.

Parts of three chapters of this book have appeared elsewhere in different forms. I thank the editors for permission to use this material.

Portions of chapter 1 were published in *ESQ* 40 (1st Quarter 1994): 27–65 and *The Explicator* 50 (Fall 1991): 21–23.

An earlier version of chapter 2 appeared in *Prose Studies* 15 (August 1992): 225–41.

A version of chapter 5 will appear in the essay collection *Emily Dickinson and Audience*, Martin Orzeck and Robert Weisbuch, eds. (Ann Arbor: University of Michigan Press, 1995).

Introduction

The Bee and the Flower

> For this is the desperate truth of the matter: it requires no art to
> seduce a girl, but good fortune is needed to find one worth seducing.
>
> —Kierkegaard, *Diary of a Seducer*

> The main problem, with honorable women, isn't
> seducing them, it's getting them behind closed doors.
>
> —Giraudoux, *Amphitryon 38*

EMILY DICKINSON LEFT behind no formulated poetics. She would prefer to have her readers believe that "Butterflies from St. Domingo / Cruising round the purple line— / Have a system of aesthetics— / Far superior to mine" (P. 137).[1] Perhaps the absence of that "system of aesthetics" is for the benefit of those readers; speculating as to its components, they can dwell in the possibility that the poet herself found such an amenable residence, a critical "House of Supposition . . . that / Skirts the Acres of Perhaps" (P. 696). Dickinson does, however, leave the trace of an aesthetics of reading. In an 1878 letter she observes that "to see is perhaps never quite the sorcery that it is to surmise, though the obligation to enchantment is always binding" (L. 565). This aside, in a letter to a minor correspondent, is hardly an aesthetic manifesto, but it does introduce the vocabulary of a Dickinson lexicon of reading—"enchantment," "surmise," "see," "sorcery." The definition and analysis of those terms will provide a useful frame for this introductory discussion.

Dickinson's favorite metaphor for the reader/text relationship is the interaction between bee and flower.[2] Often, the personal letters accompanying gifts of flowers from her garden included poems that she would similarly allude to as "flowers." The flower/poem association became a Dickinson commonplace: in one of her "flower" poems she makes it explicit:

> They have a little Odor—that to me
> Is metre—nay—'tis melody—
> And spiciest at fading—indicate—
> A Habit—of a Laureate—
>
> (P. 785)

Dickinson's alternate word choice for "melody" was, not surprisingly, "Poesy," for if flowers are poems, then poems are equally the "flowers" of her rhetoric. The interaction between bee and flower described within these poems is inevitably suggestive of sexuality. After all, a flower is more than a convenient representation of a sexual organ: it *is* a sexual organ. Pollination is frequently the central event of the poems, with emphasis on the fact that "Blossoms stand negative, / Touched to Conditions / By a Hum" (P. 1042). The respective gender assigned bee and flower is also reasonably consistent: the former is male, the latter female. One of the earliest Dickinson poems, part of a letter to her brother, Austin, makes this clear distinction:

> There is another sky,
> Ever serene and fair,
> And there is another sunshine,
> Though it be darkness there;
> Never mind faded forests, Austin,
> Never mind silent fields—
> *Here* is a little forest,
> Whose leaf is ever green;
> Here is a brighter garden,
> Where not a frost has been;
> In its unfading flowers
> I hear the bright bee hum;
> Prithee, my brother,
> Into *my* garden come!
> (P. 2)

The inviting poetic text—the paper on which the poet inscribes herself a veritable "little forest"—is a garden of eternal flowers extending the most pleasant of offers to the brother who *is* that figural bee.

Of course, the "worker" who actually collects nectar from the flower is the female bee. Dickinson was probably well acquainted with that fact because of the substantial horticultural training she received from the Edward Hitchcock science curriculum at Amherst Academy. The poet's deliberate inversion of the pollinating insect's gender and the resulting mimetic inaccuracy are therefore presumably purposeful. The major consequence of the assignation of a particular gender to bee and flower is that the exploration of their interaction often engages larger questions of sexual propriety within the vocabulary of nineteenth-century social mores. The degrees of resistance, of relative culpability, and of mutual consequence become of special concern. The following poem offers a convenient sketch of the more typical bee/flower scenario and the courtship rituals to which it so often alludes:

A Bee his burnished Carriage
Drove boldly to a Rose—
Combinedly alighting—
Himself—his Carriage was—
The Rose received his visit
With frank tranquillity
Withholding not a Crescent
To his Cupidity—
Their Moment consummated—
Remained for him—to flee—
Remained for her—of rapture
But the humility.
    (P. 1339)

In this poem, the promiscuous bee bears the trappings of gentility and the appearance of wooing to the scene of his conquest. Given his determined (and workaday) intent, that old-world civility is perhaps somewhat misleading. Elsewhere, the *assaulting* bee is associated more pointedly with the rapaciousness (the "Trains of Cars") of an intrusive commercial world:

Like Trains of Cars on Tracks of Plush
I hear the level Bee—
A Jar across the Flowers goes
Their Velvet Masonry

Withstands until the sweet Assault
Their Chivalry consumes—
While He, victorious tilts away
To vanquish other Blooms.
    (P. 1224)

On this occasion, the deceptively chivalrous insect is engaged in a direct assault on—in a neat gender inversion that is particularly "jarring"—the more immediate "chivalry" of the flowers to whom he lays siege and, ultimately, "vanquishes." Typically, a knight jousts with an opponent of equal stature and bears with him the "honor" of his lady. But in this case the honor of the lady is precisely the *object* of the bee's "tilting away." Moreover, the chivalry of his medieval "joust" is negated by the total warfare he engineers—the effective "sapping" of the flowers' walls. The monomaniac bee is here portrayed as the quintessential sweet sacker.

Because the Dickinson bee is such an inveterate seducer, a suave reprobate of always foreseeable intent, his behavioral predictability often raises questions about the potential culpability and volition of the object of his desire: "The

Flower must not blame the Bee— / That seeketh his felicity / Too often at her door" (P. 206). The fact that the success of the persuader presumes the existence of the successfully persuaded informs this meditation on the renunciatory power of virginity:

> Did the Harebell loose her girdle
> To the lover Bee
> Would the Bee the Harebell *hallow*
> Much as formerly?
>
> Did the "Paradise"—persuaded—
> Yield her moat of pearl—
> Would the Eden *be* an Eden
> Or the Earl—an *Earl?*
>
>   (P. 213)

On other occasions, however, an apparently fixed poetic gender appears rather more flexible. The provocative assertion of the narrator of poem 869 is that the relative *roles* of bee and flower may be assumed with equal facility:

> Because the Bee may blameless hum
> For Thee a Bee do I become
> List even unto Me.
>
> Because the Flowers unafraid
> May lift a look on thine, a Maid
> Alway a Flower would be.
>
> Nor Robins, Robins need not hide
> When Thou upon their Crypts intrude
> So Wings bestow on Me
> Or Petals, or a Dower of Buzz
> That Bee to ride, or Flower of Furze
> I that way worship Thee.
>
>   (P. 869)

This role-playing fluidity serves to remind us that the bee is hardly the only seducer in the typical Dickinson pollination scene. The alternative interactive scenario is the nectar-seeking insect entering, or rather being enveloped by, the nectar-heavy flower and willingly succumbing to the consequent delicious suffocation of being "lost in Balms" (P. 211). If this strange meeting, or merging, or steeping of bee in flower is Dickinson's trope for reading, her allegory of reader interaction, then it is the text that is the enchanter: its enchanting is simultaneously a delight and a dangerous spell*binding* of the reader, who is the text's would-be seducer. Indeed, that spellbinding, whether effected by the vehicle of flowers or that of poetry, is also ultimately an enchantment by the poet, who is in some sense embodied within those messages. For as we learn in another poem,

I hide myself within my flower,
That fading from your Vase,
You, unsuspecting, feel for me—
Almost a loneliness.
(P. 903)[3]

The enchantment of the reader/bee by the text/flower (and the poet who is "hidden within") is a reciprocation of the former's desire, another seduction. In this context, the word's connotations best capture the dangerous sexiness of an embedding that blurs thanatos and eros, annihilation and eroticism, experiences of loss of self that end in embalmings. Seduction (*seducere*) is a leading both on and in, an ambiguous experience of risk, promising mastery while demanding submission, perilous, yet requiring the seducee to suspend awareness of the peril. The Dickinson poem, like the alluring flower, is particularly seductive insofar as it cuts a captivating figure, an impishly posing imposition that cannot be passively received. It demands a performance from its reader. An open-ended text offers itself up to the performance that is a hedonistic reading, and the typical Dickinson text, whose linguistic strategies, as we shall see later, render it extremely open-ended, in many ways anticipates that assertively desirable text required by Roland Barthes, who demanded that "the text you write must prove to me that it desires me."[4]

Dickinson's poetic text is especially desirable to a reader because it is so *amazing*. Perhaps her most famous definition of the poet is one who "Distills amazing sense / From ordinary Meanings" (P. 448). T. W. Higginson, in the "Letter to a Young Contributor" Dickinson so admired, observed, "Literature is attar of roses, one distilled drop from a million blossoms."[5] Dickinson's art of distillation is effected by her powerful syntactic compression, a compression that, suddenly decompressed by the interpretive reading process, causes a semantic explosion for the interpreter. "Amazing sense" is a phrase itself reflective of the process it describes, since it has at least three "senses" of its own: the sense is amazing because of its own incredible logic—it is designed to take a reader beyond any "common" sense; the sense is amazing because it is beyond "normal" sensuality—and therefore appeals to some indescribable aesthetic "sixth" sense; and, most importantly, the sense is amazing in its potential for reader disorientation—a poem can be *a-mazing*. A maze is an artisan's structure, an aesthetic framework, that one enters willingly, negotiates, and quits unscathed. Although it is not necessarily a trap, the successful maze, like the successful poem, has to be intensely desirable; it must always be seductive enough to entice the reader as a stroller within its perimeters.

The mazy seductiveness of Dickinson's poems, their capacity to tease (in the sense of an unraveling "teasing out" of the reader around a linguistic center of "maybe") and thereby to elicit interactive involvement, emerges from the systematic cohabitation of a variety of possible, often mutually exclusive, meanings within them. A key Dickinson maxim is "How Human Nature dotes / On what it can't detect" (P. 1417), and there is no more powerful reader stimulus in her canon than the continually frustrated attempt to detect and fix on a missing center when there are always only possible options available. In essence, Dickinson's is an aesthetics of frustration: the potential for reader enchantment is in precise relation to that reader's inability to attain the satiated fulfillment of his or her hermeneutic desire. The poet's notorious ambiguity or duplicity is thus merely symptomatic of a larger reader-oriented strategy of indeterminacy that heightens desire by perpetually deferring fulfillment. That strategy is inevitably double-edged: a *dotage* is, after all, not just a pleasurable longing; it is also the aphasia of an imminent senility.

Not surprisingly, Dickinson discovered the condition of indeterminacy to be itself indeterminate, a placing of the reader between two receptive poles where the uncertain oscillating could be alternately sweet ("Sweet Skepticism of the Heart— / That knows—and does not know" [P. 1413]) and bittersweet ("Wonder—is not precisely Knowing / And not precisely Knowing not— / A beautiful but bleak condition" [P. 1331]). Wonder is, of course, the condition of being in the domain of an unseen, and therefore surmised, creator, and such absence-induced skepticism is the "delicious throe / Of transport thrilled with Fear" (P. 1413), a word juxtaposition emphasizing the fact that the linguistic force field that is a poem, reconciling opposites in the tense proximity of a single line, is a wondrous simulacrum of that creation. The emotional paradox that those words convey, however, an ecstatic masochism of sorts, is also precisely the reading experience that the poet's seductive rhetoric is intended to effect. For the Dickinson reader, excitement is a dynamic tension—vibration, oscillation, pulsation, a current alternating between poles. Indeed, the initial positioning of the reader between polar fields is a prerequisite for excitement to emerge, because energy vibrates within the pole markers. That excitement is contingent on uncertainty, anticipation, teasing, possibility: fulfillment, pleasure, the sense of an ending, and all other forms of satiation inevitably preclude it. As a result, the reader of a Dickinson poem can never be the dispassionate aesthetic spectator posited by Kant and Schiller. On the contrary, that reader, suspended between polar latitudes, is always a hedonistic participant in the affective domain created by the poem's syntactic tensions.

The site of a reader's exposure to indeterminacy is, to return to the Dickinson terminology of the frame letter, a scene of *surmise*. A poem can become a scene of surmise through the arabesque complexities of its narrative progression or by the unsettling insinuations of an ironic narrator, but the more effective scenes of surmise occur as specific language events within the poem at junctures of syntactic complexity. The manipulation of the reader into the textual interstices that are these poetic scenes of surmise anticipates a postmodern textual erotics that celebrates the seam or fault line. For Roland Barthes, the value of texts "would proceed from their duplicity. By which it may be understood that they always have two edges . . . what pleasure wants is the site of a loss, the seam, the cut, the deflation, the dissolve, which seizes the subject in the midst of bliss."[6] An uncertain vacillation on the surface of signification (the consequence of what Michael Riffaterre would usefully call "the infidelity of the referent")[7] will inevitably cause a reader compromising of sorts, a localized scene of seduction.

This poetic strategy is definitively seductive because it involves the mutual dependence of textuality and sexuality. Dickinson habitually associated love and poetry. One of her best-known poems explicates the connection very neatly—that both are coeval (or should that be co-evil?):

> To pile like Thunder to its close
> Then crumble grand away
> While Everything created hid
> This—would be Poetry—
>
> Or Love—the two coeval come—
> We both and neither prove—
> Experience either and consume—
> For None see God and live—
>   (P. 1247)

Poetry, love, and religion are all processes of desire, specifically, the desire of an I for the Other, be it a reader, a lover, or a god, and such desire is realized equally plausibly through aesthetics, erotics, or theology. Reading Dickinson's poetry, we are constantly reminded of the problem of placing boundaries around desire. Most alarmingly, there is no exterior to the Dickinson poetic text in the reading situation it generates, because its spatial relation to the reader is one of mutual interiority, an interaction in which the language of the text and the surmise of the reader conjoin in a peculiar temptation approximating the sexual. It is not the superior wholeness or complexity of organization that distinguishes the effects of Dickinson's poetry, but, paradoxically, its structured inducing of an experience of lack, its creation of an absence that simultaneously stimulates the reading subject's desire and facilitates its perpetually frustrated drift.

The readerly rigor required initially to spark that desire is the subject of poem 675:

Essential Oils—are wrung—
The Attar from the Rose
Be not expressed by Suns—alone—
It is the gift of Screws—

Reading is partly innate illumination ("Suns"), but the poetic "essence" is squeezed forth (e-sense) only by the labor of a rigorous mind. While overdetermination is at the heart of Dickinson's poetic strategy, determination is the major trait expected of her anticipated reader. Assuming that the voice of poem 842 is that of a poet-fox, it is her reader who is required to show the single-minded devotion to duty of the hunting hound, and the mastiff's difficult pursuit of its elusive foxy subject is reflected in the poem's teasing movement of continual qualification and restatement.

Good to hide, and hear 'em hunt!
Better, to be found,
If one care to, that is,
The Fox fits the Hound—

Good to know, and not tell,
Best, to know and tell,
Can one find the rare Ear
Not too dull—

The "rare Ear / Not too dull" is the closest Dickinson came to defining her expectations of an interpretive community.

Even more important than that community's ability to "see," however, is its participation in the subsequent "sorcery." Sorcery is Dickinson's white magic—simultaneously the *effect* of poetry and the creation *of* poetry. This complex equation is explicated in a poem that recalls the narrator's experience, as reader, of a transformingly influential text:[8]

I think I was enchanted
When first a sombre Girl—
I read that Foreign Lady—
The Dark—felt beautiful—

And whether it was noon at night—
Or only Heaven—at Noon—
For very Lunacy of Light
I had not power to tell—

The Bees—became as Butterflies—
The Butterflies—as Swans—
Approached—and spurned the narrow Grass—
And just the meanest Tunes

That Nature murmured to herself
To keep herself in Cheer—
I took for Giants—practising
Titanic Opera—

The Days—to Mighty Metres stept—
The Homeliest—adorned
As if unto a Jubilee
'Twere suddenly confirmed—

I could not have defined the change—
Conversion of the Mind
Like Sanctifying in the Soul—
Is witnessed—not explained—

'Twas a Divine Insanity—
The Danger to be Sane
Should I again experience—
'Tis Antidote to turn—

To Tomes of solid Witchcraft—
Magicians be asleep—
But Magic—hath an Element
Like Deity—to keep—

  (P. 593)

Sorcery emanates from "Tomes of solid Witchcraft": the timeless magic (the irresistible force to which the reader submits) is the poetry within those tomes.
The "Divine Insanity" produced in the narrator by her reading is the very Cole-
ridgean madness of floating hair and flashing eyes: the reaction sparked is
a frenzy of poetic activity. The reader/narrator's reactions are, in themselves,
poetic: she experiences synaesthesia ("The Dark—felt beautiful"), personification ("Lunacy of Light"), hyperbolic metaphor ("I took for Giants—practising /
Titanic Opera"), and metonymic sliding ("The Bees—became as Butterflies").
This is a poetic transformation represented *as* poetic transformations. The narrator may plead ignorance as to the precise nature of her alteration, but it is
obvious to the reader of her poem: she became herself a poet, and the "change"
she underwent while reading her precursor's poem is *this* poem. Her own poem
is not "about" the reading of another('s) poem: it is that reading *as* poem. Poem
593 does not therefore mark a reader/writer meeting, a sympathetic merging of

minds (the reader's is the only subject position involved when "Magicians be asleep"), but *is* the production, or rather reproduction, of a previous reader/ text liaison. In poem 883, Dickinson categorically restates this: "The Poets light but Lamps— / Themselves—go out." That which is vital the text alone disseminates. This is a definition of reading as a re-creational activity where the engendering of the new text is part of the original text's aesthetic of process; texts reproduce themselves in an overlapping intertextual web mapped by their readers. The new flowering of rhetoric is an anamorphosis of the primary text, but the identity of the new text lies not in what produced it but what it, in turn, potentially produces. The text that can effect this kind of transformation is a rarity (Dickinson herself noting, "How few suggestions germinate!" [L. 888]). Of such texts it can be said, "By their fruits ye shall know them." Ideally, the inducements of the text produce another text. The labor of reading a poem is therefore twofold, for it is also an ongoing site of production. In this affective milieu, the reader's task is not to analyze the text in the sense of critical explication but to elaborate (*e-labore*—work out) on that text, to creatively produce another text from within themselves, to succumb to the sublime enchantment of intertextual energies. As Adrienne Rich has perceptively observed of Dickinson, "Wherever you take hold of her, *she proliferates*" (emphasis added).[9]

This then is the Dickinson scene of reading I will elaborate in this study: the text entices the reader, leading him or her on and in, playing on the reader's desire for meaning through a process that continually thwarts it, this culminating in a successful reader/text interaction that produces another text of the reader's own making, which is, in itself, a complete poetic expression and not a mere copy of the original. In Dickinson's own terminology, it is *seeing*, being *enchanted*, being undone by *surmise*, and participating in a final *sorcery*. Now, obviously, the critical reader must take special care in this aesthetic dispensation, because the poem is frequently the textual frame within whose confines that reader may be simultaneously stimulated, exposed, and thoroughly undone. Indeed, typically, in the reading interaction elicited by the a-mazing syntax of the Dickinson poetic text, the "seduction" of the would-be interpreter is not so much an imminent possibility as it is an ongoing, and often uncomfortably self-revelatory, text-producing event. Just so, the bee, coated with the white pollen of the Indian pipe, voyages always as the bright ambassador of another's desire.

It is now standard practice (and eminently fashionable) for contemporary critical readers, who assume that meaning is produced by their applied critical grids and that hidden ideologies preclude any supposed interpretive "neutrality," to declare the politics of their reading from the outset, explicitly acknowledging the specificities of their particular reading pact. So, hardly an exception to the postmodern critical rule, I must confess immediately that what follows is a narrative of seduction. Most obviously, it is the narrative of my own seduction by the poetry and person of Emily Dickinson. The compulsion to write about the poet is the desire for repetition of an initial seduction by her poetry, and my critical narrative, structured by the continual repetition of scenes of seduction, is itself presumably determined by a primal scene of seduction, some long-forgotten moment of re-creation, poem and reader interacting intimately behind closed doors. This most pseudocritical of texts therefore might be considered a confessional script where the most conclusive evidence that poetic "seductions" occur is not to be found within the structure of its argument but rather in the space that the argumentative structure itself comes to occupy.

"Seduction" is from the outset of this critical narrative the most slippery of terms, and that is as it should be. The information that a woman has been "seduced" by a man tells us virtually nothing about the degree of their intimacy. Depending on the context and the narrator, "seduced" might be a synonym of "allured," "captivated," or, of course, "fascinated." Then again, "molested" and "raped" are equally valid alternatives, since throughout the nineteenth and twentieth centuries "seduction" has been the primary euphemism for the sexual abuse of women by men. The multiple significations of the word ensure that the narrative of a woman's "seduction" will immediately present a problematic scene of reading. Of course, the information that a man has been "seduced" by a woman is overdetermined by an equally archetypal contextuality. In this case, "seduction" is often convenient shorthand for deceit; "seduction" is that which befalls an unsuspecting male who, rendered momentarily defenseless, for whatever reason, if only by the flash of a too conspicuous anklet, succumbs to the wiles of an Eve or a Delilah or a Mata Hari or those myriad other femmes fatales of cinematic derivation. Consequently, the "seduction" of the male will present a similarly problematic interpretive scene.

In either case, because so often the desire for a specifically sexual experience can be assumed to be operative in the one seduced, "seduction" acquires the status of a fundamentally ambiguous event. Blame slips from deceiver to deceived, because there can be no seduction that does not in some way implicate the seducee. It is the fate of the seduced to confirm the seduction and thus be rendered culpable: the seducer may tempt, but it is the seducee who yields to temptation. Moreover, the mutuality of surrender is intrinsic to the act of seduction: the seducer's intention is to render weakness *in* the other; the seducee's strategy is the appearance of weakness *before* the other. There is no completely active or passive mode in seduction, no subject or object, no interior or exterior, so the word "seduction" is marvelously scored with contradiction: it alludes to notions of conquest and captivation while relying on expressions of consent or acquiescence; it compresses charm and fascination with bribery and coercion; it conflates delight and pleasure with wrongs and betrayals. It is the ultimate portmanteau word, delineating perhaps the ultimate portmanteau event.

The double problematic of reading "seduction"—the fact that both the aptitude for "seduction" and the susceptibility to it cut across gender boundaries and that the term itself typically carries a multiplicity of associations—ensures that it is also a potentially subversive event. Most obviously, "seduction" problematizes questions of agency because it can conceivably be both *of* and *by* simultaneously. In the everyday world of male/female relations, with its ritual courtship dances and attendant role playing, the doubleness of "seduction" often has unfortunate consequences. The testimony of the young man accused of date rape—which might easily be summarily transcribed as "I did not seduce (rape) her, she seduced (allured) me"—provides ample sad evidence of that fact. On the other hand, the suggestive doubleness of "seduction" as a particular discursive event, as a powerful deconstructive trope, lends it a certain critical utility as a means of analysis of gender relations. I would concur with Jane Miller's assertion that seduction is a metaphor that helps to uncover cultural patterns that permeate textual and extratextual experience and that it is also a "means by which sexual relations can be inserted into any understanding of how power is experienced in societies based on inequality."[10] Simultaneously an instrument of male hegemony and a potential vehicle for challenging patriarchal power, "seduction" both upholds and potentially undoes hierarchy. The status of "seduction" as coeval affirmation and denial of established power structures ensures a significant destabilizing potential in the representation of the "scene of seduction" in language. This is as true today as it was in antebellum New England. And this is why, throughout my own critical reading, seduction, in all its rhetorical modalities, continually destabilizes the complacencies of interpretive authority, including any complacent authority temporarily assumed by *this* critical surmise.

Of course, the ostensible focus of this critical text is the poetry of Emily Dickinson, whose challenge to critical complacencies is often sufficiently antidotal in itself. Dickinson's poetry contains unexploded bombs, smoldering volcanoes, instantaneous chills, dread anticipations, post-traumatic stress disorders. This is more than an inventory of the poetry's contents, a synopsis of its subject matter. It is equally validly a catalog of possible reader responses to that poetry; the chills, anticipations, and stresses might be physical and mental reactions to the poems, the metaphoric bombs and volcanoes vivid representations of the impacted texts that elicit those violent responses. Dickinson's poetry is, after all, most significant not in what it communicates to a reader but in what it *does* to a reader. The poet famously defined her own response to poetry as an immediate sensual reaction: "If I read a book [and] it makes my whole body so cold no fire ever can warm me I know *that* is poetry. If I feel physically as if the top of my head were taken off, I know *that* is poetry. These are the only way I know it. Is there any other way?" (L. 342a). Apparently, she shared with Freud a highly affective conception of the "effects of reading," a view of reading as an experience that could be as painful or as pleasurable (or, in her peculiarly masochistic poetic regime, both simultaneously) as bodily sensation. The continued popular success of Dickinson's poetry is, I believe, conclusive evidence of her capacity to elicit a similarly spontaneous, visceral response from her own readers, and her critical reception is the visible proof of the perpetuation of a powerful rhetorical seduction.

Chapter 1 traces one possible origin of Dickinson's affective poetic by relocating her rhetorical strategies in relation to the wider discourse of antebellum women. In particular, I claim that this poetic can be considered a subtle reemphasis of contradictions within a larger discursive formation, a rhetoric of seduction that permeated the antebellum culture within which Dickinson lived vicariously. This rhetoric of seduction, often specified or *italicized* within the sentimental "novel of seduction," is especially evident in the language of moral reform, and the moral reform movement's hyperbolic obsession with the details and strategies of seduction is, in turn, reflected in many of the local newspapers to which the poet's family subscribed. Evidently, for the typical resident of antebellum Amherst, the rhetoric of "seduction" and its discursive impact were inescapable.

Dickinson's unique manipulation of this pervasive rhetoric of seduction is evident in the personal rhetoric of her letters, especially those written to significant male correspondents. Previous critical readers of these letters have observed how the poet attempted to effect a "rhetorical seduction" of individual male readers. Chapter 2 focuses on the specific linguistic mechanisms Dickinson used and demonstrates how her letters function not as communications but as rhetorical constructions designed to elicit specific and spontaneous reactions from their recipients. Not only was the author of those letters an effective rhetorician determined to directly address and upset the social conventions and expectations of her audience through manipulations of language that forced a direct confrontation with the process of reading, but, reconsidered as linguistically impacted rhetorical devices, those same letters also become recognizable derivatives of an identifiable antebellum *ecriture feminine*.

Because Dickinson's carefully drafted, stunningly epigrammatic letters approximate prose poetry, the transition from letters to poetry within any critical narrative is easily achieved. Pursuing the argument that the letters are not so much communications as rhetorical devices, and that any critical perspective which assumes that Dickinson primarily indulged an aesthetic self-reflexivity in the writing of her poetry has failed to recognize the extent and importance of her interest in rhetorical power, chapter 3 demonstrates how the same affective concerns that underscore the letters also inform the poems. While all literature requires an element of imaginative reconstruction from its reader, Dickinson's cryptic texts exaggerate the reconstructive process and raise its interactive potentiality to an interpretive infinity. The resonant gaps in her poetry serve a primary catalytic function: the syntactic *and* semantic voids stimulate active reader involvement in a continual process of interpretive revision and replacement. Those vague referents and unspecified antecedents (the many untethered "Its" that often come to represent whatever the reader wishes to inscribe) demand the most profound of reading engagements. But the initial engagement of reader and text (or, if one prefers, the initial enchantment of reader *by* text) is simply the first strategic maneuver of a more thoroughly discomfiting "poetics of seduction."

Dickinson's antebellum poetics anticipates, in many ways, our own contemporary critical philosophies of seduction. For Jean Baudrillard, the hyperbolist of our postmodern moment, "seduction" is a strategy of appearances, a dwelling in and on the play of signifiers that flaunts its mockery of the idea of any reality beyond surfaces. As opposed to power, which is mastery of the real, seduction is the mastery of signs, and thus the site of power's inversion, or at very least the scene of its possible compromising. While the masculine is the repository of power, of a phallic sovereignty confident in its sexual identity, Baudrillardan seduction, a strategy of illusion and dissemblance that undermines discourses aimed at truth, is fated to be the domain of the feminine and its technology of subversion. This feminine seduction, eschewing the production of discourses of truth, potentially dismantles systems of sex, meaning, and power by reducing language to the play of signs that precedes interpretation. The play of signification is, however, rather more than idle female chatter, some hazily conceptualized pre-oedipal babble, for a discourse of pure appearance, a total self-reflexivity emptied of referentiality, is attractive in itself. As Baudrillard observes, "Any system that is totally complicit in its own absorption, such that signs no longer make sense, will exercise a remarkable power of fascination."[11] Not through any messages of desire they represent but by their sheer accumulation, signs effect an esoteric complicity, establish a lyrical contiguous contact, contrive their own seduction. The omnipresent possibility of that seduction might lead one to speculate that the much maligned play of signifiers posited by deconstructive theory may well have acquired, in felicitous historical eras, a subversive rhetorical import. In the central chapters of this study I indicate the specific example of Dickinson's poetic dissemblance and bear witness to the reader-implicating strategies and interpretive consequences of her localized diversionary (syn)tactics.

Baudrillard further argues that "seduction does not consist of a simple appearance nor a pure absence, but the eclipse of a presence. Its sole strategy is to be-there/not-there, and thereby produce a sort of flickering, a hypnotic mechanism that crystallizes attention outside all concern with meaning. Absence here seduces presence." Thus, the figure of the Baudrillardan seductress "constantly avoids all relations in which, at some given moment, the question of *truth* will be posed. She undoes them effortlessly, not by denying or destroying them, but by making them shimmer. Here lies her secret: in the flickering of a presence. She is never where one expects her, and never where one wants her. Seduction supposes . . . an 'aesthetics of disappearance.' "[12] We are all only too aware of how Dickinson assiduously cultivated her own uniquely seductive "aesthetics of disappearance." But the poet's vanishing beneath a series of convenient figural roles, like her choice of a literal reclusion, was strategically significant to this degree: she relinquished the power of self-definition in order to become the object of her readers' desire. Disembodied, she turned herself into a pure appearance, a useful artificial construct with which to trap the desires of the a-mazed other. This in itself would be relatively uninteresting were it not also precisely the objective of Dickinson's poetic texts: the simultaneous provocation and deception of the desire of her readers by the play of formally dislocated signs, by the flickers and shimmers of an elusive sense, by the intimate appeal of a situated reading seduction.

Cynthia Griffin Wolff, remarking that visitors to the Dickinson homestead are fascinated less by the poetry than by the woman who wrote it, wonders what "dynamic of Dickinson's interior life . . . infuses her poetry with power and passes through the verse to readers, touching so many with intimate appeal." Recognizing that the "disarming intimacy" of Dickinson is contingent on readers responding "not merely to her superb verbal artistry, but to a felt presence, her 'self,' " Wolff ponders "the reader's sense of being in touch, not with an artful set of words, but with another human being, insistent and intense."[13] This sense of insistent and intense presence is crucial to the implicating power of a Dickinson poetics within which the word indeed approaches the inscription of the body. Chapter 4 examines Dickinson's aesthetic reconsideration of the implications of the Christian Incarnation and how her faith in the possibility of textual embodiment ("A Word Made Flesh") proved to be the royal road to the later "rhetorical seduction" of her readers. For so many of those readers, "the passion of Emily Dickinson" has been deployed across the surface of a signifying body upon which have been enacted seduction scenes. Lavinia Dickinson famously described the packets of her sister's poetry as "fascicles." This chapter is designed to serve as a reminder that, in terms of the body, a fascicle defines a small cluster of muscle or nerve fibers.

The final chapters of this study trace the "seduction" of Dickinson's critical readers effected by her poetry. My concern in these chapters is to show how literary critics can become implicated in the reading *affects* of the text we are analyzing, of how metalinguistic distance may collapse and leave us no interpretive space from within which we can discuss literature objectively or, for that matter, subjectively. My thesis, that desire so infects the critical analysis of Dickinson's poetry that the poetry ultimately acts as an interpretation of its reader, derives from psychoanalytic notions of the necessarily reductive nature of any interpretation. In these chapters I argue that transference is the engine of analysis and "interpretation" the medium through which the transference is manifested. My own analysis of transference as it is enacted in the process of reading Dickinson's poetry centers on the symptomatic affects produced by the critical presumption that her poetic text is the very site where meaning and knowledge reside. Therefore, the final "seduction" is specifically the scene of psychoanalytic transference and countertransference, that interpretive space where analyst and analysand, or reader and read, or critic and text, limn routes of desire and merge, indistinguishable, in the hermeneutic space of analysis.

Dickinson once told her would-be suitor Judge Otis Lord, "Don't you know you are happiest while I withhold and not confer—don't you know that 'No' is the wildest word we consign to Language?" (L. 562). She would later pointedly note: "I have a strong surmise that moments we have *not* known are tenderest to you. Of their afflicting Sweetness, you only are the judge" (L. 750). The "afflicting sweetness" of a consummation imagined as opposed to enacted is also the (play)ground of Dickinson's aesthetic: her philosophy of "sumptuous destitution," the notion that "a secure Delight suffers in enchantment" (L. 353), permeates her poetry both as theme and as rhetorical practice. Chapter 5 examines the consequences of that cultivation of "afflicting sweetness" in the critical reader and focuses on interpretations that, consciously or otherwise, have located the poet in the position of the classic analysand, the female hysteric, the seductress who leads on but ultimately only to frustrate. Katherine Cummings has described the potential confusion caused by the "hysteric's seduction" in some detail: "Enticement scenes pose immediate problems for later readers who begin with the desire to master what they have read. The first problem is the resistance of the text. For allurement scripts are so structured that it is difficult to disentangle the seduced from the seducer, to attribute power to a single subject, or to say who has finally been taken by whom. In fact, once the boundaries are blurred between seduced and seducing subjects, as they manifestly are within allurement scenarios, seduction will assume the status of an undecidable event."[14] And just so with the allurement "scripts" and "scenarios" that are the poems of Emily Dickinson. In this chapter I explore how the possibility of transference in the reading of the poetry misshapes the critic's relationship with the text by introducing a past scene of seduction into the present context, and how the powerful, emotionally charged relationship that develops between poet and critical reader can often be detected as a rhetorical undertow within the language of the critical text.

While the penultimate chapter concentrates on critical studies of the poetry that demonstrate elements of resistance to its transferential reading affects, and how we often find, particularly in male critical readings of the poet, a certain vertigo—the loss of gravity and *gravitas*—chapter 6 examines what I have chosen to call "hysterical" readings of the poet's text. These "hysterical" readings exemplify a vivid countertransference in action. In the countertransferential text there is a distinct homology between its own prevailing critical concerns and the apparent thematic concerns of the poetic text it purportedly analyzes. This duplication is often evidenced by a series of fascinating (and fascinated) rhetorical echoes. Curiously, just such an intertextual replication seems to have been anticipated with approbation by Dickinson in her own poetic celebrations of the transformative power of the female other. In this final discussion, I also explore in more detail the possible impact of gender on the process of interpreting "Dickinson" and observe that the reading practices of female critics who address the poetry, and the reciprocal rhetorical affects the poetic text incites within their critical analyses, are often qualitatively different from those of their male critical counterparts, the intensity of whose affective responses, in turn, appears to vary considerably in proportion to the "feminist" sympathy of the individual male critical reader.

In examining critical readings of the poet, my own role is analogous to that of the psychoanalyst whose intervention analyzes a transference in order to demonstrate to the patient how his or her feelings toward and perception of the analyst are structured like a symptom. Freud argued that repressed desires lead a person to "repeat" patterns of behavior, "transferring" early childhood feelings onto the contemporary adult scene. The analytic situation triggered the transference to the extent that the analysand acted out with the analyst the repressed patterns he or she once enacted with others, a repetition that was a resistance to analysis and the clue that allowed it to proceed. The ultimate goal of analysis was to move the analysand from "repetition" to "remembering" by "working through" the transference, for an individual who "remembers" the past is no longer doomed to "repeat" it. This, I believe, has more than a little relevance for the critical study of literature. My intention in these final chapters is to demonstrate to critical readers how often Dickinson criticism has served as a mode of repetition, a repetition of the text and of the particular historical relationship of seduction that structured its initial composition.

But the fact that throughout my own "seductive" reading of "Dickinson" the positions occupied by figural seducers and victims are considered inter-changeable within a dialogic reading situation has inescapable ramifications for the rhetoric of my own critical text. It can hardly be immune to the infections of desire it traces in others. My only attempt to skirt this hazard has been to foreground each specific mode of rhetorical analysis within the critical narra-tive, thus making the particular interpretive method of each chapter a possible subject of study in itself. So while the focus of my argument remains always that "discourse of seduction" whose various manifestations and consequences I trace, each segment of its presentation is also a specific literary-critical applica-tion—new historicist, reader-response, deconstructive, feminist, Lacanian, and object-relations psychoanalytic—to the text in question. Each theoretical grid provides a temporary context for reading and a pretext for reading the theory as seduction. In this way, my own study is simultaneously a reflexive meditation on the attempted "seductions" of Dickinson's life and text by critical theory, not least by the six-part critical narrative erected within my bee/flower frame. Of course, the transgression or crisscrossing of boundaries effected by my own text, its engagement of two forms of writing in a dialogue or cross-examination, and its elision of poetic and critical rhetorics might also be considered a type of the same seduction it seeks to explore. The reader of my own reading of readings should always keep this in mind lest rhetorical replication proliferate ad infini-tum and thus obscure the always binding obligation to enchantment.

1

The Milieu of Seduction

A young woman at Amherst, of good family and of gay, vivacious
and impulsive disposition, fell a victim some while since to the
wiles of a seducer. A few weeks ago she gave birth to a child, and
the feeling that she had brought disgrace upon her family preyed upon
her to such an extent that she lapsed into periods of deep melancholy.
—*Springfield Republican*, June 14, 1872

THE POETRY OF Emily Dickinson is a superb testing ground for any literary
analysis that emphasizes historical considerations. Indeed, while recent
critical studies that attempt to relate Dickinson to her contemporary culture are
interesting and informative, it would be more difficult to argue that any are particularly revelatory.[1] I would suggest that the affinities such studies trace between the poet's culture and her text are of limited validity due to the implicit
determinism of their method. The central problem with these critical texts is
their monologic ambition. Each assumes that literary text and history can be
distinguished as foreground and background and that the devices through
which the text refracts or reflects the contextual background are therefore easily
observable for the critical analyst. As a result, these critical studies uncover (by
means of an excavation that is, at least partially, a site of construction) a series
of historical master narratives that demonstrate how Dickinson's poetry was
unequivocally determined by the culture within which it was embedded.

One of the more provocative of these master narratives has been laboriously
disinterred by Betsy Erkkila. Arguing that Dickinson's "poetic revolution was
grounded in the privilege of her class position in a conservative Whig house-
hold whose elitist, antidemocratic values were at the very center of her work"
and that "the metaphysical and linguistic space of her poems is . . . traversed by
her ideological assumptions and presumption as a member of New England's
political . . . elite," Erkkila attempts to reinscribe a social and political history effectively elided by the predominant feminist critical narrative, which
she characterizes as "the story of the daughter's revolt against a perpetually de-
monized and transhistorical patriarch and her desire to return to a preoedipal

and prehistorical mother." Erkkila's own narrative is appealingly confronta-
tional, and valuable to the degree that it is oppositional. For it *has* become all
too common in the rhetoric of contemporary Dickinson criticism simply to dismiss the uncomfortable irony that it was precisely the poet's "upper-class economic, social, and psychological status that enabled in fundamental ways her
poetic creation and the seeming radicalism of her vision," and that if Dickinson
indeed "challenged the masculine orders of authority in home and family,
church and state, it was an assault launched from within the confines and class
privilege of her 'Father's house.' " But while Erkkila's critique of the feminist
critical narrative is valid, her alternative narrative is finally no more convincing
on its own terms than the one she so pungently disputes. The notion that in her
poems "Dickinson was *in some sense* the spokesperson and representative of
older ruling class interests" (emphasis added) is hardly precise. The crucial idea
that the poet articulates "an aristocratic social ideal that had been suppressed
in the more public political rhetoric of the Whig party" surely demands a more
thorough study of this political rhetoric than Erkkila eventually provides in her
article. These assertions ultimately aspire to the same degree of ambitious reductiveness Erkkila castigates in the feminist critical narrative. Indeed, much of
the evidence Erkkila provides to support her sociopolitical thesis—a mixture of
local and family history and a series of decontextualized quotes from Dickinson's poems and correspondence—is only obliquely relevant in a critical context
where the basic theoretical premises that ground the historical analysis remain
largely unexpressed.[2]

Now, I certainly agree with Erkkila's assumption that every expressive act
is embedded in a network of material practices, but I would further assume that
literary and nonliterary texts circulate inseparably in such a way that observing
the intermingling of cultural and social events proves more problematic than a
deterministic historical approach would allow. Therefore, this study pursues decidedly more limited, essentially local ambitions: it traces one particular negotiation or exchange between the social and cultural fields of antebellum New
England by examining how a particular discursive field may have influenced
(rather than determined) Dickinson's literary and linguistic imagination. From
the outset, however, I want to acknowledge the necessary partiality of my own
historical reading of the poet. My suggestion that Dickinson's self and text
were defined by her relationship to the disciplinary power of her patriarchal
culture—that disciplinary power perfectly figured and dissolved in the trope
of seduction—is decidedly partial, both in the sense of being incomplete (as
one discursive field among many) and in being a critically constructed narrative (one to which I have myself clearly become partial). My analysis, therefore,
should be regarded as a local "negotiation" between Dickinson's poetic text and

the critical approach of new historicism or cultural poetics that, in its attempt at critical mastery, seeks to "seduce" that text.[3]

One of the more curious objects in the Strong House museum in Amherst is a cast-iron stand holding a shaped, glass bottle.[4] This waterglass "electrofying globe" is of nineteenth-century manufacture, and the mobility of the globe indicates years of refinement of the design. It was used as a lighting device, the filled globe acting as a condensing lens to concentrate the light of a candle placed behind it, thus creating a sort of spotlighting for close work. Presumably, the Strong House globe could have been useful for a woman engaged in commercial piecework for a Springfield lace company or perhaps working at home plaiting straw for the East Amherst hat factory.

Emily Dickinson's ocular problems were particularly acute in the period between 1861 and 1865. Among the symptoms of exotropia, from which she may have suffered, are blurred vision and extreme sensitivity to bright light. Dickinson wrote her poetry late at night, when the rest of the family was asleep, and the light of an ordinary lamp would have placed considerable strain on her eyes. It is therefore not unlikely that the poet was familiar with the kind of softer spotlighting provided by some type of "electrofying globe." The fact that Dickinson may have had a particular type of lamp and globe arrangement in mind (if not in front of her) when writing the following poem of 1864 helps make its metaphorical vehicle more concrete: a lamp and the globe that functions as its lens could often be found in tandem during the antebellum period.

> The Poets light but Lamps—
> Themselves—go out—
> The Wicks they stimulate—
> If vital Light
>
> Inhere as do the Suns—
> Each Age a Lens
> Disseminating their
> Circumference—
> (P. 883)

However, knowledge of this association of lamp and accompanying lens may subtly alter the poem's sense, at least as that sense has been often construed by the poem's twentieth-century readers. The waterglobe was not a visual lens: one did not look through it to focus the outline of the lamp or the light emanating from it. Instead, it was indeed a disseminating lens that spread the focused light of the lamp out over the work area. And that dissemination (the scattering of the seed of semantic possibility that later readers could bring to critical fruition) is precisely what the "lens" that is historical retrospection does to a poem. In fact, the poem's aesthetic resonance ("Circumference") is precisely in relation to the blurring of any initial signification over time. Poem 883, therefore, actually suggests that the critical reading of the historical event that is a poem from a contemporary position is inevitably flawed, but for the critical reputation of that poem this is a beneficial distortion. The fact that analysts of this poem have never considered that the poet is using a historically particular arrangement of lamp and lens as metaphor is interesting insofar as it provides actual evidence of the potentially useful dissemination of the poem by our contemporary critical lens, an enlarging of the historical circumference of the poem that is also its actual subject.

In general, contemporary critical readers need to be aware of the distortions that result when they bring their fashionable lenses to a blurry visual focus on Dickinson's poetry. It is perhaps more advisable to begin a critical study by placing a decidedly antebellum lens *before* the text that is to be analyzed. The distortions will certainly not be eliminated, but the angles of deflection narrowed, the light lines scattered more sharply to the eye, and the necessarily dialectical process of criticism more perpetually evident both to the critic and to the reader of the critical text. Such a usefully available lens here provides the necessary spotlighting for my own close work on Dickinson's poetic strategies. In this chapter, one particular page of the local *Hampshire and Franklin Express* of August 13, 1847, serves as that convenient vehicle of dissemination.

In August 1847, the sixteen-year-old Emily Dickinson was preparing to begin her first (and only) year as a student at Mount Holyoke Female Seminary at South Hadley. When on August 13 the *Hampshire and Franklin Express* published an article on the tenth anniversary commencement of that "flourishing institution," it would therefore have been of considerable interest to the young student. In that article, the *Express* correspondent declares himself most impressed by the graduating class, particularly by their display of knowledge before a discerning audience. He observes that during the pupils' public examinations "the questions were promptly and adequately answered and distinctly expressed, evincing a thorough discipline, to render them so familiar with their subjects," and that their performance as singers "gave a gratifying proof of their proficiency in music, and showed how many had cultivated it, and with what success." The public commencement examinations proved to be a fine advertisement for Principal Mary Lyon's educational establishment.

As Dickinson would have expected to participate in a similar graduation ceremony, this report might interest a scholar who chose to argue that the poet's year at Mount Holyoke was particularly significant. For example, the fact that members of the graduating class "were all plainly attired in white, without any artificial ornaments," might have some relevance to the poet's later choice of a plain, white dress as her idiosyncratic personal signature. That dress, it could be argued, was an eccentrically personal compensation for the college graduation she never had, or perhaps the sign of her individual *poetic* graduation, a surprising "collegially" conceived cosmic white election.[5] Equally suggestive might be the four major compositions written by the students that year: the "beautifully written" "The Coronation and the Execution"; the satirical "Fashion"; the cryptic "Earth had but Two—and one she gave to Fame, and one to God"; and "The Two Friends" (a piece that makes particular reference to two Mount Holyoke pupils who had died during the course of the school year). The thematic grounding of much of the Dickinson poetic canon seems to parallel the content of those student essays, suggesting that the poet's interests in crowning and transcendence, temporality and satire, renunciation and election, and death and the memory of the departed were far from peculiar to her. Clearly, the details of the *Express* report on the graduation ceremony could be used to argue that the ambience of Mount Holyoke under Lyon had an even more formative influence on Dickinson's thought than has previously been suggested.

The newspaper column that contains the report of the Mount Holyoke commencement is placed, not surprisingly, alongside those for Amherst Academy and Amherst College. But it has a more striking adjacency with a parallel column that contains a rather different narrative, one that is educational only in the most oblique sense of the word. This article, captioned in bold type "THE LATE SEDUCTION CASE IN NEW YORK," describes in detail the arrest of one Michael (or Martin) Hare,[6] a married man of twenty-eight, who had eloped with the fifteen-year-old daughter of his employer, a Mr. Fox of New York City. Since his arrest, Hare had proven himself an early adept at the technique of blaming the victim, accusing the unfortunate Miss Fox of seducing him. The *Express* was suitably outraged by this behavior and quoted approvingly, and at length, from the previous week's *New York Tribune*, which had extended its report on the affair into a full-scale editorial declaration. It is worth quoting the reprinted excerpt from the *Tribune* editorial in full:

> But the practical question in the business is this: *Shall anything be DONE to subject such villains to the wholesome discipline of Law?* Hare is now in custody, and in this city, *but seduction is not reckoned as a crime by our laws!* Attempts will be made to bring him to justice on a charge of bigamy (he having, it is said, got some sort of a marriage with his victim) or on that of larceny, in taking away the clothes of the girl. But the essential and horrible crime of violating his marriage vows, deserting her he had ever sworn to love and cherish, and seducing his childish prey from her home of innocence and love to the haunts of pollution and shame is not at all

forbidden by the laws of New York! Shall this continue? We do not remember that one of the journals now vociferous against Hare ever aided to arouse the public mind to the necessity of providing legal penalties for crimes like this. Will they *now* take hold? Will the press generally speak out on this subject? Had any hungry wretch stolen from Mr. Fox a few spoons worth twenty dollars, the law directs that the culprit shall be punished therefore by several years' imprisonment at hard labor in the State Prison; but for the most perjured and base Seduction it has no penalty whatever! Why is this? Can it be deemed uncharitable if we say it is because our law-makers are seldom thieves, in the legal sense, but *are* too generally libertines? Why else is the most flagrant crime next to murder left unpunished while minor and even venial offences are visited with merciless severity? Why is it? Why?

Like the Mount Holyoke commencement report that limns this column's left edge, this editorial is suggestive material for a Dickinson scholar, providing an arresting narrative—an antebellum fable of the Fox and the Hare—that could facilitate the historical setting of a *critical* narrative. For example, the angry polemic of the editorial (of which I shall say more later), though more usually confined to local political discourse, is not at all unusual in the *Express*. That diatribe suggests that while the refined delicacy of sentimentalism had a major place in the Hampshire County press of 1847, it was not necessarily the predominant tone. The *Express*'s use of the *Tribune* editorial might serve as a critical corrective, conveniently reminding Dickinson's twentieth-century readers that her hometown was a place where political, religious, and personal passions had been known to run high and that the occasional anger in her poetic voice might be as much an expression of her culture as is her periodic indulgence in maudlin sentiment. And it is not just the tone of the report that could correct those readers' prejudicial misconceptions about antebellum Amherst. The space assigned to this particular seduction narrative vividly demonstrates that the local Amherst newspapers were not averse to printing sensationalistic and not particularly edifying news. Such a brief perusal of the local press could modify the contemporary readers' assumption—an assumption based on the apparent thematic concerns of Dickinson's poetry—that antebellum Amherst was a repressive enclave of survivalist puritanism.

Clearly, a little critical prestidigitation of the details in these two articles could construct a rereading of Dickinson's cultural milieu that could, in turn, be connected to her later poetic strategies. While tempted by that smoke and mirrors approach to history, I have chosen a different route of access to those poetic strategies, one not quite so dependent on the dangerously assumed principle of causality. Instead, I would suggest that, for a contemporary reader, what can be learned from the narrative content of the two articles is not nearly as interesting as the questions provoked by their parallel placement on the page. Was it simply an editorial lapse that led to their striking parallel alignment? How would the antebellum Amherst reader have dealt with that strange juxtaposition of commencement and seduction narratives on the same page? Even more interestingly, how would the sixteen-year-old female reader have reacted? Would she have interpreted the adjacent columns as separate and distinct paths, as possible alternative futures for herself, as diametrically opposed fates that could befall her?

I want therefore to examine the antebellum cultural milieu that could produce the juxtaposition of these two articles. This examination will tease out a series of similarities between them that undoes their apparent juxtaposition by identifying the particular cultural discourse that both produced the editorial diatribe provoked by the Fox seduction and informed the education of the 1847 graduating class. Demonstrating the influence of that cultural discourse on Dickinson's thought, I will argue that her poetic strategies can be viewed as emerging from the interstitial space opening *between* the two articles in the *Express*. But I begin this examination with an initial qualification: the re-creation of that cultural milieu involves the construction of a seduction narrative of my own. That narrative takes a reader from Milton's *Paradise Lost* to the contents of a puzzling personal letter; from the sentimental novel of seduction to a young man being tarred, feathered, and publicly humiliated on the streets of Amherst; from the rhetorical hyperbole of the antebellum moral reform movement to the minimalist poetics of Dickinson. As this varied catalog suggests, my own narrative route is often circuitous. However, every apparent detour and digression, every limning of a circumference, returns to this ubiquitous center: the antebellum discursive formation that is "seduction."

Briefly, I want to return to the 1847 Mount Holyoke commencement and focus on one particularly rigorous examination that graduating students were expected to undergo. On the Wednesday of commencement week, the major examination of the graduating class concerned Milton's *Paradise Lost*. The details were not reported in the newspaper, but presumably this was the same examination that had been in place for the previous four years. For example, an *Express* reporter writing about the August 8, 1845, commencement describes "an examination of nearly or quite the entire graduating class in *Paradise Lost*, under the direction of Miss Lyon," during which "the poem was analyzed, some of its more striking beauties pointed out, and its agreement with scripture shown by reference to lines and texts." The reporter observes that "it must have been a thorough discipline to render the class so familiar with its structures." The commencement report for the following year, printed in the August 14, 1846, edition of the *Express*, goes into further detail about what was required of that graduating class's hermeneutic skills as they were applied to Milton's text: "The analysis of the 'Argument' was full and discriminating. It comprised a sketch of the ends designed by the Poet, and the means used to reach them, the characters that figure and the parts they act. On the learned allusions of the text, the Encyclopedia had been patiently consulted. And from the Scriptures, passages were read elucidating the theology of the classic. Evidently the young ladies had forgiven the severity of the poet to his daughters." The would-be graduate of Mount Holyoke apparently was expected to leave with as thorough a knowledge of *Paradise Lost* as she had of the King James Bible.

Paradise Lost is the quintessential narrative of seduction. In Milton's epic poem, as in Genesis, Satan is the first tempter of woman into sin: he is the epitome of successful seduction. It is Satan's subtle persuasion of Eve, his *rhetorical* seduction of her, that introduces into the discourse of humanity the possibility of using linguistic signs for the purposes of deception. And it is precisely that initial satanic cunning—the playing on a feminine vulnerability to flattery and verbal wile—that deprives the Christian search for redemption of its ultimate reliability, leaving it instead to construct a massive metaphorical and typological apparatus that can cope with the semantics of deceit initiated by the Edenic interloper. Ironically, therefore, it is also that satanic cunning, that awareness of the deceptively seductive powers of rhetoric, that first makes poetry possible. If living in a Christian dispensation of necessity requires an awareness of the dangerous power of satanic seduction, then living in a poetic dispensation requires the simultaneous awareness of the attractiveness of that seduction.

In some ways, however, Satan's rhetorical seduction of Eve is a decidedly ambiguous affair, especially when the Genesis narrative of the Fall is read through the reinterpretive lens of *Paradise Lost*. The Miltonic narrative of the Fall subtly implicates Eve herself as a candidate for the first successful seducer, for when the snake-dissembling Satan, creeping through Eden on his mission to ruin mankind, catches sight of the solitary Eve,

Such Pleasure took the serpent to behold
This Flowrie Plat, the sweet recess of Eve
Thus earlie, thus alone; her Heav'nly form
Angelic, but more soft and Feminine,
Her graceful Innocence, her every Air
Of gesture or lest action overawd
His Malice, and with rapine sweet bereav'd
His fierceness of the fierce intent it brought:
That space the Evil one abstracted stood
From his own evil, and for the time remaind
Stupidly good, of enmitie disarm'd,
Of guile, of hate, of envie, of revenge;[7]

If Eve, in all her innocence, has the capacity for "rapine sweet," then the famous scene of Eve's fascination by satanic flattery is actually the secondary scene of seduction. The pivotal point of Miltonic history is this first scene of seduction, the moment when Satan, stunned into immobility, unobtrusively observes the beauty of Eve and is thereby *tempted* to be her seducer. It is eminently possible to view Satan as a tempter tempted. Indeed, it might well be argued that from *Paradise Lost* onward, the literary representation of woman predetermines (or perhaps overdetermines) her as the agent of sin through the desire she inspires rather than through any desire she experiences.

The third seduction in Milton's Eden also depends for its effectiveness on the desire that Eve inspires, specifically that which she evokes within Adam. Eve seduces him through the medium of her own seductiveness, physical and verbal charms working in irresistible tandem:

> She gave him of that fair enticing Fruit
> With liberal hand: he scrupl'd not to eat
> Against his better knowledge, not deceav'd,
> But fondly overcome with Femal charm.[8]

As every subsequent literary seduction scene can be read as an allegory of the Fall, we must be alert to the ambiguities implicit in these first lapsarian seductions. In particular, the Edenic seductions of *Paradise Lost* complicate questions of blame insofar as they implicate the victim's subtle culpability, since she appears to be already susceptible to the straying. What makes Eve such a fascinating character is her paradoxical doubleness: she is the seductive seducee. Whatever Milton's narrative intention, his representation of an Eve who, even in her passivity, powerfully controls male figures might be far from negative for the woman reader of his text. Indeed, the figure of a latently subversive Eve, the first "fallen" woman, proved particularly useful to the antebellum woman writer seeking a suitable model of empowerment. After all, Eve's disobedience is the first challenge to patriarchal authority: a direct challenge to God and man. Feminist critics propose that Victorian novels by women are subtle rewritings of the Fall myth that conflate women's sexuality, power, and hunger in a new literary order of transgression.[9] In general, the notion of trespass comes to represent a significant source of power for the woman writer. More specifically, Eve's desire, which of course includes her *desirability*, often comes to represent that decentering power. Of course, the appropriation and rewriting of the Fall myth was especially necessary for women poets of the era, who had to confront Milton's bogey—the fact that he is the most dangerous of poetic precursors—as a direct threat to their corporeal *and* aesthetic autonomy.[10]

In the Miltonic universe of *Paradise Lost*, the Fall has major consequences not only for the users of language but also for language itself. In order to effect any physical seduction, the would-be seducer must first "produce felicitous language."[11] In other words, the successful seducer must be an exemplary rhetorician. Indeed, a rhetorician might well be defined as a seducer of language, for in the etymological sense of "seduction" (*seducere*) the rhetorician purposely leads language astray. Throughout *Paradise Lost*, the fallen Satan is an exceptional rhetorician, an exemplary seducer, a prototypical poet. Similarly, as the fallen Adam and Eve soon learn, the immediate consequences of eating from the Tree of Knowledge are the death of humankind *and* the birth of rhetoric. Milton's Fall is therefore also metaphorical to the degree that it signifies a fall *into* metaphor. What enters the lapsarian world with death is the deviation of language into a series of seductive possibilities: language as an unnecessary but delicious ornament; language as the means to covert insinuation; language as a means to the use and manipulation of others; language as rhetoric pure and simple. For Milton, language determined by rhetorical intention is corrupt because rhetoric necessitates the deviation of words from their originally perfect correspondence with nature into a misleading, inherently evil entity.

The attitude of Milton, the religious poet who found the uses of rhetoric intrinsically satanic, toward his own poetry is therefore distinctly paradoxical.[12] That paradox is implicit in *Paradise Lost*, which often seems to be the epic narrative of its author's regret that poetry is possible. While Milton's doubled attitude toward rhetoric can easily be overlooked by the reader predisposed to religious orthodoxy, it was blatantly apparent to the later romantic poets, who, more committed to problems of art than problems of faith, would willfully misread the epic poem as Milton's troubled satanic manifesto.[13] This might lead one to suspect that a young, quasi-romantic poet, herself a distinctly unorthodox Christian, who was probably quite familiar with the text of *Paradise Lost* and its deviations from the original Genesis text, would be tempted to read the poem in a similarly critical light.

And Dickinson appears to have done just that. During her year at Mount Holyoke the significance of the text might well have been instilled in her. It was probably unavoidable. Certainly, there was a copy of *Paradise Lost* in the Dickinson family library from which the poet directly quoted in a number of letters. As Jack Capps observes, "On two separate occasions [in L. 304] she refers to Eve's reluctant departure from Eden, and both instances seem closer to Milton's description of the expulsion than the concluding verses of the third chapter of Genesis."[14] It is likely that Dickinson did just what a Mount Holyoke student was expected to do: reinterpret the King James Bible through the filter of its Miltonic rewriting.

What Dickinson seems to have derived most from Milton is a paradoxical attitude toward her own art, a sense that her calling as a poet was simultaneously an invitation to sin. This attitude is most evident in her frequently troubled identification with the figure of Eve. Of course, it was in a distinctly playful vein that Dickinson confided in an early letter, "I have lately come to the conclusion that I am Eve, alias Mrs Adam. You know there is no account of her death in the Bible, and why am I not Eve?" (L. 9). But the recurrence of Eve imagery elsewhere[15] makes it one of her most significant tropes. The Eve figure often emerges in epistolary contexts that associate a "calling" to poetry with a dangerous external temptation ambiguously resisted. This is the religiously heretical Dickinson who observes that "I dont wonder that good angels weep— and bad ones sing songs" (L. 30) and who famously comments on what we may well assume is her poetic vocation, "I have dared to do strange things—bold things, and have asked no advice from any—I have heeded beautiful tempters, yet do not think I am wrong" (L. 35).

The image of the "beautiful tempters" is reworked in other vividly exploratory letters of Dickinson's late adolescence:

> I think of the perfect happiness I experienced while I felt I was an heir of heaven as of a delightful dream, out of which the Evil one bid me wake & again return to the world & its pleasures. Would that I had not listened to his winning words! . . . But the world allured me & in an unguarded moment I listened to her syren voice. From that moment I seemed to lose my interest in heavenly things by degrees. (L. 11)[16]

In this letter, Dickinson imagines herself a type of the tempted Eve, an identification repeated in a letter to her friend Jane Humphries: while charitable works, she writes, may provide the opportunity

> for turning my back to this very sinful, and wicked world[, s]omehow or other I incline to other things—and Satan covers them up with flowers, and I reach out to pick them. The path of duty looks very ugly indeed— and the place where *I* want to go more aimiable—a great deal—it is so much easier to do wrong than right—so much pleasanter to be evil than good. (L. 30)

This is an Eve susceptible to the direct seductions of rhetorical possibility, the latent poet slowly surrendering to her daemon. Moreover, she seems virtually incapable of resisting the seductive temptations of the world. Even when she does succeed in resisting a specific temptation, the victory is, to say the least, ambiguous:

> A friend I love *so* dearly came and asked me to ride in the woods, the sweet-still woods, and I wanted to exceedingly—I told him I could not go,

and he said he was disappointed—he wanted me very much—then the tears came into my eyes, tho' I tried to choke them back, and he said I *could*, and *should* go, and it seemed to me unjust. Oh I struggled with great temptation, and it cost me much of denial, but I think in the end I conquered, not a glorious victory Abiah. . . . I had read of Christ's temptations, and how they were like our own, only he did'nt sin; I wondered if *one* was like mine, and whether it made him angry—I couldnt make up my mind; do you think he ever did? (L. 36)

In the same letter, a Dickinson deadly serious in her playfulness asks her correspondent "Where do you think I've strayed, and from what new errand returned? I have come from '*to* and *fro*, and walking up, and down' the same place that Satan hailed from, when God asked him where he'd been, but not to illustrate further I tell you I have been dreaming, dreaming a *golden* dream, with eyes all the while wide open."

Interestingly, she chooses to analyze her reprobate condition in the terms of an interpretive problem that she cannot solve and that leaves her "one of the lingering *bad* ones." She continues, "So do *I* slink away, and pause, and ponder, and ponder, and pause, and do work without knowing why . . . and I ask what this message *means* that they ask for so very eagerly, *you* know of this depth, and fulness, will you *try* to tell me about it?" (L. 36). This process of continual pausing and pondering, of asking what the message means, seems not unlike the process the poet requires her readers to pursue. But what makes Dickinson's association, in this letter, between the inability to interpret and the satanic persona so fascinating is its recurrence in other letters of the same apprentice period. In another letter to Abiah Root, Dickinson engages in a poetic whimsy and then says, defensively, "Now my dear friend, let me tell you that these last thoughts are fictions—vain imaginations to lead astray foolish young women. They are flowers of speech, they both *make,* and *tell* deliberate falsehoods, avoid them as the snake, and turn aside as from the *Bottle* snake, and I dont *think* you will be harmed" (L. 31). In the course of discussing her various "mistakes" and her tendency to "sin," Dickinson essentially demands that Abiah, in turn, play the role of Eve to her own female Satan, whose final signature will be, appropriately, "Your very sincere, and *wicked* friend." There is an assumption of complicity here—an assumption that the initially tempted can and has duly become the tempter of another. In a letter written during approximately the same week, Dickinson emphasizes the contagion of her art to another correspondent: "You are out of the way of temptation—and out of the way of the tempter—I did'nt mean to make you wicked—but I was—and am—and shall be—and I was with you so much that I could'nt help contaminate." At the same time, she empha-

sizes the sheer inevitability of her surrender to the process to which she has succumbed: "Is it wicked to talk so Jane—what *can* I say that isn't? Out of a wicked
heart cometh wicked words" (L. 30).

In many of these early letters, as Margaret Homans has observed, Dickinson moves easily between Eve and Satan as equivalent metaphorical figures. The
assumption is that Eve is Satan's accomplice and therefore a tempter in her own
right—in short, the tempted temptress. As such, she is a significantly doubled
figure, an affirmatively subversive presence, and perhaps attractive to the woman
poet for precisely that reason. The attractiveness of the Eve figure to the woman
poet is that her seductiveness, while potentially her undoing, is simultaneously
the means to an equally powerful seduction of her own. At the heart of her apparent powerlessness, at her weakest point of surrender, is a significant genera-
tor of power. And the passive power of luring, delighting, and pleasing need not
signify weakness if it eventually confers the power to persuade actively. This
entire seduction scenario, of course, also offers a significant commentary on the
possibilities of language. According to Homans's analysis of the Fall myth in
Dickinson, "Adam becomes the traditional symbol for literal language in which
words are synonymous with meaning, but Eve is the first to question that synonymity, the first critic, the mother of irony. It is in this sense that she is similar
to Satan, and in making tempter and tempted synonymous Dickinson is recognizing this aspect of her inheritance from Eve."[17]

What emerges from that early Dickinson correspondence concerned with
her poetic vocation is an almost Miltonic association of poetry, or of rhetoric in
general, with intrinsic evil. Since the motor of poetry, metaphor, is the giving
to an object a name that belongs to something else, the art of poetry is the art
of the lie. In any Christian dispensation, "beautiful tempters" must be the off-
spring of Satan, the Father of Lies. In choosing to be a poet, Dickinson comes
to see herself as a Mother of Lies, a necessary return to Eve. This is a consistent
Dickinson, the same who enjoys reporting a nephew who "tells that the Clock
purrs and the Kitten ticks" because "he inherits his Uncle Emily's ardor for the
lie" (L. 315), and who delights in the successful dupings of the commercial
world. Commenting on her father's suspicion that he has been defrauded by the
local steel market, she says, "I cannot stop smiling, though it is hours since, that
even our steelyard will not tell the truth" (L. 311). Perhaps this celebration of
the lie is what lends such resonance to the story Dickinson told T. W. Higginson
of her brother concealing Longfellow's *Kavanagh* under the piano cover for her
in order to deceive their father.[18] It seems such a characteristic, appropriate gesture that it is not difficult to imagine the young poet reveling in such a deception. Indeed, either way her narrative is one of deception: if the story is true, her

father was her dupe; if not, the dupe is Higginson. We would do well to remember, as Dickinson's readers, that the enjoyment of deception is prerequisite not merely for the poet but also for the love of poetry.

Of course, there were more immediate examples of specifically literary seduction available for Dickinson's recreational perusal in the family library. While the underlying plot structure of many ballads concerns an archetypal demonic figure who tempts, seduces, betrays, and victimizes women, the seduction trope is most crucial to romanticism. The romantic seducer is, interestingly, not necessarily gender specific; if the lineage of Satan incorporates the male seducer, the Dons Giovanni and Juan, Eve's legacy is doubled: the female seducer is exemplified by Keats's La Belle Dame Sans Merci and Coleridge's Geraldine, the female seducee by Hawthorne's Hester Prynne, Eliot's Hetty Sorrel, and, later, Hardy's Tess D'Urberville. The romantic seducee, who proves always all the more seductive to her seducer through the fact of her innocence, is the naive twin of her perniciously active other, and their differentiation is often only the matter of a problematically assignable intentionality.

Joanne Feit Diehl notes that Dickinson's poetry, which is variously preoccupied with the self's relation to nature, the imagination's power in the presence of death, the psychic voyage, and the heroic questing, is firmly grounded in the romantic tradition and observes that "implicit in the Romantic view of the poet as quester is a self that pursues the dangerous, seductive female." Diehl discusses the problem of how the female poet deals with "the desire for and resentment of the seductive female"[19] by adapting the terminology of Harold Bloom's "anxiety of influence" and arguing that since for Dickinson both precursor poet and muse are inevitably male, there is detectable in her poetry a composite figure, a masculine erotic other equivalent to Keats's muse or goddess, that she anxiously deflects and invites simultaneously. Dickinson's poetic tautness, her rhetorical power, is a consequence of the tension between her rejection of precursor authority figured as male and her need to tap the resources of a passionate inspiration that she unconsciously identifies with the assertive power of male sexuality. Ultimately, Diehl's Dickinson comes to occupy the position of both seducer and seducee in order to create an adequate field of power: "She entices her lover-adversary into death so that she may achieve dominance; she becomes, through her reassuring her prince, a beguiling murderess at last able to assert her own supremacy."[20]

Diehl's study is valuable and does partially explain the shadowy male figure detectable in so many of Dickinson's poems. However, her adapted Bloomian theory does not place Dickinson firmly enough in the romantic tradition, especially the romantic obsession with seduction. That would require a more systematic study of the ultimate fruit of romanticism, the modern novel.

In particular, it would require an analysis of the influence of Richardson's *Clarissa* on a host of American imitators. In early-nineteenth-century America, novels invariably reproduced the classic Richardson scenario, each prose narrative tracing the dangerous mating dance of the villainous seducer and the virtuous maiden to its denouement in marriage or death. But the fact that both the character portrayals and the early plots of sentimental fiction center so often on seduction also suggests that the representation of the act itself was evidence of a more specific female discontent regarding the condition of American society.

In her analysis of the postrevolutionary American novel, Cathy Davidson notes the particular significance of the printer's advertising technique in the publishing of William Hill Brown's early novel *The Power of Sympathy* (1789): "Even a casual glance at the Thomas's typography . . . registers the prominent placement of the word 'SEDUCTION.' This key word is centered in the middle of the page; occupies an entire line; and is written in the darkest, clearest, boldest type on the page. Even the spacing between each letter gives further prominence to the word. What we have here is another graphic illustration (literally and figuratively) of the role of the printer in the creation of the American novel and in the 'seduction' of the American reading public."[21] But "seduction" is not merely a key word that helps us understand the techniques of commercial printing and advertising in the selling of the postrevolutionary novel: it is also the essential *keyword* toward any comprehension of the major fictional strategies of woman writers from the postrevolutionary through the antebellum period. Seduction became the focal point of so many early American sentimental novels because it was a succinct metaphor for the gender power inequalities of the contemporary society. As Davidson neatly puts it, "Seduction spun so many of these sentimental plots precisely because seduction set forth and summed up crucial aspects of the society—the author's, the characters', the contemporary readers' (especially if they were women)—that did not have to be delineated beyond the bare facts of the seduction itself. Seduction thereby becomes a metonymic reduction of the whole world in which women operated and were operated upon."[22] The fictional portrayal of sentimental seduction, almost always represented as the temptation of the central female character, with narrative suspense generated by the threat of her succumbing to the charms of the predatory male, is never merely a sexual interaction. A primary economic component is also implied in the fictional seduction: the eventual success of the seducer depends on his superior social status, and therefore on the greater economic and educational prospects of the middle-class American male. The scene of seduction is invariably a scene of inequality, and its fictional portrayal implicitly critiques the distribution of power and evaluation of worth in nineteenth-century bourgeois culture.

The social critique implicit in the so-called novel of seduction produces fundamental ambiguities in the reader's response to the genre.[23] Not least because the central female character (in postrevolutionary sentimental fiction often a representation of irresistible innocence, in later antebellum sensationalism more likely a model of unfathomable deviousness) inevitably establishes a field of fatal attraction not only for the novel's male characters but also for the female reader. This raises the interesting question of who is being seduced by whom and points to a complex ambiguity at the heart of any sentimental novel that turns on the plot mechanism of seduction: to maintain the sympathy of the reader, the victim of the attempted seduction has to be *seductively* attractive to that reader. This leaves the reader uncomfortably occupying an extratextual location that duplicates the seducer's position within the text. The ambiguous position of the reader vis-à-vis such a text, empathizing with the powerless while participating in an exercise of power, both seducer and seducee, is paradoxical in the extreme. It is precisely this reader-implicating ambiguity that permits the novel of seduction its subversive subtext, its suggestive critique of social hierarchies.

Of course, for the unmarried young women who were their initial audience, sentimental novels that turned on the plot mechanism of seduction also fulfilled a precise social function: they allowed their readers a preliminary testing of the possibilities and dangers inherent in the courtship process by presenting the diametrically opposed twin poles of choice—seduction or marriage. However, the actual message of the fiction is hardly univocal; the "weak" woman may succumb to the seducer, but the portrayal of her circumstances can elicit significant sympathy for her from the reader. Moreover, while seduction ostensibly represents female powerlessness, the representation of that powerlessness in a fictional setting, combined with an intimate portrayal of the female character's choices in the charged world of courtship, permitted a vicarious identification with the character from the reader's paradoxically powerful position of shared authorial omniscience. Thus, the reader of sentimental fiction could acquire a degree of power through her covertly sympathetic identification with a scene of powerlessness. The "sentimental" female reader really could have it both ways. The seduction novel's oblique social critique reinforced the appeal of the genre to its female audience. The novel's subversive subtext was its subtle questioning of the societal rules apparently textually affirmed by the fall of a female character and by its analysis of the sociological or socioeconomic dimensions of a seduction that signified an unfairly unequal hierarchy of social power and, by extension, social worth. Its implicit critique of a more generalized cultural misogyny was bolstered by the hint of possible reform; such inequalities could be rectified by legally enforceable punishment of the seducer and, even more importantly, superior education for women.

The basic ambiguities implicit in literary seduction would become explicit in the antebellum period. Such early American novels as *The Power of Sympathy* (1789) and its best-selling seduction-centered successors, Susanna Rowson's *Charlotte Temple* (1791) and Hannah Webster Foster's *The Coquette* (1797) (the latter two sustained their incredible popularity throughout the antebellum period), were superseded by a stream of more sensational literature whose agendas included nothing remotely covert. Although the seduction plot virtually disappeared from sentimental fiction by 1818, its basic concerns survived in the later sensational design. The very titles of Alice Cary's novels *Hagar, a Story of Today* (1852) and *Married, not Mated* (1859) clearly delineate a concern with the assumption of extramarital power by their central female characters. Meanwhile, the latent agenda of many early novels of seduction (that the seducee could become a potent seducer in her own right) was realized in later novels such as Lillie Devereux Blake's *Southwold* (1859), whose heroine, Medora Fielding, attracts men in order to destroy them, and Louisa May Alcott's *Behind a Mask; or, A Woman's Power* (1866), whose heroine, Jean Muir, wreaks vengeance on the male sex after first attracting them through her apparently transparent innocence. David Reynolds notes that in many sensational novels of the period, "the fallen women became a fantasy figure of vindictive violence and unrestrained sexuality. It was taken for granted that a woman, once seduced and released from the constrictions of female propriety, was capable of becoming more ferocious and more sexually aggressive than a man."[24] In these novels we can glimpse a repeated paradigm: the assumption that seduction, far from being an incontrovertible disaster for the female victim, could be a highly ambiguous boon insofar as the surrender of a false, socially legislated vulnerability could accommodate the release of untapped power and vital strength from within the main female character. When D. H. Lawrence claimed that "the greatest triumph a woman can have, especially an American woman, is the triumph of seducing a man,"[25] he may have been closer than he knew to a fundamental truth of American literature, at least as it had been written by and for women.

The fictional scene of seduction was thus always double-edged. Seduction, conventionally the representation of female weakness before rapacious male sexuality, could simultaneously be associated, through a subtext reinforced by the reading experience, with the exercise of female power. If seduction "served as both metaphor and metonymy in summing up the society's contradictory views of women,"[26] then those contradictory views, inevitably internalized by the middle-class female reader, found an expressive outlet in the paradoxical scene of fictional seduction, a male/female power interaction of fundamental ambiguity. Moreover, the paradox of the scene of seduction must have been all too evident to the woman writer, whose sentimental novel *of* seduction also had to *be* seductive, her fiction's success depending as it did on the rhetorical seduction, the linguistic enticing, of its reader. The novel of seduction, so often attempting to reinforce a moral lesson, could only do so through an enticing series of episodes that duplicated the condemned immoral center, the sequential unraveling of those episodes effecting a narrative seduction of the reader that effectively undermined the desired moral message. The social ambiguities of the scene of seduction were therefore probably heightened in the woman writer by the very fact of her being a writer in the first place. And the positioning of the woman writer would also simultaneously increase her awareness of the fluid connections between the "real" and "fictional" rhetorics of her society. Often, as in the overlapping of the novel of seduction and the moral reform movement, the writer must have found those rhetorical worlds uncannily paralleled.

The mutual interpenetration of printed text and social structure is everywhere apparent in antebellum society. In her excellent study of the period, *Confidence Men and Painted Ladies*, Karen Halttunnen examines how the images of the "confidence man" and the "painted lady" became a cultural personification of the pervasive duplicity of an emergent nineteenth-century middle-class and notes that "in the classic antebellum tale of seduction, he [the confidence man] . . . leads the youth into a gorgeous theater—the seducer's natural habitat, for he himself is a skilled actor."[27] Halttunnen argues that an attempt to counter societal duplicity, once more figured as potential seduction, by embodying sincerity in cultural forms collapsed, inevitably, into formalized rituals of insincerity and that "the sentimental demand for a true courtesy that would betray no stage effect ultimately contributed to the theatricality of social life in the parlor."[28] A pervasive cultural concern at the potential insincerity of everyday life became a fascination with the theatrical art of everyday life. The evolution of acceptable theatrical frameworks produced as its finest ritual construct the dramaturgic structure that was the "genteel performance," an essentially fictional code of behavior sufficient to support the duplicities of the contemporary society. This social "performance," although thought "natural," was actually derived primarily from the fictional behavior portrayed in the myriad style manuals that were necessarily perused by the middle class in the interests of achieving and maintaining social acceptability. By 1850 the codes that supported middle-class society borrowed significantly from fiction and inevitably included the rhetorical code of seduction, now to be played out more overtly in the "gorgeous theater" that is the scene of antebellum life.

In many ways, society and the socioliterary had established a certain equilibrium in the antebellum period. Society was effectively represented in a sentimental literature that, in time, through its pervasive commercial appeal and obvious popularity, came to influence the social structures that initially inspired it. The line between fiction and reality was especially transitive as regards seduction; if the fictional seductions of the sentimental novel were primarily a metaphor for larger power inequalities in postrevolutionary society, then the moral reform movement, for example, suggests the active reemergence or effective literalization of that fictional rhetoric into the discourse of antebellum society. Of course, the similarity between the goals of the moral reformers and the concerns of a spectrum of women novelists before and during the antebellum period is scarcely coincidental. They shared an interest not only in the social inequities figured in the scene of seduction but also in the potential rearrangement of the power dynamic that seduction offered.

Barton St. Armand is surely correct when he asserts that "only by charting Dickinson's debt to her own time can we truly be sure how she may have anticipated current aesthetic and philosophical concerns."[29] In *Emily Dickinson and Her Culture*, he usefully links the poet's aesthetic and philosophical concerns with the contemporary dogmas and cults of Calvinism, transcendentalism, Gothicism, occultism, and Ruskinism and examines how Dickinson may have taken aspects of popular culture and through "a process of personalization, internalization, exaggeration, and inversion"[30] come to "italicize" them. It is therefore surprising that St. Armand does not pursue that process of Dickinsonian bricolage into an examination of her use of the available cultural vocabulary provided by contemporary reform movements, in particular the moral reform movement. It may be more than a little useful to pursue David Reynolds's thesis that "moral reform literature offered a wealth of imagery and themes . . . precisely because, in its most imaginative forms, it was, paradoxically enough, immoral and ambiguous," and his observation that some moral reformers used "didactic rhetoric as a protective shield for highly unconventional explorations of tabooed psychological and spiritual areas."[31] Although Reynolds argues that there was a stylization of reform devices by antebellum writers who took the reform impulse and reform imagery as rhetorical materials for their own art, and while he elsewhere discusses contemporary female influences on Dickinson's poetry, he does not connect the two by discussing the possibility of any specific influence of female moral reform rhetoric on the poet. This is unfortunate, because an analysis of Dickinson's rhetoric as viewed through the contemporary lens provided by the moral reform movement can shed considerable light on her habitual poetic strategies.

The moral reform movement was most active in the period from 1830 to 1860 and primarily aimed to eliminate seduction from contemporary society.

This aim required that the movement focus on a double target, as there were clearly two subjects in need of moral reforming: the actual or potential female victim and the actual or potential male seducer. To that end, the movement advocated not only the abolition of prostitution, which was regarded, somewhat naively, as purely a consequence of seduction, but also the exposure of male seducers, who were viewed not simply as perpetrators of acts of seduction but also the root cause of myriad social ills.[32] Originally founded in 1834 as the New York Female Reform Society, within five years the movement "boasted some 445 female auxiliaries, principally in Greater New England."[33] The voice of the Female Reform Society was its journal, the *Advocate of Moral Reform*, which by 1837 was publishing 20,000 copies semimonthly. That relatively large readership was neither disinterested nor passive, but a primarily female audience that responded enthusiastically to the journal's appeal for correspondence that would recount specific instances of seduction and name the male seducers involved. This strategy influenced the popular press of the day. For example, to return to the Amherst locality, the *Hampshire Gazette* reports the case of a hysterical young woman found wandering the streets of Williamstown and notes that "the unfortunate heroine of the mysterious affair . . . is probably another of the thousand victims of seduction." The following week's issue follows up the story by observing that "the Pittsfield papers state that the betrayer of the artless girl is Edward Bulger. As no statute law can probably reach him, it is proper that the public press should herald his infamy, the whole length and breadth of the land." In so doing the *Gazette*, and the public press in general, not only reproduced the cause of the moral reform movement but also, by assuming the typical rhetorical flourishes of that movement's literature—"the thousand victims of seduction," "betrayer of the artless girl," "herald his infamy"—duplicated the typical rhetoric of its journal mouthpiece.[34]

The movement's enthusiastic female audience would find in each issue of the journal a petition demanding that seduction and adultery be punished as crimes. In time, the dedicated campaigning of that readership would achieve significant results. After major petition drives, and having earned the support of liberal male reformers such as *New York Tribune* editor Horace Greeley, the movement won passage of antiseduction laws in New York and Massachusetts. In 1848, that year of significant political upheaval elsewhere in the world, the movement's political agitation resulted in the passing of a bill in the Albany legislature. "The Act to Punish Seduction as a Crime" stated that "any man who shall under promise of marriage seduce and have illicit connection with any unmarried female of previous chaste character shall be guilty of a misdemeanor, and upon conviction shall be punished by imprisonment."[35] As the legal punishment of the seducer was one of the primary goals of moral reform, the passage of such an act is proof of the success of the movement's agitation and its ability to mobilize its membership as a political force. It also provides evidence that the pervasive influence of the moral reform movement in antebellum society should not be underestimated.

The predominantly middle-class women who made up the membership of the moral reform movement in the cities did most of their active campaigning in lower-class areas where prostitution was rife. Unlike the earlier male reformers, who typically portrayed the prostitute as a source of depravity and a threat to public health, these women claimed sympathy with the "fallen" woman, who was not be condemned but uplifted, restored to true womanhood. The attack on female depravity had metamorphosed into a challenge to male licentiousness. In working-class neighborhoods, the bourgeois reformers were to experience the culture shock of coming into contact with women whose acquaintance with male abuse was especially vivid. They therefore, of necessity, confronted a societal ill previously unrecognizable from within the enclosure that was their assigned sphere in middle-class antebellum culture. Studying the causes and effects of prostitution, the reformers became objective observers of their own condition and, in due course, participant-observers who recognized that the inequities of antebellum society pervaded all social classes. The prevalent sexual double standard was simply *italicized* in working-class prostitution. If prostitutes were forced into selling themselves as a commodity as compensation for obvious economic inequities, those same inequities were evident in the reformers' own situation. Indeed, they had become initially involved in the moral reform movement *because* there was virtually no other socially sanctioned outlet for their political abilities and talents. The prostitute was the most visible embodiment of the pervasive double standard and thus an effective symbol of a subjugation of women that transcended social class. Prostitution, signifying sexual victimization and female powerlessness, was a convenient representation of the more general antebellum female condition. It was not necessarily the case that in the prostitute the moral reformer caught a glimpse of herself subtly reflected; rather, in the figure of that "fallen" woman the reformer was surprised and horrified to recognize the oblique mirroring of her own essentially powerless situation.

There was a great deal at stake in the redemption of this "fallen" woman. The ideal of female moral superiority that dominated prescriptive literature addressed to middle- and upper-class women in the earlier part of the nineteenth century had necessarily exiled the older image of the seductive Eve. As D'Emilio and Freedman note in *Intimate Matters*,

> In a reversal of the traditional western European view that woman—like Eve, the temptress—embodied carnal desire . . . early-nineteenth century moralists suggested that women had fewer sexual desires than did men.

... The new ideal of sexually pure womanhood created an antithetical model: the so-called fallen women who defied female nature or failed to resist men's advances. In popular culture, seduction could be literally deadly. American folk songs, unlike earlier British ballads that tended to celebrate women's sexual independence, stressed the sexual vulnerability of women. Those who were seduced by men would ultimately die, often at the hands of their lovers.[36]

D'Emilio and Freedman point out that popular ballads published in American almanacs after 1799 dealt with the issue of women seduced by men in understanding terms, and that in New England magazines of the late eighteenth century, both fiction and nonfiction writers had sympathized with women who, either through force or ignorance, had illicit sexual relations. But the female transgressor who could once—like her male counterpart—have repented and been reintegrated into the community was now tainted for life by the shifting paradigm of a nineteenth-century culture that had redefined her fall as being from a higher plane than that allegedly occupied by man and that had thus rendered her, literally, irredeemable. In this way, the prevalent social ideal of female purity was essentially enforced by the extreme social stigma attached to the woman who "fell." Attacking the stigma potentially demolished the ideal. The moral reformers' activist redemption of the "fallen" woman was the means of exhuming the larger subterranean legacy of Eve, and of female sexuality in general, in the further interest of redefining an increasingly stultified "female nature."

The moral reform movement's straightforward commitment to eliminating the sexual double standard (at its most basic, the assumption that men could be promiscuous while women had to remain chaste or face the direst of consequences) therefore concealed its unwritten manifesto, an agenda of reform that would culminate in equality for women. Even though seduction implies a degree of mutuality, notions of choice are complicated when power centrally defines the relationship between the participants (many of the sexual encounters that nineteenth-century reformers considered "seduction" would today be categorized as a rape annulled by an ambiguous assertion of consent). Only through exposure could the male seducer be placed on the same level as his victim. That subtle emphasis on leveling and equality explains how so many suffragists began in the ranks of the moral reform movement. Middle-class women used the movement as the first socially acceptable outlet for their own frustrations and resentments; it was a socially permissible means of publishing brutal narratives of male abuse and sympathetic catalogs of female suffering and, simultaneously, urging a society-wide restitution that had subtle applicability to their own condition.[37] At the same time, the movement's focus on an ill that befell working-class others also permitted the protective distancing of the reformers from the wider cultural implications of their own powerful social critique.

The rhetoric of moral reform—the movement's recognition of "deep laid schemes of treachery against female innocence"; its urgings of society to "brand the seducer with the infamy that he deserves"; and its typically hyperbolized warning, "Admit him not to your house, hold no converse with him, warn others of him, permit not your friends to have fellowship with him, mark him as an evildoer, stamp him as a villain and exclaim, 'Behold the Seducer' "—was the verbal manifestation of a widespread female anger at social powerlessness, and it directly addressed the existing power dynamic of antebellum society.[38] For while the narratives of the movement represented women as passive victims of male lust, the language of moral reform evoked the possibilities of female power: a power to avenge seduction (by publishing the name of the male responsible); a power to control the consequences of seduction (by treating the victim as precisely that, with no stigma of blame); and a power to reform the root cause of seduction itself (by creating a more equitable society that would circumvent the power hierarchies that facilitate its operation). Thus, while "seduction" came to function for the moral reform movement as a complex metaphor representing the hierarchical male/female relations that supported antebellum society, the actual scene of seduction, activating as it did those inequities, could be transformed into an assertion of female power. The message of the moral reform movement, and its own literal example, was that a powerful female voice could make itself heard, even from the depths of male-instituted corruption. It was the recognition that at the ultimate limit of female powerlessness lay a reservoir of energy that could be tapped and expressed as female power. Of course, the submission of the self to a superior force as preliminary to vital self-assertion is an essentially Christian message. The moral reform movement reproduced that message but rewrote it more politically as a morally secular aesthetic of assertion, combining the vocabulary of religious conversion and the scene of seduction in a potent fusion of powerful intent.

Perhaps unfortunately, the protofeminist assault on societal inequalities contained within the rhetoric of moral reform occurred within the constrictive frame of an already-given fictional vocabulary of female victimization. Tales of innocent women forced into prostitution were a cultural commonplace, and the seduction of poor, innocent girls by salaciously evil aristocratic rakes was one of the most popular themes of nineteenth-century melodrama. Antebellum literature offers a thousand examples of the female character whose reputation is ruined by a villainous male, the characterization of whom, over time, assumes stereotypical proportions. As moral reform "feminists" fixed inexorably on the

familiar, recognizable Victorian image of the male seducer and the female innocent, the corrupter and his unfortunate victim, they had, of necessity, to deal
in literary stereotypes. The depraved seducer, motivated purely by lust, playing
on the naive trust and innocent romanticism of his intended victim, is something of a literary stock figure, the Lovelace of Richardson's *Clarissa* perpetually
recontextualized. So while seduction was an all-too-real fact of antebellum life,
the figure of the seducer presented by the moral reform movement was essentially a fiction, at least in his generalized portrayal in the movement's literature.

Of course, it would be erroneous to assert that Emily Dickinson was in any
way directly influenced by the *cause* of moral reform. Indeed, it might be more
plausible that her poetry was sometimes a reaction to contemporary reform
movements for which she often expressed nothing but disdain. The fact that her
father was the respected Amherst executive officer of the Hampshire County
Temperance Union in the 1850s probably only exacerbated a more general cyni-
cism obvious in the gleeful sarcasm of her personal correspondence: "The Sew-
ing Society has commenced again—and held its first meeting last week—now
all the poor will be helped—the cold warmed—the warm cooled—the hungry
fed—the thirsty attended to—the ragged clothed—and this suffering—tumbled
down world will be helped to it's feet again—which will be quite pleasant to
all. I dont attend—notwithstanding my high approbation—which must puzzle
the public exceedingly" (L. 30). That same tone comes through more interestingly in her poetry, most memorably in poem 401:

> What Soft—Cherubic Creatures—
> These Gentlewomen are—
> One would as soon assault a Plush—
> Or violate a Star—
>
> Such Dimity Convictions—
> A Horror so refined
> Of freckled Human Nature—
> Of Deity—ashamed—
>
> It's such a common—Glory—
> A Fisherman's—Degree—
> Redemption—Brittle Lady—
> Be so—ashamed of Thee—

Indeed, this poem's attack on the "Dimity Convictions" of the typical woman
reformer might well be targeted precisely at moral reformers and their particular concern with the "assault" and "violation" of young, innocent women. Part
of the effectiveness of Dickinson's irony in this poem is her insinuation of the
substantial distance between the reformers and the objects of their reforms. To

put it bluntly, Dickinson seems to suggest that the women concerned need not worry that the circumstances affecting other members of their sex will directly impact them in any more vividly personal way. In other words, these "Gentle-women" will scarcely merit the attention of any seducer.

Another poem that can be interpreted as an oblique critique of moral reformer is the often-discussed poem 315:

> He fumbles at your Soul
> As Players at the Keys
> Before they drop full Music on—
> He stuns you by degrees—
> Prepares your brittle Nature
> For the Ethereal Blow
> By fainter Hammers—further heard—
> Then nearer—Then so slow
> Your Breath has time to straighten—
> Your Brain—to bubble Cool—
> Deals—One—imperial—Thunderbolt—
> That scalps your naked Soul—
>
> When Winds take Forests in their Paws—
> The Universe—is still—

The fact that the referent to the pronoun "He" is never identified is a significant problem for the reader of this poem.[39] Previous critical readers have plausibly suggested that "He" is a representation of an effective preacher of the latter-day hellfire school.[40] This sermon, evoking images of physical violence and sexual violation in its audience, is clearly the property of a minister who would seek to ravish his congregation into heaven. The major criticism of the earlier male preachers who founded moral reform was that they implicated themselves in the sins they condemned, wallowing in the very iniquity they sought to correct. Their typical strategy was not unlike that of our own tabloid newspapers, which editorialize against the same corruption that sells their copy, apparently unaware of internal contradiction. In this poem, the viciously violating power of the preacher's rhetoric may well be subverting the content of his address, ironically unraveling the power of its moral message.[41]

The influence of the actual cause and agitations of the moral reform movement on the poetry of Dickinson is therefore negligible. Any traces of possible influence are negative ones; the cause of moral reform provided simply another occasion for Dickinson's perpetual irony, the possibility of another studiously satirical exercise. Yet the hyperbolic rhetoric of the moral reform movement was a pervasive part of the discourse of antebellum Amherst, a discourse within which Dickinson, for all her protested renunciation of society, was inescapably embedded.

To establish moral reform rhetoric as part of the discourse of antebellum Amherst, I might begin by referring the reader back to the Fox seduction case of 1847. The editorial jeremiad excerpted from the *New York Tribune* is a classic example of the power and strategies of moral reform rhetoric. In that editorial we clearly see the ambitious momentum of the movement's rhetoric. What begins as a selective exposure of the conduct of an individual seducer builds to a broad attack on the hypocrisy of the entire male political establishment and the corrupt system that establishment upholds. Of course, it might well be argued that the Fox case is a primarily an example of New York moral reform agitation and therefore, despite its reprinting in a local newspaper, of limited applicability to Amherst. But that particular example is only one among many. The "seducer," a stock figure of the larger antebellum cultural imagination, was often conveniently localized in the Hampshire County press. A number of Amherst seduction narratives prove this point more than adequately. The following discussion begins with one such local narrative.

On a wet Friday evening in September 1845, Ransom Guillow left East Amherst for the second time in forty-eight hours. Although we can only speculate as to what was on his mind, it is safe to assume that he was in good spirits and that the turn in the weather did not depress him unduly. Indeed, Guillow must have been considerably relieved that this second departure from the Grant homestead had begun with minimal drama, unlike his leave-taking of the previous day. On Thursday, this itinerant shoe salesman had taken what might well have been the biggest gamble of an already eventful thirty-six-year-old life. It was then that he had eloped with Ester Grant, a young resident of Amherst, whom he had only known for some three days previously. On the morning of September 1 he had come back to town, journeyed once more to the Grant homestead, and asked her father's permission for the imminent marriage. Presumably, under the circumstances, given the necessity of protecting his daughter's reputation, and despite the fact that Guillow, who had spent time in the state prison, was hardly the most desirable son-in-law, Mr. Grant would have had little option. Permission for the marriage was duly "granted," and the father gave his reluctant blessing to the union. For that reason alone, it is surely highly probable that Guillow was in an upbeat state of mind, presumably more relaxed, perhaps even already indulging himself in the comfortable anticipation of a late-summer wedding, when he set out once more to leave the Amherst area on that rainy September night.

Unfortunately, both for Guillow's state of mind and for his physical well-being, good times came to an abrupt end on the outskirts of the town. It was there that he was ambushed by a mob of angry Amherst residents. They tarred and feathered him and apparently abused him enough to elicit the promise that he would leave town and never return. Probably, in his situation, most of us would have pledged something similar. The entire proceedings, except the important fact that Mr. Grant had given permission for the marriage, were reported, without anything remotely resembling a censorious comment, in the following week's local *Hampshire Gazette*, published in nearby Northampton. That report read, in part, "Ransom Guillow, who eloped with Ester Grant, a guileless girl, on Thursday last, returned to East Amherst the next day. In the evening some 40 persons collected, rode him on a rail, gave him a coat of tar, and made him promise to leave and never show his face in town again. The whole transaction is causing considerable excitement in Amherst."[42] I assume that everyday life in the Amherst of 1845 was not quite so dull as to elevate the soap operatic events of September 1 into the major local entertainment they seem to have become. What I therefore want to do is examine for a moment the nature of that "considerable excitement" and suggest one possible historical explanation as to why the Grant elopement and its feathery denouement generated such an "excitement" in the first place. In developing that explanation, I will show how what transpired that night was part of a larger structure of activity in antebellum Amherst, and also, if I may be permitted a small play on Dickinson's words (a play she herself would have surely indulged), to examine traces of connection between the details of that particular historical "transaction" and the poet's rhetoric—in short, to find where "There's Ransom in a Voice" (P. 1251).

But before I preside over my own strictly rhetorical marriage of Ransom Guillow and Emily Dickinson, it should be understood that a variety of similar "transactions" might provide us with an equally convenient, if not identical, historical lens. The Guillow/Grant affair was, after all, only one episode within a larger narrative, periodically visited by the local Amherst area press, that was concerned with the temptation of some naive young woman by a more experienced male concealing villainous intent. In particular, during the 1840s the narrative of seduction was strikingly popular. The "Arrest of a Seducer"[43] was always newsworthy material, and tales of elopements and the designing and deserting villains responsible for them were as much part of the fabric of the local newspapers as were their catalogs of railway accidents and their most recent gossip about the singer Jenny Lind. For example, in the course of the next four months the subscriber to the *Gazette* could read of the substantial damages awarded another father, more obviously irate, the plaintiff in a court case, whose daughter was the victim of an "aggravated case of seduction,"[44] or of the conviction at Dedham of one John Cook for "abducting an unmarried woman with purposes of seduction."[45] In the years that followed, that same reader would learn the precise nature of the damages awarded. If, in May 1849, one Lawrence Boxer recovered $1,000 damages from Phillip W. Ingalls for "seducing" his daughter, and then, by November of that year, Daniel S. Dickerman went to New Bedford court to recover $2,800 damages from Samuel W. Graves for the "seducing and debauching" of his wife, an inflationary spiral of sorts seemed to be pushing up the price of practicing seduction.[46] That is, if it were not simply the case that a wife was a more valuable antebellum possession than a daughter and that the added "debauchery" of a spouse could justify the significant monetary difference in the "compensation" awarded.

While the costs of his actions to the convicted seducer could usually be measured in financial terms, the costs to the seducee tended to inscribe themselves on her body more directly. A typical portrayal of the seducee's sad fate appears in an 1849 article entitled "The Prostitute's End—Crime and Remorse," a bleak narrative that begins, "Two young and beautiful women whose beauty had made them a mark for the seducer, were suddenly stricken with death yesterday afternoon. An elder sister decoy'd them from their home and made them prostitutes." Interestingly, the actual cause of the deaths in this case is never specified. Presumably, it did not have to be; the expected premature end of the seducer's "mark" scarcely needed further detailed elaboration into a distinctly immoral territory that could be visited adequately through the reader's imagination.[47]

My favorite example of this particular newspaper genre is from the *Hampshire Gazette* of April 7, 1846:

> About a year since, a young man named Warren D. Tobey, came to Northfield with high recommendations from the Seminary at Wilbraham as a Methodist preacher, and was stationed at the Methodist Church in Northfield. He became attached to a worthy young lady of that church, by the name of Stratton, and their affection for each other soon apparently ripened into love. Under protestations of the most ardent affection for her, and with assurances that they were already married in the sight of heaven, the confiding girl yielded to the wiles of the seducer. Having accomplished his iniquitous purposes, he left Northfield.

What is so striking about this particular tale of seduction is the extent to which it mirrors many of the narratives imposed on the life of Emily Dickinson by her later critical readers. Replace the names Tobey and Stratton with Wadsworth and Dickinson, develop at some length, with ample quotations from the poetry, the concept of being "already married in the sight of heaven," and one would

have duplicated the narrative explored by a number of Dickinson critics, rang-
ing from George Whicher in the 1930s to William Shurr in the 1980s. The fact
that twentieth-century critics have tended to impose a distinctly nineteenth-century narrative on the life of the poet is a highly curious phenomenon and reason
enough to make the explication of the curious nature of that retrospectively contemporary imposition one of the major goals of this study.

Dickinson was still a teenager in the mid-1840s, and it might plausibly be
argued that she was then too young to be directly affected by such tales of seduction. However, as Dickinson matured there was virtually no way for her to
escape the local newspaper fixation on the contemporary seduction of naive
young women. For example, even in 1871 Amherst exhibited "considerable excitement" about a case that, in many of its details, paralleled the Guillow/Grant
affair of a quarter century before. Indeed, the later affair very nearly had the
same conclusion, with, at one juncture, an irate uncle threatening to raise a mob
of 250 students to tar and feather the villain, who intended to marry his niece
without the consent of her family. Amherst's "considerable excitement" ex-
ploded in a gossip that ran through all social strata. In a letter to his wife concerning what had come to be known as the Count Mitiewicz/Miss Lester affair,
J. Leander Skinner noted that "Amherst was never so much excited, from the
President to the sots, nothing else has been talked of or thought of for several
days."[48] The general interest in the case noted by Skinner is borne out by the
considerable coverage and commentary in the local press. The *Amherst Record*
characterized the incident as a "first class sensation," observing, "We do not remember ever seeing so many of our citizens so excited by any local occurrence
as during the past week." The *Hampshire Gazette*, under the caption heading
"Great Excitement over a Love Romance," also noted that the town of Amherst
had been "very much excited for ten days past." Meanwhile, the *Springfield Republican* reported in detail on "facts exciting enough to set romantic hearts pal-
pitating and excite the distrust and anxiety, if not the indignation, of all sober
minded and respectable people."[49] "Excitement" was clearly the adjective of
choice, just as in the late summer of 1845.

The facts in the case seem relatively straightforward. Carrie Lester, the niece
of a Professor Tyler of Amherst College, had fallen in love with one Eugene
Mitiewicz. The latter claimed to be a Russian count, although his lineage was
apparently closer to that of the Polish peasantry than of the Russian nobility.
What Mitiewicz could claim to be with some justification was an adept confidence man. There was already substantial evidence that he had financially
cheated a number of gullible individuals (often women whose affection he cultivated) in other locales and that he had spent time in prison, both in America
and England, as a result. The fact that the art of the confidence man appeared

to work so well in Amherst exasperated the *Amherst Record*, which observed that the "utter lack of decorum and good manners" displayed by Mitiewicz "in all his performances here shows not only that some people like to be gulled, but also that some people do not know when they are gulled."[50] The behavior of Carrie Lester provoked similar exasperation. The *Hampshire Gazette* confined its comments to the observation that "the love of the young lady is simply a case of infatuation, for she knows all the previous facts about his previous love and criminal life, and yet seems to love him more than he does her, and will insist on throwing herself away upon him"; the *Amherst Record* judged simply that she was "under a sort of infatuation which she seemed as powerless to resist as a bird under the charms of a basilisk." The *Springfield Republican*, however, used her infatuation as the basis for a more general comment on the vagaries of the female sex: "It is distressingly discouraging to those who want to believe in the right and capacity of woman to take care of herself, when an intelligent and well bred American girl gives herself so unreservedly, and against the advice of all her best friends, to a man so unworthy."[51]

The newspapers did reach consensus on one matter: as the *Hampshire Gazette* remarked, while marriage "would be the proper and regular termination of the affair in a novel . . . facts are sometimes dreadfully unromantic." That disparity between fact and fiction led the local press to hope earnestly that "the dreadful calamity—which to any well ordered family would be darker than death—may in some way be averted."[52] But despite the general disapproval of the print media, the marriage eventually did take place in Amherst in May 1872. The church was filled to capacity in only ten minutes, which, since none of the bride's family was present, further reflects the continued excitement in Amherst about the affair, an excitement sustained for more than a year.

The contemporary fascination with the affair seems primarily focused on the character of "the count," an individual generally recognized as "a man of decidedly doubtful character."[53] The precise nature of that fascination is evident in a narration borrowed by the *Amherst Record* from a New York newspaper. It describes the count's typical technique as practiced in his previous charming of another young woman, a distraction that also permitted him to appropriate her diamond ring (he later pawned it): "Artistically twirling the ring in the sunbeams, with an apologetic air, the nobleman placed it on his little finger. . . . He was good looking. He was fashionably dressed. He was fascinating. He was deferentially affectionate."[54] While this media portrait casts the "count" as the confidence man so fascinating to the American public of this time, it also recalls the earlier antebellum seducer, a prior version of the charming individual who led young women astray in order to appropriate their most valuable possession—be it their diamond ring or their virginity—with an equally charming facility. The fact that traits of an earlier seducer persona cluster around the figure of the "count" reveals them to be of still evident appeal to a later audience.

Between 1845 and 1871 there does appear to have been a declining interest in the seducer as an individual phenomenon. The local newspapers, for example, reported considerably fewer tales of seduction after the Civil War. But perhaps that apparent decline is partially explicable by taking into account how the art of seduction was subtly recontextualized: the seducer took on a different form, the form of the confidence man as exemplified in the person and techniques of the "count," who is simply a latter-day seducer of a different type, a stylistic variation on the original. At the same time, the media treatment of Carrie Lester would suggest that society recognized that the woman of the 1870s wielded more power over her choices, whether those choices were ultimately for good or ill. This would imply a subtly different attitude toward the probable seducee, too: she was held more accountable for her actions than was her antebellum predecessor. Therefore, the most important evidence provided by the Mitiewicz/Lester case is that the basic "seduction" formula, structurally updated and adapted, had not only survived but maintained its appeal: the fine art of "seduction" still had the same capacity to generate "considerable excitement" in Amherst that it had a generation before.

Less plausible is the argument that the newspaper treatment of the Mitiewicz/Lester case shows how seduction, reported as a matter of life and death in the 1840s and 1850s, had become more of a passing amusement, a media circus, in the 1870s and 1880s. Evidence that public concern and outrage had not dissipated into public entertainment is provided by the *Springfield Republican.* One month after the newspaper reported the denouement of the Mitiewicz/Lester affair, it (deliberately?) offered a bizarre alternative coda to the scene of seduction. On June 14, 1872, the *Republican,* under the capitalized heading "SAD AFFAIR AT AMHERST," noted, "A young woman at Amherst, of good family and of gay, vivacious and impulsive disposition, fell a victim some while since to the wiles of a seducer. A few weeks ago she gave birth to a child, and the feeling that she had brought disgrace upon her family preyed upon her to such an extent that she lapsed into periods of deep melancholy. . . . [S]he managed in some way to get possession of a small quantity of strychnine, and swallowing it was soon a corpse." Significantly, this young woman of Amherst fell prey to the same "wiles of the seducer" that had been the downfall of Miss Stratton some twenty-five years before. What this series of newsworthy stories reveals is another narrative of exceptional relevance to the antebellum period, one that clearly lingered after the Civil War. That narrative concerns the activities of the seducer, a figure who stalked the young women of Amherst for those twenty-five years in a variety of guises. Less a reality than an effect of the cultural imagination, catered to by the salacious tendency[55] of the local media, the character of the seducer was realized by, or perhaps draped upon the shoulders of, such (un)worthy locals as Guillow and Mitiewicz. In reality, however, such a role could perhaps only be played to clinical perfection by that unnamed seducer whose successful seduction took the equally anonymous young woman's life.

The events of the 1870s cast significant retrospective light on the activities of a generation before. When Ransom Guillow came back to town on that particular September day in 1845, he had not the slightest conception of precisely what he was coming back to, or rather whom he had *become* in the eyes of the Amherst community. Guillow had strolled into the mantle of a recognizable persona and been effectively metamorphosed: the smooth-talking shoe salesman had surrendered his individuality, had been subsumed beneath the convenient cloak of an antebellum archetype. This explains the "considerable excitement" in the Amherst locality on that late-summer evening. It was not Ransom Guillow who set out to leave town that night, and it was not Ransom Guillow that the townspeople tarred and feathered: instead, it was the figure of "the seducer" literalized momentarily by Guillow, that most unfortunate inter(e)loper.

It should by now be evident that many of the surprisingly sensational narrative scenes that critical analysts can plausibly extract from Dickinson's poetry—the seductions, the elopements, the corruptions of young women, the suicides that follow abandonment—were not necessarily gleaned by her from reading available literary texts but were actualized in her local newspaper sources. Of course, whether Dickinson did or did not read, or even have access to, the *Hampshire Gazette* and *Springfield Republican*[56] on certain days is not critical. Given the fact that Amherst was small enough for gossip to spread like wildfire, and that Dickinson showed no disinclination toward sharing gossip with her closest female confidantes (indeed, much of Dickinson's correspondence with Mrs. Holland assumes a mutual and thorough knowledge of the contents of that particular week's *Springfield Republican*), she may well have been familiar with the content of the news stories from other sources. What clearly is important is that there was considerable local public interest in the figure of the seducer as a specific regional phenomenon. Dickinson would not have needed to hear of specific seductions for the scene of seduction to form an integral part of her psyche when, through the popular cultural imagination of Amherst, for a period of some twenty-five years, strolled the wily figure of "the seducer" of guileless young women, a very plausible bogeyman for the adolescent female, or a suitably nightmarish familiar.

I would argue that seduction rhetoric influenced Dickinson's poetics by making available to her certain rhetorical structures. The pervasiveness of such rhetorical structures helped create an antebellum milieu in which seduction was a prevalent thematic center, not simply as a narrative subject but also as a linguistic, rhetorical category. For nineteenth-century women, the act of seduction, whether fictional or real, came to be a metaphoric and metonymic representation of their subject position in society—a "structure of feeling," in Raymond Williams's felicitous phrase. "Structure of feeling," despite its empirical vagueness, captures the necessarily unconscious element in their awareness, their sense more of a brooding insistence of significance, a fleeting sensation of indefinite relevance to their life in a tropic structure, rather than any concrete realization and comprehensive understanding, clearly impossible for them from within the confined circumstance of their patriarchally defined "women's sphere." Due to a complex combination of factors—in particular, the sustained dominance in the literary marketplace of popular sentimental fiction, a dominance evident not only in the art of the "genteel performance" required by a heavily codified bourgeois society but also in the language and rhetoric of popular activism in the moral reform movement—the rhetoric of seduction had become a significant residual cultural formation. For any woman writer who began writing in the 1850s (as Dickinson almost certainly did, only beginning to compile her fascicle arrangement through redrafting later), this cultural rhetorical code was available; for a writer with the courage to adopt a more liminal position within that culture, as Dickinson chose to do, it was adaptable. Moreover, essentially reflective of the power dynamic operative in antebellum society, it was particularly attractive, as a rewritable discursive formation, to the woman writer who sought to rechannel rhetorical power.

Dickinson manipulated this rhetorical code, this "structure of feeling," more advantageously than any of her contemporaries. She did, of course, succinctly avoid the more obvious problems those contemporaries confronted. Mary Kelley, in her study of the public and private writings of the so-called literary domestics, offers an obliquely persuasive explanation of Dickinson's chosen seclusion as the necessary means to an end. The new educational advantages that permitted at least the theoretical expansion of the female mind could not overcome the severely internalized restraints imposed by society. This often led to an acute confusion in the mind of the woman writer, who was a public figure in a society where the sphere of domesticity was the only identifiably acceptable female arena. The consequence for the literary domestics was an identity crisis of sorts: "Because the gulf between a private domestic existence and a public literary career was immense, they found themselves in a world they did not know and that did not know them . . . most significantly, they struggled in their tales to assess and place a value on women's lives while disparaging and dismissing their own literary efforts."[57] Finding themselves in a paradoxical situation, the literary domestics had a consequently ambiguous reaction to their own status as writers. Dickinson, choosing seclusion and a personal mode of publication, turned the paradox of her situation as a woman writer into a private aesthetic.

It was to Dickinson's advantage that she occupied a liminal position in her society. Carroll Smith-Rosenberg notes that single women were "institutionally marginal to the increasingly nuclear family of the bourgeoisie, and ideologically marginal to Victorian social beliefs."[58] Such marginality was not without its costs; the composite picture of the single female held by the culture was scarcely flattering, and dialect humor such as the Widow Bedott papers, with its satirical portrait of the widow/spinster as poet, sold 100,000 copies.[59] Similarly, in many of the plots of the early sentimental novels the very threat of spinsterhood was sufficient motivation to force the sentimental heroine to succumb to the seducer's flatteries. But the strengths of a liminal positionality could more than outweigh the disadvantages. By exacerbating the enclosure of her own life, Dickinson found the time to write without compromising her art to society's expectations of the woman writer and in so doing found an element of the freedom previously reserved for the male writer. Her liminality facilitated the exploration of a male potentiality from the margins of a female deprivation.

That self-location between male and female worlds constituted an at best transient liminality: Dickinson's allegiance was ultimately to women's sphere, which social circumstances would not allow her to vacate for long. For if what came to be known as women's sphere was an enclosure, it was not merely the bounded area of the exaggeratedly hallowed circle of domesticity, it was also a circumscribed mental space. Dickinson could not escape the bell jar; she could only explore its limits, tracing the perimeter of an epistemological sphere, charting its circumference in the knowledge that the boundaries set by a society are precisely the bounds of knowledge itself. But occupying her marginal position did allow her a more perceptive, because objective, insight into the workings of rhetorical mechanisms of control and limitation that fashion and demarcate the territory of a sphere. In particular, that insight was into the favored rhetorical structures of woman's sphere—the language of its own recreational (in a double sense) fictions. Dickinson biographer Richard Sewall remarks that "many of her poems appear to be her end of conversations struck up with what she found on printed pages."[60] The most crucial of those pages belonged to the sentimental novel because the rhetoric of those pages was particularly reflective of, if not

constitutive of, the society that produced it, that society, itself a tissue of sentimental rhetorical codes, increasingly the most elaborate of fictions.

If the poet could not think herself out of a discursive formation, she could
engage it actively through the rewriting of its possibilities. Dickinson's most obvious manipulation of an available rhetorical structure is her use of the Gothic
scene as a suggestive, if far from concrete, framework for the scenelessness of
her poetry.[61] The implied Gothic scene, lurking in the recesses of the poem, is
all the more provocative and terrifying for its lack of specificity. But in *The
Nightingale's Burden* Cheryl Walker shows just how many of Dickinson's poems
are actually subtle rewritings of the paradigmatic structures that inform a contemporary antebellum women's poetic. Walker identifies three thematic stances
for the woman poet: "identifications with power, identifications with powerlessness, and reconciling poems that attempt to establish a ground for power in the
midst of powerlessness itself."[62] Using an existing thematics of frustrated longing and hopeless aspiration, Dickinson manipulates such topoi as the forbidden
lover and the secret sorrow to new effect, and her infusion of those topoi with
her peculiar religious and aesthetic concerns, combined with her parallel generation of a subversive disorganizing humor, ensures that these hackneyed cultural themes acquire a more telling contextual resonance.

But Dickinson's most significant rhetorical restructuring concerns seduction. An avid reader of sentimental fiction, a skeptic only too aware of the masks
worn by the orthodox, and, to say the least, a radically unorthodox Christian,
Dickinson was perfectly situated at the juncture of many of the major cultural manifestations of seduction rhetoric. Given her liminal positioning, she
could restructure that rhetoric, particularly within the grounds of the "reconciling poem" concerned with establishing power at the heart of powerlessness.
Thus, while Dickinson's contemporaries, the literary domestics, were continually readapting the seduction theme as a cultural given, part of an inherited
discourse, essentially treating it as a textual element that could be integrated
into their fictional content, Dickinson absorbed it into her poetics, the code at
once becoming part of the form and inhering in the very structure of her poetry.
Rewritten, the code became a new rhetoric, a new poetics of power.

Obviously, this study is now seriously impinging on the most crucial and
yet problematic area of literary and cultural analysis. Although I think it is safe
to assume that there is a certain interrelatedness between all elements in a social
formation, the more difficult questions concern the nature of the relationship
between the formal analysis of a poem and its social ground, and how, in a particular analysis, the critic can establish any *mediation* between the two structural

levels or texts. In this particular case, how far can one go in setting about establishing any mediation between the antebellum poetic text of Dickinson and the "text" of the culture that produced it? Particularly useful (although with the always necessary reservation that the use of such a critical lens is inevitably distortive) for the purposes of examining Dickinson's rhetorical strategies is Fredric Jameson's suggestion that a literary text is also an intrinsically symbolic act—that is, that the text presents a symbolic resolution to a particular contradiction within the particular society in which it is written. As Jameson elaborates,

> The type of interpretation here proposed is more satisfactorily grasped as the rewriting of the literary text in such a way that the latter may itself be seen as the rewriting or restructuration of a prior historical or ideological *subtext*, it being always understood that that "subtext" is not immediately present as such, not some common-sense external reality, nor even the conventional narratives of history manuals, but rather must itself always be (re)constructed after the fact. The literary or aesthetic act therefore always entertains some active relationship with the Real; yet in order to do so, it cannot simply allow "reality" to persevere inertly in its own being, outside the text and at distance. It must rather draw the Real into its own texture.[63]

If the literary work is thought of as creating within its own formal structure the situation to which it is actually a reaction ("drawing the Real into its own texture"), then the aesthetic act will always be an inevitably ideological one. My assumption here is that Dickinson's poetry can be thought of as ideological in these terms: that it does not symbolically resolve a contradiction in the larger patriarchal society, but is instead an attempt to resolve a contradiction at the level of the early and inadequate prefeminist response to the problem of women's role in antebellum society, a response figured in the rhetorics of the moral reform movement and of the early sentimental novel and implicit in the very existence of that particular political movement and in the continued popularity of that particular literary genre. Consequently, Dickinson's lyric poetry is far from private and ahistorical in its wider implications, and her poetics might be viewed as an attempt at a complex restructuring of seduction rhetoric in the ultimate interests of a persuasive rhetorical power. It is not that the personae within the poetry represent either seducer or seduced, nor that the language of the poems is, in some metaphorical sense, seductive; it is rather that the poem does not so much become seductive as become the *apparatus of*, or the *means to*, a seduction. The target of that seduction is the reader's habitual structures of response. The seductive mechanism is an often elaborate one, with a complex evolution in Dickinson's own writing. That evolution can be traced in both the poetry and the letters, as the distinction between poetry and prose was for Dickinson always tenuous. Perhaps the fact that so many of the early novels of sentimental fiction that included the seduction plot (*Clarissa* being the most obvious example) were epistolary explains Dickinson's assumption of an elaborate rhetorical seduction in her letters to important male correspondents. Certainly, reading those letters we are all too soon aware that it was not just the *Advocate of Moral Reform* that "merged epistolary style and melodrama to create a uniquely American and female composite."[64] The technique of rhetorical seduction evident in the uniquely American and female composite that is the theater of Dickinson's correspondence is the subject of the next chapter.

2

Seduction and the Male Reader

I am glad it is over, & a boy. The girls are getting rather the better of us, & we need recruits. I give him welcome, & enlist him for the war.

—Samuel Bowles to Austin Dickinson on
the birth of the latter's son, August 1875[1]

I'm so glad it's a little boy, since now the little sisters have some one to draw them on the sled—and if a grand old lady you should live to be, there's something sweet, they say, in a son's arm.

—Emily Dickinson to Mrs. J. G. Holland on
the birth of the latter's son, December 1859

THE LETTER, inscribed in a communicative circuit, is determined by external social contexts, most obviously a specific audience. The fact that Emily Dickinson communicated effectively with a large circle of correspondents refutes the notion that she was unable to adapt her modes of discourse in cooperative conversation because of her entrapment in some Wittgensteinian private language. But we must be wary about the quality of that communication and aware of the static that disrupts the communicative circuit established by those letters. Within them, Dickinson frequently laments that the written word is an unreliable mode of communication. In particular, she despairs that the written text fails to carry necessary information about the qualitative feelings of an emotional self and that, as a result, the language used and the language user are always quite separate entities. Letter writing is a confinement both spatial— "tell the man who makes sheets of paper, that I hav'nt the *slightest respect* for him!" (L. 77)—and temporal—"my pen is not swift enough to answer my purpose at all" (L. 9). Often, she asserts the primacy of a speech for which writing is an inadequate substitute—"so long as a bodily interview is denied us, we must make letters answer" (L. 8). Speech is the *"warmer* language" (L. 96), whose soothing quality ensures that "we bruise each other less in talking than in writing, for then a quiet accent helps words themselves too hard" (L. 332). The written text has orphaned words by depriving them of a voice, and that loss—of intonation, rhythm, and stress—is irrecoverable in graphic form. It is therefore the construed tone emerging from the formal arrangement of words that is their potentially hurtful power, rather than the meaning they convey.

Dickinson describes an even more fundamental inadequacy of writing in an often-quoted letter to T. W. Higginson: "A Letter always feels to me like immortality because it is the mind alone without corporeal friend. Indebted in our talk to attitude and accent, there seems a spectral power in thought that walks alone—I would like to thank you for your great kindness but never try to lift the words which I cannot hold" (L. 330). Writing ("thought that walks alone"), although an almost spiritual "power," is nonetheless unable to convey the powerful physicality of experience and emotion. More precisely, written language can convey things, but not the complexity of imaginative thought: "When I seek to say to you something not for the world, words fail me" (L. 94). Dickinson is often exasperated by mere "symbols traced upon paper" (L. 15) and continually asserts "how vain it seems to *write*, when one knows how to feel" (L. 73). On occasion, she informs her readers that her best letters are written by "pens which are not seen" (L. 175) or "with that spirit pen—and on sheets from out the sky" (L. 30). Those readers, however, "*would* paper, and ink letters" (L. 30) rather than the more spectacular imaginative variety. In one early letter this frustration leads to a bizarre authorial stratagem: Dickinson leaves a blank space at the top of the page and informs her reader, "That is'nt an *empty* blank where I began—it is so full of affection that you cant see any—that's all" (L. 32).

Dickinson's concern that writing required the physical absence of a necessarily present speaker led her to suspect the perlocutionary effectiveness of any written message. It may be in playful vein that she informed her brother Austin that "the Horse is looking finely, better than in his life, by which you may think him *dead* unless I add *before*" (L. 49), and "Mrs Cutler wished me to tell you that she thought she would soon be off . . . dont know whether it's to be understood literally or figuratively—cant tell" (L. 167), but it is also hardly surprising that Dickinson repeatedly assured her early correspondents that she would "see you soon and tell you all those things which seem obscure when written" (L. 47). Eventually, of course, few were given the privilege of that clarifying personal interview.

Despite, or perhaps because of, all her apparent doubts, Dickinson took exceptional care over the actual construction of her letters, so much so that she felt the need to comment when a letter was "truly extempore" (L. 165). Her redrafting was hardly in the cause of precision or clarity: it was a telegraphic honing and paring, the concise exclusion of all superfluities, sometimes the inadvertent exclusion of the essential. When Helen Hunt Jackson was confronted with this impacted comment on her imminent marriage,

Have I a word but Joy?
    E. Dickinson,
    Who fleeing from the Spring
    The Spring avenging fling
    To Dooms of Balm—
        (L. 444)

her understandable response was "I do wish I knew just what 'dooms' you meant, though!" (L. 444a). The telegram is designed to have an immediate impact on its audience. If writing is "spectral," it is also, more importantly, a "power" (L. 330). Such power, the immediate authority to summon (or to grant) an audience, was positively regal, and the poet was "happy as a queen to know that while I speak those whom I love are listening" (L. 45). Crucially, that loving audience could at least be relied on to listen even while they were failing to comprehend the royal decree.

Dickinson's letters thus continually demonstrate her belief that in the complexity of intersubjective relationships, unmediated expression was impossible; the intended and actual expressions would not, indeed could not, coincide. In an epistolary context where the writer's consciousness is not the expression of self but rather her semiotic intercourse with others, through a language that does not so much express a self as fictively create one, role play is not a temptation: it is inevitable. The commitment of self to language made Dickinson as much a "supposed person" (L. 268) in her prose as in her poetry. Readers who seek her in the letters should therefore prepare for a bumpy ride. In a letter to Austin, the poet claims to be the fox and he the hound and then elaborates her metaphor to describe the foxhunter's reading process thus: "If you've stumbled through these two pages of folly, without losing your hat or getting lost in the mud . . ." (L. 110). The reading *experience* here clearly supersedes the message: what happens to the reader is more important than what the writer says. This interest in the affective rather than the expressive qualities of her prose is suggestive. If some of Dickinson's more significant letters are not self-expressive but reader directive, then they function as rhetorical devices that demand of the contemporary critic a careful rhetorical processing. No longer viewed as personal missives that are read over the shoulder of the intended recipient, the letters instead would be more usefully read as literary texts designed to be experienced in such a way as to elicit specific aesthetic responses within their readers.

In this chapter I focus only on the rhetorical strategies Dickinson devised within her letters to male correspondents, because these strategies were frequently a response to her situation as a woman writer and thus directly address questions of rhetoric, gender, and power in a social relationship. The authority denied Dickinson as a woman writer had to be covertly appropriated, and that appropriation could be facilitated by the strategic *rhetorical seduction* of a male correspondent. In these letters of seduction we discover a particular antebellum socioliterary context producing a female discourse of linguistic disruptiveness as a very specific act of rebellion against dominant patriarchal structures of communication. It is therefore not the case that *ecriture feminine* is the contemporary critical lens through which I have chosen to read these letters: rather, it is the lens through which Dickinson's pioneering anticipation of gender disruptive strategies demands that her prose be read.

It has become entirely customary for critics to associate Dickinson's prose with her poetry. David Higgins finds the prose "as unmistakable as her poetry. In both she tried to condense thought to its essence in epigram"; Richard Sewall blurs the distinction by stating that "in her letters as in her verses she was a poet all the time"; and Cristanne Miller observes that "her letters may be as elliptical syntactically and metaphorically as her poems."[2] By contrast, David Porter emphasizes that the "fragmented discourse" of the poems offers a contrast to the occasional clarity of the prose and that "she was demonstrably capable in her letters of extended and coherent writing."[3] I would have to agree. But if the poetic function is defined (following Jakobson) as a focus on the message for its own sake, the creation of a syntactic texture by the motivated usage of a patterning over and above that required by the language's referential function, then the prose/poetry association is also valid in specific instances: the letters of Emily Dickinson are, without question, exceptionally poetic on occasion.

Reading these syntactically textured letters as prose poems may help elucidate elements of Dickinson's unformulated "sensationalist" poetics, in particular the foreseen role of an impressionistic reader. Suzanne Juhasz has suggested that Dickinson's letters are "always love letters" and a "seduction carried out by flattery, so that the compliment serves as the essential rhetorical act."[4] To this valid reading it should be added that the letters are rhetorical seductions, grammatically contrived. Dickinson's seduction involves more than the ability to "produce felicitous language" in order to compliment a reader: the etymological root of seduction, *seducere*, which suggests both a leading on and a leading in, is also a convenient metaphorical description of the grammatical demands that the letter makes of that reader, of the means by which the text leads him or her into a series of syntactic ambiguities that frustrate any comfortable interpretive processing. As complex poetic messages, these letters demand a more rigorously attentive reading than even Dickinson's best critics have been willing to grant them.

Such an attentive reading of the letters might subtly qualify recent critical work particularly concerned with the affective nature of Dickinson's poetics. For example, Gary Lee Stonum has brilliantly argued that the basis of that poetics is Dickinson's personalization of the romantic sublime. But while Stonum realizes that the poet's "work performs a sort of jiujitsu on the poetics of mastery, drawing much of its strength from the resources of domination, submission, and the intersubjective rivalry underlying them," he also finds Dickinson's a "superlatively autoeffective art" and concludes that, "according to Dickinson's affective understanding of poetry . . . the assertiveness of a writer's style plays a crucial role in provoking the reader's response. Beyond any momentary aggrandizement of the authorial self, it contributes centrally to a network of textual relations *in which the author's part is never finally that of the master*" (emphasis added).[5] This conclusion is not dissimilar to that reached from the more overtly feminist perspective of Margaret Homans, who has argued that Dickinson's predominantly metonymic poetic strategy substitutes for a hierarchical masculine metaphoric economy a feminine perspective that privileges nonhierarchical "pleasure."[6] By adopting such a strategy, Homans implies, Dickinson reveals herself to be an eminent precursor theorist of *ecriture feminine*. What the different theoretical approaches of Homans and Stonum toward Dickinson's poetic project share is the assumption that she was a passive rhetorician, that she could successfully engage and undo hierarchical textual structures without imposing any rhetorical mastery of her own.

I would suggest that this assumption is not borne out by the evidence of Dickinson's personal correspondence. If history is an ongoing struggle for control of the script, then those letters are often a subtle strategic attempt to wrest that script away, at least temporarily, from male hands. That correspondence is occasionally the site of a scrimmage for control of language and the apparent logic of a letter often masks a real concern with issues of power and desire. While it is true that within individual letters Dickinson creates a new field of power, attacking principles of mastery and difference by forging a new pattern of authority that, transposed to the horizontal, the medium of one-to-one correspondence, is far from hierarchical, it is also apparent that the agonistic nature of a personal correspondence, particularly when that letter is a text, a rhetorical device mediating directly between Dickinson and her reader, often demonstrates how the undoing of the reader's position of male authority often became the means to a direct assertion of the female writer's power.

Dickinson's conception of writing was inextricably connected with rhetorical notions of power: "What is it that instructs a hand lightly created, to impel shapes to eyes at a distance, which for them have the whole area of life or of death? Yet not a pencil in the street but has this awful power, though nobody arrests it. An earnest letter is or should be life-warrant or death-warrant, for what is each instant but a gun, harmless because 'un-loaded,' but that touched 'goes off'?" (L. 656). The letter—a carefully arranged series of signs—is, in itself, harmless until activated (or, more accurately, detonated) by the decoding reader. To pursue that metaphor for a moment, swept on the crest of the hyperbole that is so prevalent in Dickinson's letters, it is the reader who loads the gun and slips the hair trigger—the paradox of the suicidal reader submitting to the whim of the writer terrorist. While reading Dickinson's letters is perhaps not danger-ous, it can be a distinctly unsettling experience for their reader. There is evi-dence that the cultivation of this uneasiness is deliberate—that selected letters were designed as linguistic booby traps for specific male correspondents. Such letters are very much directed toward the individual male correspondent, and the relationship with that individual is crucial to their internal construction. As that orientation toward a reader is the constitutive feature of rhetorical dis-course, the letters function primarily as rhetorical devices and, far from good-will messages, are designed to be a rhetorical force acting on their reader. The evolution of Dickinson's letters as rhetorical devices displays how, in order to be taken seriously, she had to fashion her address toward a predominantly male audience of advisors, editors, and publishers.[7] Seduction is a necessarily dia-logic process, and many of her letters were intended to effect a rhetorical seduc-tion of their male reader through their implicit linguistic strategies. This rhe-torical seduction was the means to a delicate inversion of the gender power hierarchy figured in the social relationship of Dickinson and her male corre-spondent.

To comprehend that rhetorical seduction requires that we ourselves read the letters rhetorically. That rhetorical reading must be based on an initial theory of noncommunication. More precisely, it is a search for that which is *indirectly* com-municated within the letters. Actually, one of Dickinson's poems may describe exactly what is being sought:

> Going to Him! Happy letter!
> Tell Him—
> Tell Him the page I didn't write—
> Tell Him—I only said the Syntax—
> And left the Verb and the pronoun out—
> Tell Him just how the fingers hurried—
> Then—how they waded—slow—slow—   [stammered]
> And then you wished you had eyes in your pages—
> So you could see what moved them so—
>   (P. 494)

A rhetorical reading puts the "eyes in your pages" by assuming that the reader's experience of processing the letter should be of primary importance. Such a reading assumes that Dickinson sought power over her immediate audience, despite her realization that the perfect speech act was no guarantee of perlocutionary effectiveness. Her awareness that meaning was ineffectually conveyed through the attitudinal and cognitive functions of language led her to develop alternative and compensatory linguistic strategies that shifted the reader's focus toward his or her own actualizing participation, the concretizing of the letter as poetic text. It is therefore the reader's response, line by line, that is of primary importance. As we shall see, an analysis of two highly rhetorical letters to two male correspondents provides ample evidence of this strategy in action as a rhetorical technique.

Not coincidentally, that rhetorical technique is accompanied, or rather duplicated, by an inordinate degree of personal posing. Much has been written about the poses Dickinson adopted before the men in her life. She *is* terribly coy, and *does* practice the disembodied flirting celebrated by Karl Keller.[8] Dickinson's seductive posing, however, is linked to her struggles with a language that creates a persona in words (poses) and, simultaneously, entangles an audience (the leading *in* rather than *on*). Again, there is no Dickinson "identity" in her letters, for the commitment of "self" to language made her as much a "supposed person" (L. 268) in her prose as in her poetry. In her letters to specific male correspondents, therefore, Dickinson assumes femininity as a deliberate masquerade, flaunting the conventional signs of the feminine in order to frustrate any appropriation of her actual self. Such a deliberate assumption of the feminine role is a means of converting a form of subordination into an affirmation. The psychoanalyst Joan Riviere observed how in certain circumstances a woman who wishes to appropriate for herself a masculine authority may put on a "mask of womanliness," where the assumption of this masquerade is "an unconscious attempt to ward off the anxiety which would ensue on account of the reprisals she anticipated from the father-figures after her intellectual performance."[9] The masquerade as a necessary strategy of subversion has clear applicability to Dickinson's letters to significantly powerful male correspondents. Suzanne Juhasz has already observed that while Dickinson's tactics of seducing male correspondents are stereotypically feminine, the motivation behind the seduction was the perhaps stereotypically masculine one of having a career as a poet. The feminine masquerade is thus Dickinson's subtle means of deflecting her reader's attention away from her more significant project and ultimate poetic ambitions. Dickinson intuitively chose the men who were most suitable to participate in her stereotyped script; they were essentially father figures with whom she could impersonate a seduction, engage in harmless rhetorical flirtation.[10] Reassured by her "masculine" intelligence, these men knew that nothing more tangible than the game itself would be demanded of them by *this* coquette.

However, if Dickinson's letters to male correspondents require a strategy of self-presentation (the masquerade) that is subversively doubled (the feminine approach of submissiveness, the masculine intent of poetic self-affirmation), then that self-presentation is presumably duplicated in the rhetorical strategies of those letters. For Juhasz, that rhetorical doubleness is present in the compliment itself, "a form complex enough to carry both overt and covert messages; Dickinson uses it for critique as well as praise, aggression as well as submission."[11] But it is perhaps more accurate to say that the strategy of doubleness is ultimately dependent on more specific *rhetorical* effects designed to discomfit the reader of the prose. It is precisely those rhetorical effects that I want to trace.

To that end, what follows is my reading of two Dickinson letters sent to male correspondents. Any reading of these letters is, of course, historically contingent and politically situated within a larger cultural context. Ideally, therefore, I would discuss the historical readers of the letters—Higginson and the "Master"—in terms of their own horizon of expectations, identifying their membership in historically specific interpretive communities. That, I repeat, is the ideal. But since I can only conjecture as to the actual expectations of that audience, I must, of practical necessity, privilege the aesthetic dimensions of reception and my own response, positing myself as the ideal reader of the letters in question. In so doing, I partially elide the historically specific conditions by which reading proceeds. But not completely, at least insofar as I recognize my own implication in a system of historically specific strategies that, in all likelihood, constitute the textuality they propose to describe, my own reading embedded within its own particular historical field of discursive practices, epistemic frames, and interpretive codes. My reading of the letters, therefore, must itself be read within the rhetorical context of its production and reception; the all-too-obvious focus on the temporal dimensions of textual processing renders that rhetorical context—a scene of seduction enabled by the rhetorical practice of reader-response theorists Jauss, Fish, Booth, Iser, et al.—more than apparent. To facilitate their reading, I have divided the letters, rather arbitrarily, into sections. Though hardly systematic, this division does help isolate their developing patterns of ambiguity, which, I will assert, are the result of Dickinson's upsetting of the normal codes of communication and the key component of the attempted rhetorical seduction of her reader.

It was to Higginson that Dickinson reiterated her deepest doubts about the writing process. A simple misunderstanding could cause a letter to "scuttle" and "sink" (L. 1007), and, she reminded Higginson, such misunderstanding may be inevitable when the written has primacy over the spoken—"A Pen has so many inflections and a Voice but one, will you think it obtuse, if I ask if I quite understood you" (L. 470)—particularly in a language system already unable to embody the unspeakable, where "the broadest words are so narrow we can easily cross them—but there is water deeper than those which has no Bridge" (L. 413). The first letter chosen for analysis is the third that Dickinson wrote Higginson (L. 265).

> Your letter gave no Drunkenness, because I tasted Rum before—Domingo comes but once—yet I have had few pleasures so deep as your opinion, and if I tried to thank you, my tears would block my tongue—

This letter, like so many of the poems, opens with an abrupt, stunning image. A letter is the metaphorical container (bottle or flask) that holds the intoxicating language (Rum) that is to be imbibed by the reader. The hazard is that it may send that reader reeling. The metaphorical suggestion is a common one in Dickinson's poetry about letters; in poem 169, the purpose of reading an old letter was "to con the faded syllables / That quickened us like wine," and in poem 636 the joy of any letter is that "for transport it be sure." In this particular letter, the recipient of Higginson's letter suggests that she has developed a level of tolerance, perhaps predictable for someone addicted to language. The squeezing of the word "me" from behind the verb may imply, however, that Higginson's letter may have a similar effect on another reader. In a somewhat oblique sense, therefore, Higginson's letter's failure to produce a more generalized "Drunkenness" is evidence of its potential disappointment.

The word "yet" marks the first of many sudden shifts required of the reader of this letter. The disorientation produced by this shifting is primarily a consequence of Dickinson's semantic choices. Why, for instance, was the verb "have" chosen to describe "pleasures," when "felt" seems more appropriate in the context? The word choice emphasizes a possible syntactic doubling[12] reminiscent of the poetry; there is now a temptation to read "deep" as the adjective before "opinion" rather than "pleasures." There is an immense space of irony in the semantic opening between the report of a deep pleasure experienced by the reader of the letter and the comment on a deep opinion held by the writer of that letter. The startling image of the tear-blocked tongue reinforces the sentence's strangely muffled sense, and that muffled sense consolidates the consistent image that the writer offers to her reader as one who feels deeply but, dramatically overcome by the depth of her own emotion, cannot communicate that fact.

> My dying Tutor told me that he would like to live till I had been a poet, but Death was much of Mob as I could master—then—And when far afterward—a sudden light on Orchards, or a new fashion in the wind troubled my attention—I felt a palsy, here—the Verses just relieve—

The phrase "My dying Tutor" seems designed to intrigue. The reader (Higginson no less than myself) can have no concrete knowledge of whom she refers to.[13] Of course, Dickinson is often deliberately factually vague in the Higginson correspondence, but this particular biographical evasiveness is reinforced by a simultaneous syntactic evasiveness. The compression "Death was much of Mob," which elides an article, leaves the reader wondering if death is the mob or merely part of it, in which case what is the mob?[14] And is that capitalized "Death" a general experience of mortality, or a specific reference to the dying of her "Tutor"? The syntactic shift to "then" confuses the writer's relationship to "Death" even more; is the word "then," imprisoned ambiguously as it is within dashes, the last word of the preceding phrase, the first word of the succeeding phrase, or both? And does the phrase mean that she could master death *then* and imply that now she cannot, or that *now* she can?

Even more disconcerting is the comprehensive failure of deixis[15] that is the writer's feeling "a palsy, here." Does "here" mean the present moment, in the sense of today, or does the reader have to imagine a physical gesture by the writer, a pointing to the body? Given that failure of deixis, a more suggestive reading is that "here" is the written page and that the "palsy" is most evident in the writing itself.[16] The final phrase is irritatingly ambiguous too; if the "Verses just relieve," does that mean, in dismissive fashion, that that is all they do, or do they merely or barely (in the sense of "just and no more") ease? As it stands, the relief of the writer can be understood as both desperate and dismissive simultaneously.

> Your second letter surprised me, and for a moment, swung—I had not supposed it. Your first—gave no dishonor, because the True—are not ashamed—I thanked you for your justice—but could not drop the Bells whose jingling cooled my Tramp—Perhaps the Balm, seemed better, because you bled me, first.

The most obvious question here is who (or what) "swung," for if that describes Dickinson's response to the letter then it directly contradicts the earlier assertion that she felt no drunkenness. What follows, in fact, seems symptomatic of just such a verbal inebriation. Not only does the punctuation by dash become increasingly random and erratic as the letter proceeds, but the little alliterative run of "the Balm, seemed better, because you bled me, first" positively stutters. The sense appears to be that the first action of Higginson, performing the asked-for "surgery" on her poetry, was to "bleed" that poetry, but implied therein, by that apparently random comma before "first," is the insinuation that he was the first to bleed *her*, an assertion that places Higginson in the role of the ravishing deflowerer of her poetry, the first to touch its innocence, and a far from gentle lover. This almost subliminal suggestion plays off earlier words in the passage—"True," "dishonor," and "ashamed."

I smile when you suggest that I delay "to publish"—that being foreign to my thought, as Firmament to Fin—
If fame belonged to me, I could not escape her—if she did not, the longest day would pass me on the chase—and the approbation of my Dog, would forsake me—then—My Barefoot-Rank is better—

The simplest reading of that first sentence is that for Dickinson to publish would be the equivalent of taking a fish out of water—publishing is the "Firmament," and the "Fin" is Dickinson's thought. Language (recalling her earlier metaphor of rum) is fluid, but the dry land of publication is a stability she does not, or cannot, seek. Indeed, the entire letter up to this point has emphasized the liquidity of her thought process, if not her own instability. Her self-presentation has been as the outsider, the fringe-dwelling gypsy with the jingling bells of verse. The reader's awareness of absences—be it the absence of factual information or of the words that complete a syntactic phrase—and of suggestive semantic ambiguities is significant; his consequent inability to pin down meaning irrevocably, to control the written discourse, is easily transferred to the writer of that discourse and explained in terms of the *writer's* lack of control. The control of language becomes inextricably associated with self-control. In a paradoxical inversion equivalent to Dickinson's assertion that to own fame is to be captured/imprisoned by fame, it is *her* thought that comes to strike a reader as "foreign."

You think my gait "spasmodic"—I am in danger—Sir—
You think me "uncontrolled"—I have no Tribunal.
Would you have time to be the "friend" you should think I need?
I have a little shape—it would not crowd your Desk—nor make much Racket as the Mouse, that dents your Galleries—
If I might bring you what I do—not so frequent to trouble you—and ask you if I told it clear—'twould be control, to me—
The Sailor cannot see the North—but knows the Needle can—
The "hand you stretch me in the Dark," I put mine in, and turn away—I have no Saxon, now—

By now it is clear that Dickinson is using a vocabulary given to her by Higginson in his previous letter. It was Higginson who used the words "spasmodic" (presumably in reference to the spasmodic school of poetry) and "uncontrolled" to describe her poetry. This reply is her willful misinterpretation of his words, a response that is her justification of uncontrol. If the poems were uncontrolled, well, so is the prose and, significantly, the palsy-prone writer of that prose. Higginson thinks that she "should" need a friend, and, in this context, that "should" seems extraneous: that this is what he *should* think is her message to him. The sudden lapsing into meter in this central section is hardly accidental. The apparent incoherence of the letter has been an elaborate appeal for control; it is as though the very contemplation of his help has given her a semblance of that control within the letter.

But, of course, that control has been evident throughout the letter as an irony-charged ambiguity. In this final passage, Higginson is the compass needle that gave her the necessary maritime directions (the passage is full of nautical imagery—water omnipresent as the language itself), but also the needle that bled her, that necessary purgation described earlier in the letter. Indeed, the statement "I have no Saxon now" takes the letter full circle, for, now overcome with the emotion she said she would avoid, the writer's language is ineffectual and the tongue is blocked. The letter has had a carefully constructed, not to say positively poetic, development.

The letter concludes with a poem (P. 323) interesting only in its contextually hyperbolic flattery, part of an appeal that culminates in her question to him (and, at this point, a question is not merely an interactionally powerful utterance but the coda of an entire rhetorical process): "But, will you be my Preceptor, Mr Higginson?" There can only be one answer if her rhetorical strategy has been successful.

The components of the rhetorical strategy within this letter can be briefly summarized. The letter is Dickinson's response to Higginson's description of her poetry as "spasmodic" and "uncontrolled." As such, it is her (re)turning of his language in a reply that itself proves suitably uncontrolled in a variety of ways. This message is consolidated by role play, and the most obvious lack of control revealed is the writer's presentation, as if normal, of her own hyperbolic responses to stimuli, an "inadvertent" self-revelation of an emotional intensity that borders on mental fragility. Dickinson presents this role through suggestive self-description. Moreover, a role structure analysis of the letter would reveal her grammatical self-presentation to be essentially passive. She is never the agent of an action but remains passive throughout: she effects little, while things happen to her, disrupting the static equilibrium of her patient state.

More importantly, the sense of written "uncontrol" also emerges through the reading process: the reader, clearing a path through the dense Dickinson prose, must impose a logical development by replacing syntactic deletions. That reader, making sense, must impose a control, a missing order, on an apparent chaos of fragmentation. But this is not always possible when the multiplicity of potential choice—and the reader's consequential inability to fix on one univocal meaning—renders the discourse itself uncontrollable. The "uncontrol" is part of the signifying process, and that signifying process itself has become the central means of communication. It is through the constant slipping and dispersing of meaning that the reader experiences the lack of control over language of which Dickinson was accused by Higginson.

Of course, the language used, or rather returned, in this letter is that of Higginson, the intended reader. Dickinson's reply has been a demonstration of the uncontrol latent in his own controlled language, of the potential for referential aberration that is in the actual language system. Simultaneously, she demonstrates her control over the uncontrollable: her presentation of an uncontrolled language becomes a persuasive power that is potentially perlocutionarily effective. That reinforced persuasiveness is a significant rhetorical power that far surpasses any obtainable through the cognitive function of language alone. It is also a power that in its brilliant exercise leaves no doubt as to who is in control of the correspondence.

Richard Sewall has observed that Dickinson "seems to have made a separate world of each of her major correspondents."[17] The question a rhetorical reading must ask is whether those worlds are also separate linguistic universes that can be mapped, their distinctive geographies plotted, and their divergences one from another traced. For example, a letter to a different correspondent can present a subtly different strategy from that used in the Higginson letter. The notoriously rhetorical first "Master"[18] letter (L. 187), a concisely crafted twelve sentences, is a suitable example. My assumption is that the question of whether or not it was sent is irrelevant: it was clearly initially written by Dickinson with a specific reader in mind.

> I am ill, but grieving more that you are ill, I make my stronger hand work long eno' to tell you. I thought perhaps you were in Heaven, and when you spoke again, it seemed quite sweet, and wonderful, and surprised me so—I wish that you were well.

The first sentence of this letter, unlike the majority of her epistolary openings, does not seem designed to stun her reader. It is even a little weak rhetorically. It is certainly ambiguous. The ambiguity is a result of the frustration of the reader's valid grammatical expectation that the comma will follow "but." This may be a simple punctuation error, but it also alters the sense in a significant way; the apparent sense is, "Although I am ill, my concern for you overrides that illness," but the placement of the comma emphasizes the sheer bluntness of "I am ill," and the subsequent compression of "but grieving more" emphasizes the aggravation of the writer's illness. Her concern for the reader, by the placement of the punctuation, might well exacerbate the reader's concern for her. Just as the colloquially shortened "eno' " seems purely chosen for its open vowel sound, so other words seem to have been chosen for their sibilant indistinctness: "perhaps . . . seemed . . . wonderful . . . surprised me so." It surprises a reader to see Dickinson qualify with "quite," for her a most unusual vagueness.

I would that all I love, should be weak no more. The Violets are by my side, the Robin very near, and "Spring"—they say, Who is she—going by the door—

Indeed it is God's house—and these are gates of Heaven, and to and fro, the angels go, with their sweet postillions—I wish that I were great, like Mr. Michael Angelo, and could paint for you. You ask me what my flowers said—then they were disobedient—I gave them messages. They say what the lips in the West, say, when the sun goes down, and so says the Dawn.

This rhythmic passage exemplifies the sense of the incantatory that permeates this letter. Word choice seems primarily determined by consonance or assonance: "lips . . . West . . . say . . . Sun . . . so"; or for their near ("down . . . Dawn") or actual rhymes ("to and fro . . . go . . . Michael Angelo").[19] It is not, therefore, just Dickinson's lapsing(?) into her habitual meter that gives the passage its poetic quality; the sunset is here personified as the mouthing of a red-lipped sky. And, as is so often true of Dickinson, where there is poetry there is also an accompanying irony.

As in the Higginson letter, the message seems complexly ironic both in individual syntactic detail and in the apparent intentionality of the whole. Does "all I love" refer solely to the "Master" (is he her "all"), or is the phrase a move toward a generalization that would gently undercut the individual approach of the first paragraph? If the phrase does refer to the "Master," then the choice of the word "weak" as opposed to the less ambiguous "ill" could be ironic. That irony is elsewhere suggested in the letter by Dickinson's assigning the social signification "Mr." to Michelangelo. Whatever the opinion of her art held by her baffled recipient, the artistry of this letter is sufficient evidence that creativity has nothing to do with gender. The largest irony of all is that if the recipient has been unable to comprehend her poetry (and I assume literal flowers were accompanied by poetic ones)—a series of word paintings that spoke, apparently, of sunsets and sunrises, of beauty, of time, of nature, of life, death, and resurrection—what hope did he have of deciphering a highly poetic letter that presents interpretive problems such as the "postillions" of the "angels"?

Listen again, Master. I did not tell you that today had been the Sabbath Day.

Each Sabbath on the Sea, makes me count the Sabbaths, till we meet on shore—and (will the) whether the hills will look as blue as the sailors say. I cannot talk any more (stay any longer) tonight (now), for this pain denies me.

How strong when weak to recollect, and easy, quite, to love. Will you tell me, please to tell me, soon as you are well.

This letter, too, displays a failure of deixis. The phrase "this pain denies me" is powerful, but what does it mean—precisely what pain is the referent? "Denies" is not a synonym for "stops" or "prevents," but means "refuses." The reader cannot possibly know if this is a specific or general, physical or mental pain. Or is it a spatial suggestion that the actual writing is responsible for the pain? Dickinson cannot continue to write, not because some "pain" stops her but because the writing itself, and not the act of writing, is that pain. The notion that the writing is itself a process of pain is reinforced by the repetition of the word "Sabbath" three times and the repetition of six other words within this letter; it is as if Dickinson, wearing a prose straitjacket, had access only to a scant vocabulary.

There is ample evidence of how the pain is the writing. The simplicity of the language, dazzling in its gentle lyric repetitions, does not make the letter any less opaque. What emerges is not any clear "message," but an awareness, on the part of the reader, of the writer's weakness. Dickinson says she is ill, that she is physically weak. This weakness is shown to extend to her mental faculties, to her organizational abilities, and inhibits her ability to construct an effective letter. Her role playing, this time an exaggerated deference and submissiveness, is that of a fundamentally weak person. Here, suffering is the seduction of the critical, rejecting other: the self-denigration of extreme submissiveness is the means of avoiding retaliation, the appeasement of the targeted reader.

In this letter, too, the experience of reading consolidates the message; the repetitions do not so much facilitate reading as cause gentle resistance to it— this might well be the "wading" experience referred to earlier. The letter becomes a strength-sapping voyage for its reader. More importantly, what was displayed in the Higginson letter as symptomatic of the writer's lack of control, the opening of ambiguity and the consequent dispersal of meaning, is in this letter a verbal manifestation of her weakness. In fact, it is again unclear whether the weakness is hers or the language she uses, as that weakness is primarily communicated through the signifying process, the repetition of words suggesting that synonyms are either unavailable or ineffectual. The simplicity of the vocabulary, in the simplest of sentences, still provides endless allusiveness/elusiveness.

The letter to Higginson was a (re)turning of his language, and a similar process is at work in this letter. I assume that the "Master" informed Dickinson of two things—that he was ill (weak) and that he failed to understand the poetry she had sent him previously. This letter is therefore concerned with communication failure, the inability to achieve a communion that was physical, spiritual, and artistic. "Listen again" says the writer, for the reader comprehensively failed to grasp the first time. Dickinson is the teacher (the "Master" an errant child) repeating (the repetition of individual words itself a metaphor) a message emphatically. This letter is the scene of a power struggle: the question is *who* is to be master.[20] If, in the Higginson letter, Dickinson demonstrated the interchangeability, or at least mutual interdependence, of "control" and "uncontrol," in this letter the terms are "weakness" and "strength." The "Master" confesses a weakness that is physical and—given his failure to comprehend the poems—imaginative to a writer whose response is an exaggerated representation of that weakness. This weakness emerges not merely through the writer's reporting of some (unspecified) physical ailment, or through her playing the exceptionally deferential role of social (and sexual) inferior; it manifests itself primarily as an intrinsic linguistic weakness, as part of the signifying process. The paradox—and it is no paradox for Dickinson—is that her presentation of that powerlessness is evidence of an intrinsic strength, of linguistic power.

Dickinson's poetic language in these letters, containing elements in excess of meaning and signification, is obviously quite distinct from any spoken language whose basic function is communication. Such letters are best read as poetic texts. The critic Julia Kristeva has theorized that within a poetic text there is a dialectical interplay between the *phenotext*, constituted by a system of social, cultural, syntactical, and other grammatical restraints that ensure communication, and obeying rules of communication that presuppose a subject of enunciation and an addressee, and the *genotext*, an unconscious rhythmic undertow, process rather than structure, that renders language partly unintelligible because it is *not* restricted to the limited informational relation between two subjects. The foregrounding of the genotextual elements of language results in the subversion of textual unity and authority in a communicative structure. It is clearly tempting, though perhaps historically invalid, to draw analogies between Kristeva's theory and Dickinson's practice in these two letters, where the poet has clearly set about dislocating typical communicative restraints through the poeticization of her prose. Indeed, it is amusing to consider that any parallel that could be made would have to be qualified by the assertion that Dickinson's practice apparently goes farther than the theory would allow. The poeticizing of Dickinson's prose is for her the very conscious means to an end: it is the deliberate exercise of a rhetorical power that, through its incremental inversion of an assumed gender hierarchy, eventually reinforces her authority as a writer.

While it may be problematic to apply contemporary literary theory to these letters, it is difficult to dismiss their subversive edge, the sense that something is going on beyond straightforward communication. Clearly, the reader of the letters is never permitted the leisure of command, any sense of complacent authority. Indeed, both letters demand to be read as unreadable. Not only do nonrecoverable syntactic elisions[21] leave individual utterances undecidable, but the only spatiotemporal situation available to grammar, the deictic system, is fractured at key moments. Dickinson obviously wants to explode the normal structures of reception in order that, for her reader, meanings cease to be constative and become performative. As a result, that reader must, of necessity, assume a more participatory role, must directly engage the signifying process of language itself. The writer's rhetorical choices are therefore ultimately made in the interest of maximum persuasiveness; the potential for effective communication with an audience is actually dramatically increased by the reinforcement of the message through the signifying process. In an 1881 letter to Mrs. Holland, Dickinson praised just such a communicative method: "Your sweet light-hearted manner informed me more than statements, that the Doctor was better—*the inferential Knowledge—the distinctest one*" (L. 685, emphasis added).[22]

Interestingly, the tremendous, almost subliminal, infusion of "inferential knowledge" in these two letters is often an obvious manifestation of the writer's increasing control over not only the signifying process but also the reader who finds himself implicated in it. Ultimately, the main effect of Dickinson's dual assumption of a persona *and* of an affective rhetorical strategy is a subtle manipulation of the correspondent, for whom both are particularly devised. In both of the letters examined, Dickinson creates a linguistic space of irony for her persona to occupy, and the most obvious manifestation of that irony is that "the page she didn't write" often proves to be the contradiction of the message by its practice. In creating the subversively ironic space into which authority is lured to the scene of its own destruction, Dickinson does not merely engage mastery, she uses the mechanism of rhetorical seduction to wrench control away from her correspondent in order to personally assume it. This is a Dickinson who is an active rhetorician and therefore a woman with a purpose. For this reason alone, her letters demand the same careful scrutiny as her poems, and, as critics of her prose, we would do well to heed the advice that she gave one of her correspondents on the surface of an envelope—"open me carefully" (L. 94).

While it has become customary for critics to associate Dickinson's prose with her poetry, that association usually conceals an understandable tendency to privilege the poetry at the expense of a prose that can eventually be categorized as similarly poetic. As the subject of this analysis has been Dickinson's subtle rhetorical inversion of an established power dynamic, it might be useful to conclude by speculating on the consequences of a similar inversion of the critical power dynamic that has established an apparent hierarchy between Dickinson's poetry and her prose. If, rather than considering the prose poetic, one were to regard Dickinson's poems as having a proselike function, as being essentially rhetorical devices, that would most certainly posit a challenge to Stonum's assertion that Dickinson's is "a poetry designed more to stimulate responses in the reader than to control them or instruct the reader's imagination."[23] Indeed, one might well be led to conclude that Dickinson's interest was precisely in the controlling and the instructing of that reader. Reading her poetry through the critical lens provided by her rhetorical prose style might also prove her a more aggressive precursor of feminism than even the most sympathetic of feminist critics have succeeded in making her. In opposition to Homans's argument that Dickinson's poetic strategy was the undoing of hierarchical structures, essentially a process of leveling, it could be argued that Dickinson's particular concern was the inversion of hierarchical structures in order to appropriate and assume the rhetorical power held by the Other; in other words, that the authority of a Dickinson poem is dependent on its destabilization of the authoritative position of its reader. However, the primary intention of my analysis of these letters has not been to urge a more attentive critical reading of Dickinson's prose in order that it might provide some fascinating insight into Dickinson's poetry. That would be to reestablish precisely the type of poetry/prose hierarchy of which we (like Dickinson before us) should be particularly suspicious. Rather, my intention has been to suggest that it is perhaps only by studying the affective rhetorical techniques within her prose as well as within her poetry, and then proceeding to establish a series of mutual equivalences between the two linguistic models, that we may finally be able to generalize about Dickinson, not as a poet or a prosodist but as a *writer*.

Reading Dickinson's correspondence is clearly a tricky business. For those who would attempt to use that correspondence as an excavation site, as the archaeological dig for some palpable evidence of the poet's personality, the reading of the extant letters can be an especially circuitous process.[24] In the usual scenario, a superficial literal reading of the letters, ahistorical to a fault, is presented as supporting evidence for the psychological profile that predetermined its initial premises. This demonstrates the reflexive suppleness of a particular critical reader but tells us nothing about the real Dickinson, whomever she may have been. Unfortunately, reading the letters within their cultural context provides no panacea; it is ultimately no more likely to give readers a privileged, unmediated access to the poet as she really was, for while it may be true that any attempt to find the personality of the letter writer must begin by reading the letters in the historical context of their composition, the antebellum codes of correspondence argue that the typical mannered epistle is anything but a biographical key.

Establishing the context of the correspondence can facilitate the demolishing of some of the more stereotypical Dickinsons of our imagination. Karen Halttunnen's cultural criticism proves especially useful for the purposes of contextualizing the poet's letters and serves to definitively correct, for example, any notion that the letters are further evidence (the first being the thematic content of the poetry) of an unnatural obsession with death, of some pathological personal morbidity. From a twentieth-century perspective, such a diagnosis would seem validated by the inordinate number of sympathy letters the poet sent to the bereaved. But Dickinson is not at all ghoulish—unless, that is, we feel comfortable applying the adjective indiscriminately to the mores of antebellum New England. For the typical middle-class sentimentalist the mourning process was an intensely self-conscious experience, a self-analysis in the tradition of Puritan self-examination. Dickinson's predilection for the rhetoric of condolence is simply representative in a context where, for average bourgeois women, "in their sentimental scheme of social status, the capacity to experience deep grief demonstrated true gentility. For the same sentimental reasons, they were almost equally obsessed with the art of offering sympathy to those who mourned."[25] The assumption that Dickinson was an excessively morbid individual actually elides her cultural identity. Concerned primarily with gentility, and manifesting a high, perhaps alarming, degree of sentimental ideality, Dickinson was often the most exemplary of antebellum bourgeois women.

We might also tend to overstress the sense of separation anxiety evident in the letters. It is certainly true that her correspondence displays the delicate personal balance Dickinson felt between the worlds of relationship and separation, and that it suggests a need to stay close to others, if not an almost obsessive concern with sustaining and maintaining often frayed ties of affection. But even aside from the fact that maintaining such webs of communication is, contemporary psychologists would argue, a more general female concern from infancy, it is all too possible to overemphasize Dickinson's neediness and the depth of her particular imposition upon her correspondents. The equivalent of Dickinson's plaintive pleading can be found in much of the female correspondence of the period.[26] The exaggeration of an expressed desire for an immediate reply to one's own letter was part of the rhetoric of sentimental excess that pervaded the culture. This was not evidence of an insatiable demand on the part of the writer, but rather part of an epistolary code signifying an affectionate concern. In fact, not only was Dickinson incredibly successful in eliciting replies from her correspondents—particularly after the normal, and often painfully slow, demise of early childhood friendships—but those correspondents, in turn, frequently begged *her* for replies to their letters. Often, Dickinson has to apologize for the tardiness of her response to a previously received letter. This mutuality of demand would have been self-evident if the letters she received had not been destroyed by her sister, Lavinia. We can assume that the female recipients of her letters, in particular, would have responded to Dickinson's fervent appeals with a rhetorical excess the equal of her own. Epistolary excitability was not at all unusual, and, in this at least, the emotionally demanding poet of our conjecture appears a paragon of normality.

Of course, since it is in social contexts that personal identity emerges, and because letters became Dickinson's primary field of social interaction, it is only natural that we should demand that the poet's correspondence reveal her identity in all its mysterious glory. But it is not just the case that certain personality traits—pathological morbidity and hysterical codependence—are invalidly superimposed on Dickinson's prose persona by the clumsy surmises of historical retrospection. Rather, *any* judgments we make about her self based on her personal correspondence are probably equally deluded. Austin Dickinson, who knew her best, cautioned that in her letters to Higginson she "definitely posed." And Dickinson experimented with the definitive pose often in the letters: one of the more memorable of her late-adolescent poses was assumed before Austin Dickinson himself. This cultivation of epistolary disguise drew upon the major undercurrents of a society where the art of performance had become crucial. Halttunnen claims that in the antebellum period "the sentimental dread of hypocrisy was yielding to a new appreciation for the aesthetic value of personal disguise."[27] The decay of the sentimental ideal demanded an awareness of the power of the social mask and of the necessity of skillful social performance. In the 1850s and 1860s, this led to an increasingly theatrical attentiveness to the social presentation of the self. The Dickinson family, notorious Amherst snobs, were always concerned with appearances. The long concealment of the Mabel Loomis Todd–Austin Dickinson affair from curious scholars and Martha Dickinson Bianchi's subsequent editing of the poetry in the interests of constructing a family myth are obvious evidence of the tenaciousness of that concern for a later generation. Dickinson did not need to travel far beyond her father's grounds to recognize the artistry in an adept social performance and the necessity of maintaining appearances.

The poet's appearance (and infrequent public appearances) in the 1860s was marked by her famous white dress. Halttunnen, commenting on the semiotics of antebellum clothing, notes that "within the sentimental ideal, dress had been regarded as an index of character, a mirror of the soul, an outward revelation of inner moral qualities. But, now, in the 1850's, the art of dress was the art of projecting a particular personal style, and this new concept of style was increasingly confused with character itself."[28] Critical interpretations of Dickinson's choice of dress tend to demarcate it as either "an index of character" or "a revelation of inner moral qualities." But if style and character were quite discrete during the antebellum period, it will not do to confuse the two. Replaced in its historical context, Dickinson's white dress, as a vivid manifestation of personal style, seems more likely one very contrived component of an individual theatrical performance.

And this performance finds its quintessential expression in the personae and style the poet developed for the theater that is her social correspondence. In general, the predominance of style over substance in the presentation of the self had important consequences for the antebellum letter writer. For example, the existence of letter-writing "style manuals" was an obvious manifestation of the society's inbuilt contradiction regarding the compatibility of gentility and sincerity:

> For the sentimentalists who instructed the American middle classes on epistolary etiquette, writing a letter was an act of emotional self-expression. At the same time, letters, like manners, were a critical aspect of the genteel performance. . . . In many guides to polite letter-writing, as in all American etiquette manuals of the period, sentimental demands for sincere self-expression lay side by side with bourgeois demands for civilized emotional self-restraint. Although the avowed content of the polite letter was heart-felt sentiment, the form was rigorously self-restrained, stylized, and most significant, standardized.[29]

The extremely mannered letters of Dickinson's adolescence are saturated with sentimental rhetoric, standardized in their own way. However, her later letters, especially those written after a mid-1860s watershed, are more personally stylized. Finding her voice in the interstice between social form and sentimental content in the standardized mode, it may be the case that the friction or tension evident in Dickinson's epistolary rhetorical apparatus is partly the consequence of her adaptation, rather than resolution, of an existing paradox. Whatever the cause of that rhetorical tension, it serves to reinforce the suspicion that the poet's prose is only indirectly a revelation of personality, that being the personality of the recipient of the individual letter insofar as it can be reconstructed from the expectations Dickinson had of him or her as a reader. Ultimately, as Sharon Cameron has observed, Dickinson's letters "tell us more about the postures that replace relationship than about the relationships themselves."[30]

Dickinson's culture encouraged in the letter writer the assumption of formal disguise and of an affected, rhetorical prose style. In order to elicit a specific reader response, Dickinson apparently took both processes to a hyperbolic extreme. Her manipulation of the formal mask is evidence of her awareness of the limited options available to women in a sentimental culture, where the best survivalist technique was precisely the cultivation of role-playing prowess. Her rhetorical prose style evidences her simultaneous construction of a subversive authority from within the confines of the assumed pose.

Dickinson has recourse to rhetorical seduction of Higginson and the "Master" because issues of power are integral to her correspondence with both men. The complex rhetorical mechanisms she devises to effect that seduction are a means of inverting the hierarchy implicit in the typical male/female social relationship. I call the process "rhetorical seduction" because there are parallels between this rhetorical strategy and other representations of seduction in the discourse of antebellum women. For a woman living in a mid-nineteenth-century culture defined by sentimentalism, seduction had a potentially duplicitous signification. The evidence of the moral reform movement and of the sentimental novel was that the scene of seduction opened a rhetorical space within which could be effected the temporary upsetting of the prevailing gender power structure. The scene of seduction was the cultural expression of female powerlessness and, simultaneously, a means of access to the existing cultural power dynamic. It offered the possibility of situational subversion and therefore reconnection to the conduit of cultural power. Within the letters studied we find Dickinson's stylistic adaptation of antebellum women's cultural figuration of the scene of seduction. While her self-presentation appears particularly submissive and her chosen language structures imply an intrinsic powerlessness, her tentative deference toward the male correspondent is ultimately a sham in a context where the actual presentation—personal and linguistic—of that deference is concurrently the powerful expression of her own authority as a writer (and the authority that comes with being a superior writer) as it comes to be vividly exercised over that same correspondent in the form of rhetorical control.

However, the exercise of an authority accessed through the strategic seduction of the reader is not just rhetorical, and it would be misleading to confine the poet's capacity for enticement to a linguistic effect. Like all the best, or at least all the most memorable, seductions, Dickinson's is also a seduction *of the body*. In her reading of the letters, Suzanne Juhasz only tentatively makes use of the word "seduction" and reminds us that Dickinson "always uses language to represent herself, and language is never a body."[31] But as Juhasz notes in her discussion of Dickinson's letters to Austin, "the letters *as a body* are constructed to seduce him" (emphasis added).[32] I would suggest that the letters can—and not necessarily metaphorically—function as a textual embodiment of sorts, an embodiment that confirms Dickinson's seduction as being of palpably physical intent.

Kristevan theory demarcates poetic language as the overlapping of the physical and the rhetorical. As distinct from any spoken language whose function is communication, poetic language contains elements in excess of meaning and signification. It is not a departure from any norm represented by communicative language, but instead foregrounds an otherness of language, an unconscious of language. The poetic text is the effect of a dialectical interplay between the conscious and unconscious dispositions of language, what Kristeva classifies, in her radical reinterpretation of Lacan, as the "symbolic" and "semiotic" registers. Art can be defined as the successful semioticization of the symbolic, an infusion of the repressed unconscious of language into the normal communicative structure. The dialectical interplay between the symbolic disposition of language (which makes up the phenotext) and the semiotic disposition (which makes up the genotext) in a sense *is* the poetic text. More specifically, the genotext, which is an "unmediated physical presence" of prelinguistic bodily drives that articulates only nonsignifying structures, finds its actualization through poetic language. Poetic language is therefore always to some extent an inscription *of the body* as a sequence of basic rhythms and drives that subvert textual unity and authority.

As I observed earlier, Kristeva's descriptions of the textual consequences of genotextual effects have application to Dickinson's impacted prose: language acquires the depth of materiality as opposed to transparency; syntax, as a guarantee of consciousness, disintegrates because of disturbance of sentential completion; ellipsis causes an endless array of possible syntactic applications; as a result of nonrecoverable elision, terms are linked together in a potentially endless multiplicity; the meaning communicated is undecidable because the signified is either multiple or incomprehensible; and the signifying apparatus is itself foregrounded and centrally displayed for the reader.[33] But what makes Kristeva's theory especially suggestive is that the reader of the poetic text is a participant. As semiotic operations are dependent on bodily drives, the response to poetic language is an exercise of the reading subject's desire, where sexuality is implicated in an attentiveness focused on the subliminal prelinguistic rhythms of the text. If the poetic text is the writing of the body, then reading subjects process that body through the inscription of their *own* bodies. Therefore, if we are to claim that Dickinson's letters upset normal communicative structures through their subversive infusion of the semiotic disposition of language, the primary evidence of that fact would be their effect on the physical disposition of their readers. Of course, few of the letters written to the poet in reply to her own survived the posthumous destruction of her papers. Higginson's remark that Dickinson displayed in her letters to him "skill such as the most experienced and worldly coquette might envy" is, however, decidedly suggestive. We will have cause to revisit Higginson's "worldly coquette" in future chapters concerned with critical responses to the poetry.

Despite Dickinson's occasional rhetorical separation of the terms "prose" and "poetry"—for example, her assertion to Sue Dickinson that "all the rest are prose" and her poetic lament "They shut me up in Prose— / As when a little Girl / They put me in the Closet— / Because they liked me 'still' " (P. 613)—she often seems to have had no separate public (letters) and private (poems) language. Not only are poems integral parts of her letters, but the rhythms of the prose meld into the hymn meter of the poetry at emotionally heightened moments within those letters. So if at times the prose approximates poetic communication, it seems equally the case that poetic communication, as communication, also had, for Dickinson, a proselike function. Thus, while the prose assumes the texture of poetry, the poetry is rhetorically conceived as the functional equivalent of a personal letter. Gary Stonum notes that Dickinson imagines poems as being like letters insofar as "the speech-act situation of poetry [is] like the sending and receiving of letters."[34] Of course, it has always been possible to think of a Dickinson poem—on and using her own terms—as "my letter to the World / That never wrote to Me" (P. 441). It may even be possible to consider her poems concerned with the act of reading letters as exemplifying a general model of ideal Dickinsonian reading. The necessary rigor that ideally accompanies an attentive reading is, for example, demonstrated by the (hyperbolically amused) letter-reading narrator of this poem:

The Way I read a Letter's—this—
'Tis first—I lock the Door—
And push it with my fingers—next—
For transport it be sure—

And then I go the furthest off
To counteract a knock—
Then draw my little Letter forth
And slowly pick the lock—

Then—glancing narrow, at the Wall—
And narrow at the floor
For firm Conviction of a Mouse
Not exorcised before—

Peruse how infinite I am
To no one that You—know—
And sigh for lack of Heaven—but not
The Heaven God bestow—
    (P. 636).

This letter reader requires complete separateness, an absolute privacy that verges on self-imposed imprisonment. Locking the door is the prerequisite for unlocking the letter, an unlocking that is not merely the tearing open of an envelope but also the slow deciphering of the contents. The ritual of reading is conducted with religious solemnity: there is a communion of reader and text here. On this occasion, however, to the reader's disappointment, transport proves less than sure ("sighed for lack of Heaven") and the text too prosaic for enchantment. In poem 412, one of Dickinson's pseudo-Gothic narrators, a prisoner reviewing her own capital sentence, *does* find a text worthy of intimate perusal: "I read my sentence—steadily— / Reviewed it with my eyes, / To see that I made no mistake / In its extremest clause." In the circumstances, attentiveness is only to be expected, but the abrupt last line of the poem—"And there the matter ends" (where the matter in question is also the poem itself)—recalls the significant play on the word "sentence": this has been the narrator's reading of *her* sentence presented to the reader of the poem as *another* sentence to be read. The duplicity of this signifier is a reminder that the rhetorical seductions of Emily Dickinson find their exemplary expression in her poetry. The question that both prefaces and informs my discussion of that poetry in the next chapter is therefore this one: to what extent do the subversive rhetorical strategies of address identifiable in the letters similarly inform the poetry?

3

The Poetics of Seduction

Risk is the Hair that holds the Tun
Seductive in the Air—
That Tun is hollow—but the Tun—
With Hundred Weights—to spare—

Too ponderous to suspect the snare
Espies that fickle chair
And seats itself to be let go
By that perfidious Hair—

The "foolish Tun" the Critics say—
While that delusive Hair
Persuasive as Perdition,
Decoys its Traveller
—Dickinson, *Poem 1239*

CRITICS OF DICKINSON's poetry have often been intrigued by what Joanne Dobson characterizes as a "particularly intense constellation of images, situations, and statement in her poetry [that] reveals an intriguing preoccupation with masculinity, and, more particularly, with a facet of masculinity that is perceived as simultaneously omnipotent, fascinating, and deadly."[1] Indeed, this obvious preoccupation led Clark Griffith to suggest that Dickinson "stood in dread of everything masculine, so that one of the bogies she fled from was nothing less than the awful and the implacable idea of *him*."[2] Griffith correctly points out that although Dickinson's poetic victims and victimizers assume many guises, the former are usually feminine figures and the latter invariably masculine—the female child is molested by a male sea (P. 520), or equally tormented by a male God (P. 476); female flowers are blasted by a male frost (P. 391), while the female morning is betrayed by an uncaring male sun (P. 232); the female narrator is sent scurrying by a phallic snake (P. 986), or driven to eternity by a ghostly coachman (P. 712)—all apparent evidence that Dickinson came to regard "cosmic depredations as depredations practiced by one sex upon the other."[3] Griffith observes that "far too often to be either chance or coincidence, the 'loved one' arrives on the scene to alarm as well as to delight; his actions threaten even as they gratify, and the possibilities he extends are always somehow double-edged, so that love shades off into pursuit, betrothal can easily become seduction."[4] Certainly, in Dickinson's poetry the reader frequently finds a female speaker whose narrative emphasizes her own passivity, weakness, and insignificance. That speaker is locationally dwarfed by proximity to the powerful presence of a clearly superior masculine force. When that force is personified and directly addressed as God, Lover, Father, King, Emperor, Lord, or Master, the speaker's relative powerlessness invariably defines the relationship. Within such a system of established hierarchy, the speaker often characterizes herself as the tiny daisy juxtaposed to the "Immortal Alps" (P. 124) and the "Himmaleh" (P. 481), or unflatteringly paired with the "Great Caesar!" (P. 102) who is her "Her Lord" (P. 339).[5]

Dickinson's experience of antebellum culture must have provided ample evidence of the ways male power had been codified, not only in patriarchal religion and the institution of marriage but also in an essentially masculine poetic tradition. The exercise of power—whether social, religious, or aesthetic—and the assertion of masculinity were virtually simultaneous activities. Given that fact, Dobson has chosen to interpret the masculine figure in Dickinson's poetry as a composite image of appropriated power: the poet's desire for a power that she inevitably associated with the masculine impelled her to reconstruct a male archetype that could effectively symbolize that power. Readers of the poetry, according to Dobson, witness a complex figuration of Dickinson's imagined relationship to a male muse, or Jungian animus, a relationship she often regarded as one of potential threat and probable subordination and tinctured with hints of ecstatic masochism: "Most—I love the Cause that slew Me" (P. 925). Dobson's conclusion parallels that reached by a number of her critical predecessors—most obviously, Adrienne Rich, Joanne Feit Diehl, and Arthur Gelpi—who have variously asserted that the hierarchical relationship between Dickinson's poetic narrators and a variety of male others does not necessarily express or examine a relationship between individuals but instead meditates in quintessentially romantic fashion on the relationship between the poet and her creative imagination.[6]

Though interesting, this critical perspective is distinctly limited in its ability to recognize (or to offer) any more overt social critique. Most obviously, confining the male/female relationship figured within the poems to an internal agon of the female psyche presumes the poet's relative disinterest in the more significant external male/female power dynamics that contributed to her particular aesthetic problem. Such a critical reading assumes that Dickinson was primarily an exponent of an art-for-art's-sake aesthetic that happened to have a passing gender nuance. It is both more interesting and more plausible to argue that while the male figure within the poems is indeed a "composite figure" of power, he is also a recognizable derivation of a more specific and identifiable sociohistorical "character." In fact, Dobson suggests as much herself, albeit inadvertently, when she asserts that "the Death as Lover configuration that is such an inextricable part of Dickinson's mythos of masculinity is vitally relevant to the understanding of this *seductive* aspect of her negative animus" and that "Because I could not stop for Death" (P. 712) and "Death is the supple Suitor" (P. 1445) are "explicit in their assignment of this characteristic of the *masterful seducer* to the death figure" (emphasis added).[7] Dobson is perfectly correct (as was Griffith) in characterizing the composite male figure as seductive, not least because he derives in large part from the cultural image of the "masterful seducer" that, as we have already seen, was a fixture of the discourse of the antebellum period as a significant residual cultural formation.

The familiar seducer is a fixture of Dickinson's poetry. Poem 1053 offers us a paradigmatic demonstration of his technique:

It was a quiet way—
He asked if I was his—
I made no answer of the Tongue
But answer of the Eyes—
And then He bore me on
Before this mortal noise
With swiftness, as of Chariots
And distance, as of Wheels.
This World did drop away
As Acres from the feet
Of one that leaneth from Balloon
Upon an Ether street.
The Gulf behind was not,
The Continents were new—
Eternity it was before
Eternity was due.
No seasons were to us—
It was not Night nor Morn—
But Sunrise stopped upon the place
And fastened it in Dawn.

This poem, like so many of Dickinson's that feature an unspecified male figure, has a potentially significant double reference.[8] That vague pronoun "He" clearly refers to some male force that could completely efface the world as it was previously known to the speaker. The pronoun could therefore quite plausibly signify yet another of Dickinson's personifications of Death as cosmic travel courier. Similarly, "He" might be the God who requires a Christian, especially as one of the Calvinist elect, to turn away from mundane concerns. However, the poem resonates with the possibility of a secular equivalent, an earthly transformation of a woman speaker by a male figure that is of sufficient magnitude to ensure that "Eternity it was before / Eternity was due." This figure takes her not "*Beyond* this mortal noise" but "*Before* this mortal noise," a significant difference. Establishing the "seductive aspect" of the deathlike masculine figure who strikes the speaker dumb when "asked if I was his" is therefore of particular importance. It is worth recalling that the antebellum woman who succumbed to the wiles of the seducer would, in a real sense, have comprehensively destroyed her world. That destruction went considerably beyond social ostracism and isolation: the succumbing to the seducer, at least in its fictional representation, was inevitably considered a prefiguring of the seducee's death. Therefore, it was not only God whom none could see and live: for an antebellum woman, the same was often true of the seducer.

The personification of the frost as a particularly effective seducer in poem 391 provides another example (among many)[9] of how the gendered participants in a typical Dickinson poetic narrative might have proven particularly evocative of other seductive situations for an antebellum audience:

> A Visitor in Marl—
> Who influences Flowers—
> Till they are orderly as Busts—
> And Elegant—as Glass—
>
> Who visits in the Night—
> And just before the Sun—
> Concludes his glistening interview—
> Caresses—and is gone—
>
> But whom his fingers touched—
> And where his feet have run—
> And whatsoever Mouth he kissed—
> Is as it had not been—

In the rhetoric of moral reform, unspoiled young women were often delicately flowerlike: "Oh! that we who are mothers, may become doubly diligent!—watch over the precious plants entrusted to our care, and endeavor to secure them 'from the wild beasts of the desert' of this world."[10] The fact that Dickinson tended to represent not just Frost but also God, Christ, and Death as seductive male figures who demand of her narrators the willing surrender of their entire being is not likely to be coincidental. Indeed, that fact might remind us of the extent to which the social ramifications of seduction were presumably more significant determinants of the Dickinson psyche than was her fearful approach toward the symbolization of a Jungian animus. The unspecified "He" whom the reader of Dickinson's poetry can variously find fumbling at the victim's soul before scalping her (P. 315), snapping the belt around her life as a preliminary to folding her up (P. 273), finding, setting up, and adjusting her being (P. 603), touching her in particularly memorable ways (P. 506), and, in general, living a life of ambush in anticipation of her passing (P. 1525), is, I would suggest, somewhat more than an all-purpose, protean "Burglar! Banker—Father!" (P. 49) male figure. While sometimes "He" may be identifiable as God or Death or Lover or Father, what can always be said with some certainty is that his typical actions and strategies are those of a first-rate seducer.

The evil seducer identified by moral reform rhetoric was also a shape shifter. Carroll Smith-Rosenberg observes that in the movement's literature he is variously described "as an 'animal,' a 'wild beast,' a 'serpent's coil.' He was 'brutal,' a 'hideous monster,' a 'master demon.' He existed between states, outside of categories and boundaries. He was alien to women's world, beyond her control—and dangerous."[11] In Dickinson's poetry, that alien force is often conceptualized as a simultaneously inviting and encroaching sea. That sea is, of course, also the poet's favorite symbol of eternity, and the drowning of an individual or the sinking of a ship therein—representing, one supposes, the dissolution of self the seeker of spiritual truth need experience in integration with the divine—is the subject matter of many Dickinson poems. But in what is often an ironic simulacrum of a death-tinged mating dance, the sea's seductive technique, his proffering of that "glittering Embrace" to his intended, itself seems *the* subject of particular interest to the poet:

Escaping backward to perceive
The Sea upon our place—
Escaping forward, to confront
His glittering Embrace—

Retreating up, a Billow's height
Retreating blinded down
Our undermining feet to meet
Instructs to the Divine
    (P. 867)

The equation of repeated futile attempts to escape and/or retreat from a threatening sea with an understanding of the divine is a typical Dickinson flirtation with blasphemy. But the curt humor is undercut by the further suggestiveness of the metaphorical vehicle and its intimation of other flirtations punishable by death. The final line may affirm the speaker's sustained faith in "the Divine" and her acceptance of its instruction, but the terror of the preceding lines is never completely dispelled. The price of surrenders secular and divine is the bliss that encroaches on an imminent fatality. The overtones of sexual seduction in this speaker's mingled fear of and desire to be consumed by the powerful Other reappear in other poems of marine threat. In this seductive context, the conclusion of poem 520's memorable (and often-examined) tidal pursuit requires no further elaboration:

> But no Man moved Me—till the Tide
> Went past my simple Shoe—
> And past my Apron—and my Belt
> And past my Bodice—too—
>
> And made as He would eat me up—
> As wholly as a Dew
> Upon a Dandelion's Sleeve—
> And then—I started—too—
>
> And He—He followed—close behind—
> I felt His Silver Heel
> Upon my Ankle—Then my Shoes
> Would overflow with Pearl—

Poems that appropriate the terms of a preexisting rhetoric of seduction for situational deployment in their basic narrative reveal the most common adaptation of the basic seduction motif in Dickinson's poetry. As inoffensive a jingle as poem 91, for example, concerning the narrator's secretive plucking of a flower, acquires further resonance when considered alongside contemporary accounts of the seducer's plucking of the flowers of femininity:

> So bashful when I spied her!
> So pretty—so ashamed!
> So hidden in her leaflets
> Lest anybody find—
>
> So breathless till I passed her—
> So helpless when I turned
> And bore her struggling, blushing,
> Her simple haunts beyond!
>
> For whom I robbed the Dingle—
> For whom betrayed the Dell—
> Many, will doubtless ask me,
> But I shall never tell!

The narratives of the female flower gatherer and the male seducer overlap provocatively here. Mary Loeffelholz comments that, "imagining nature as female and herself as a sexually ambiguous raptor," Dickinson "replays and parodies romantic errands into nature."[12] That may well be true, but by assuming the position, power, and voice of the male seducer Dickinson also "replays and parodies" the dialectic of power in antebellum culture. This was a culture, after all, within which young women could frequently be found "hidden in the leaflets" of the sentimental and romantic novels. The seduction represented in poem 91 is, however, something of an exception to a more general rule. Dickinson's narrators rarely assume the voice and superior position of the seducer within the poems. Usually they do not have to resort to strategies of mimicry or parody; instead, they set about directly appropriating the seducer's powers by destabilizing his established position of rhetorical authority within the actual framework of the poem.

In the usual scenario, a female speaker establishes a scene of seduction within which she assumes the role of antebellum seducee. In earlier chapters I noted how the role of antebellum seducee was not without its possibilities when deliberately and consciously assumed. In the antebellum period, the scene of seduction had become for women the convenient representation of the existing gender hierarchy and the act of seduction the effective symbolization of their own relative powerlessness. However, the fictional or rhetorical rendering of a scene of seduction by a woman writer, offering as it did the potential both to address and expose that hierarchical power structure, was frequently preliminary to an attempt at upsetting the gender dynamic. The re-creation of that power structure in writing—which amounted to the fictional representation of a role that was itself already figural—could be the means of access to a power grid that could be rerouted. This process is evident in Dickinson's poetry. When an identifiably female narrator appears to establish and validate a traditional male/female hierarchy within the scene of seduction, she is often simultaneously engaged in a subtle questioning of and sometimes an inversion of the very same power coordinates that support the hierarchy. Indeed, this subversive process occurs frequently enough to suggest that the examination and dismantling of the power dynamic between the speaker and her male addressee is the primary theme of the poems.[13]

The typical strategy of seduction in such a poem is figured in the apparently submissive female speaker's address to a significantly more powerful male reader/addressee. In the course of that address, however, it is precisely the relative power of the two subjects that is increasingly called into question. In recent years, the subversive edginess of address in poem 106, for example, has helped make it a touchstone text for feminist criticism of Dickinson:[14]

The Daisy follows soft the Sun—
And when his golden walk is done—
Sits shyly at his feet—
He—waking—finds the flower there—
Wherefore—Marauder—art thou here?
Because, Sir, love is sweet!

We are the Flower—Thou the Sun!
Forgive us, if as days decline—
We nearer steal to Thee!
Enamored of the parting West—
The peace—the flight—the Amethyst—
Night's possibility!

Margaret Homans observes that the daisy and the sun are alike insofar as they share a minimal visual resemblance implicit in the daisy's name (day's eye). The daisy's deferential address to a sun beside whom she finds herself unfavorably comparatively defined is at the same time her subversive strategy for the bridging of the tremendous discrepancy between their relative powers. That bridging is achieved "through a strategy of mock humility" that "gently dismantles the sun's pretensions to absolute power." Finding that "she can increase her power only by decreasing his," the speaker invokes a transcendent third term—"Night's possibility"—beyond both the daisy and the sun, which permits an escape from a closed system of opposed and relative power and not only "removes the basis of their relationship (visual resemblance and optical illusion)" but also "requires the absence of the beloved sun himself."[15] In Homans's reading, the undoing of the specific male-sun/female-daisy hierarchy established within the poem is facilitated by the dismantling of other male-imposed hierarchies, which she identifies as the conventional structure of romance and the privileging of metaphor as rhetorical trope.

Homans's reading of "The Daisy follows soft the Sun" is a bravura critical performance.[16] But the same scenario is played out in many other poems. Poem 481, another daisy poem, is representative:

The Himmaleh was known to stoop
Unto the Daisy low—
Transported with Compassion
That such a Doll should grow
Where Tent by Tent—Her Universe
Hung out its Flags of Snow

Initially, the reader's assumption is that "The Himmaleh" is male. However, the poem's ambiguous conclusion (centered on that problematic feminine possessive) implies that either the mountain is female or the "Universe" is the province of a significantly more powerful daisy. As Cristanne Miller points out, "Because Dickinson's mountains in her flower poems are usually male, and because *Himmaleh* is so suggestively masculine, we conclude that the universe is probably the daisy's."[17] If that is the case, the fact that the mountain stoops with compassion and therefore deferentially is clearly ironic. The implication of the poem is that his stooping should rather be one of respect for the extent of her dominion (the "Flags of Snow" she drapes around his summit) over a "Universe" of which he is merely a part. Of course, the ambiguous syntax of the first two lines also problematizes this reading. Can we really decide that it is the daisy that is adjectively "low" or whether that describes the *extent* of the stooping that she requires the mountain undertake? Our inability to establish any interpretive hierarchy in the reading of this poem is therefore the appropriate consequence of its sustained questioning of hierarchy.

Both "The Himmaleh was known to stoop" and "The Daisy follows soft the Sun" do not so much effect a significant power inversion as suggest its imminent possibility. Apparent subservience conceals strategies of aspiration and affirmation: complacent omnipotence is liable to become the first principle of dependence. The mutual implication of power and weakness—the fact that power not only defines itself in relation *to* the powerless but requires that it be recognized as such *by* the powerless—ensures that the sudden inversion of hierarchies is always a possibility. Many of Dickinson's poems announce the imminence of such an inversion in memorably paradoxical first lines, such as "She rose to His Requirement—dropt" (P. 732) and "I rose—because He sank— / I thought it would be opposite" (P. 616). In such poems, subject/object confusion is a predictable rite of passage: "He was my host—he was my guest, / I never to this day / If I invited him could tell, / Or he invited me" (P. 1721). Indeed, it is decidedly inadvisable that "he" should be a host, as that would frequently be to a particularly parasitic "she." The extraterrestrial metaphor of poem 909 elaborates the principle of variable dependency and relative power that is implicit, if habitually unrecognized, in any relationship structured by gender:

> I make His Crescent fill or lack—
> His Nature is at Full
> Or Quarter—as I signify—
> His Tides—do I control—
>
> He holds superior in the Sky
> Or gropes, at my Command
> Behind inferior Clouds—or round
> A Mist's slow Colonnade—

But since We hold a Mutual Disc—
And front a Mutual Day—
Which is the Despot, neither knows—
Nor Whose—the Tyranny—

In these poems, this alternative scene of seduction operates on a "see/saw" principle—the female speaker's rise is simultaneous with the male addressee's related fall, and, in the process of that positional interchange, the readers of the
poem can no longer *see* what they once *saw* in the poem. As the actual etymol-
ogy of the word implies, Dickinson's verse (versus) is often the site of the pivotal
activity, of oppositions in mutually informed movement.

Of course, the limitation of this particular rhetorical seduction is that its
effects are confined to the participating subjects—the speaker and her fictional
addressee—within the framework of the actual poem. Poem 124 appears to be
an allegorical meditation of sorts on precisely this limitation:

In lands I never saw—they say
Immortal Alps look down—
Whose Bonnets touch the firmament—
Whose Sandals touch the town—

Meek at whose everlasting feet
A Myriad Daisy play—
Which, Sir, are you and which am I
Upon an August day?

The final question the speaker poses—whether it is she or the addressee who is
either the mountains or the daisies—is precisely the question that the poem continually calls *into* question. The poet's epistolary identification with the name
"Daisy" might imply that it is the speaker who is the "Myriad Daisy." Dickinson did, after all, assume her "Daisy" persona (most obviously in the "Master"
letters) in order to defer to a male reader, and in this poem the implied reader
is clearly male. However, if the "Sir" addressed in this poem is to assume that
he is, metaphorically, the "Alps," then he will have to explain away his accou-
trements, as "Bonnets" and "Sandals" are decidedly feminine accessories. So
perhaps it is the speaker who is the "Immortal Alps," since she is a poet, and
timeless stature is the province of the artist. In which case, there can be scant
quantitative satisfaction in her addressee's being a *"Myriad* Daisy." An August
day signals the imminence of the daisies' late-summer death, and mortality is
inescapable, however myriad of them contest it. The poem's final image also
problematizes the hierarchy that would place the immortal speaker/mountains

above the addressee/daisies. "August" is a duplicitous adjective; this is not merely a late-summer day but also an *august* one, inspiring awe and reverence, one that is magnificently imposing and worthy of respect because of its age, dignity, and stature. If "Night's possibility" was the transcendent third term in "The Daisy follows soft the Sun," then in this poem it is the August day—one that proves more magnificent than the mountain basking in its light. Of course, the sun that perfects that August day is also the singular day's eye (daisy), so what magnificence then in "Myriad Daisy"? Hierarchy has here become so confusing, or at least so relative, as to be meaningless.

But at the same time, the playful speaker recognizes that the power inversions and mutual equivalences she imagines are possible only "In lands I never saw." Having no personal knowledge of the existence of such lands, she must rely on the knowledge of others, on what "they say." The invocation of the authority of a generalized other within a Dickinson poem is usually a vicious irony, and this is no exception. The poem's opening line undercuts what follows: the playful see/saw inversion of internal hierarchies is dependent on a more significant authoritative external hierarchy of power/knowledge, which its poet-speaker has little capacity to challenge. The fact that her poem itself constitutes just such a hierarchy-neutral "land" is scant compensation to the speaker in the context of her larger locational dependence, that greater relational powerlessness. The speaker's qualification is Dickinson's own. The dismantling of hierarchy within a poem is an ineffectual strategy when it has been sanctioned by a more immediate manifestation of that same hierarchical authority. The question is how a poet could ever set about dismantling those more significant established hierarchies.

The poems I have examined so far can be separated into two related groups. The first group adapts an existing thematics of seduction. The recognizable antebellum characters of seducer and seducee are deployed in the poems' basic narrative as occupied subject (and object) positions in a scene of seduction. The second group expands the possibilities of the situated seduction scenario. These poems depict the formal subversion of male/female power hierarchies that the scene of seduction typically offers the antebellum woman writer: within these poems we witness the inversion of an assumed male/female power structure conceived as hierarchical difference. In this case, the scene of seduction occurs between the female narrator and a metonymically addressed male "you" from whom the reader, assuming a certain ironic distance, can choose to disassociate. However, both these scenes of seduction can ultimately be viewed as second-order representations of, or decoys for, the poet's most significant scene of seduction, one continually effected in the reader/text interaction itself. Many of Dickinson's poetic texts posit enticement scenes, but all of her poetic texts enact them.[18]

The manipulation of the reader's interpretive processing of the poems—or *poetic rhetorical seduction*—is particularly evident in Dickinson's enigma poems. The enigma poem seems to describe a specific mental experience, but one that is communicated only with exceptional difficulty, and in highly abstract terms, by its narrator. So, although the poems' subject matter could be (and has been variously critically identified as) depression, desperation, despair, and madness, what seems more important is the fundamental incommunicability of the central experience. In poem 937, for example, the narrator attempts to describe a specific mental experience through an abstract terminology that impedes a straightforwardly referential communication. The aesthetic supposition behind this poem would appear to be that, paradoxically, words can arouse senses that words themselves cannot explain. At the same time, the dissolution of context becomes a means to a poetic end, the description of the reaction to an incident, but not the incident itself, producing a strange effect of immensity:

> I felt a Cleaving in my Mind—
> As if my Brain had split—
> I tried to match it—Seam by Seam—
> But could not make them fit.
>
> The thought behind, I strove to join
> Unto the thought before—
> But Sequence ravelled out of Sound
> Like Balls—upon a Floor.

This poem is frequently interpreted as evidence of a personal dysfunction: Dickinson's unspecified mental trauma objectified by poetic language. But, like the many similar poems that also discuss this experience of internal difference or distancing, the abstract narrative reveals a speaker's attempts to cope linguistically with an experience that defies symbolization. Inevitably, such poems are both the most unfathomable and those that most often invite critical explication. A plausible explanation for their provocatively attractive difficulty is that they are a complex allegory of a crucial experience of difference that is not merely reported by the poems but *evoked* in their processing by a reader. Frequently, as in this poem, the attempt to convey this baffling experience of mental difference in linguistic terms concludes in an abstract image ("Sequence ravelled out of Sound") only imaginatively conceivable in language itself.[19] Such a conclusion seems useful not in eliciting the reader's empathetic understanding of that mental splitting through its representation as a concrete image in language, but in *actively reproducing* that sense of difference in the reader venturing an interpretation of that language.

Similarly, the distinction that the speaker attempts to make in poem 305 also defeats effective representation in language. This poem, too, is therefore most usefully read as a complex reading allegory of that distinction:

> The difference between Despair
> And Fear—is like the One
> Between the instant of a Wreck—
> And when the Wreck has been—
>
> The Mind is smooth—no Motion—
> Contented as the Eye
> Upon the Forehead of a Bust—
> That knows—it cannot see—

This poem's development is baffling until the reader realizes that its progress is not the careful pursuit of a detailed analogy. In fact, it is a misreading of the first stanza to anticipate the establishment of any one-to-one correspondence between "Despair" and the "instant of a Wreck" and "Fear" and "when the Wreck has been," or, allowing for an inverted syntax, vice versa. The poem is not an analysis of *a* difference but a meditation *on* difference, and the opening stanza does not establish any subtle analysis of the measurable difference between two separate emotional states, but instead traces the interstice between those two states as an end in itself. The interpretive problems that emerge in the course of reading are purposeful insofar as they cause a *replication* of difference as an instantaneous interpretive gap in the mind of the reader. The major interpretive problem is the frustration of the reader's search for the completion of the analogy apparently begun in the first stanza. The second stanza's continued analysis of the state of mind that is the difference between two abstract emotions through an even more abstract analogy, a metaphorical representation of that difference through the image of the bust's eye, is unexpected to say the least. But because of the unexpected content of that second stanza, the reader must confront the specific seam that separates the two stanzas, or, more precisely, their *difference* one from the other. Instantaneously coping with that difference comes close to replicating that state of being "between" that is the poem's subject. This embodiment of difference in the reading process itself recurs in the particularly apt final image of the bust "That knows—it cannot see." The knowledge that one cannot see is also the acquired knowledge of the reader of a poem that frustrates perception by making the awareness of a frustrated perception its central concern.

The experience of difference (not least from oneself) is also the subject of poem 721:

Behind Me—dips Eternity—
Before Me—Immortality—
Myself—the Term between—
Death but the Drift of Eastern Gray,
Dissolving into Dawn away,
Before the West begin—

'Tis Kingdoms—afterward—they say—
In perfect—pauseless Monarchy—
Whose Prince—is Son of None—
Himself—His Dateless Dynasty—
Himself—Himself diversify—
In Duplicate divine—

'Tis Miracle before Me—then—
'Tis Miracle behind—between—
A Crescent in the Sea—
With Midnight to the North of Her—
And Midnight to the South of Her—
And Maelstrom—in the Sky—

This poem offers many interpretive problems to its reader. As is so often the case in Dickinson's poetry, obscurity is the excess, not deficiency, of meaning. That excess is a result of the poem's momentum as a process that continually separates and duplicates the central terms of its argument. For example, in the first stanza the words "Eternity" and "Immortality," although clearly distinguished by the speaker, are insufficiently separated for the reader. Although "Immortality" is certainly more reflective of general eschatological concerns, the fact that both terms refer to an unending expanse of time, and that those mirroring expanses of time symmetrically surround the speaker, makes them virtually indistinguishable within the poem. Indeed, by the third stanza both terms will be collapsed as "Miracle." Moreover, the personal cosmic location of the speaker as "Myself—the Term between" complicates the sense of "term" (and, by implication, all "terms"). Referring both to a finite and elapsing pocket of time *and* to the word that forms part of a larger equation, "Term" must be understood by the reader as itself double, as two distinct terms. The first stanza's closing image is therefore most apt. That metaphorical comparison of death and a promised afterlife to sunset and sunrise traces the point of a specific transition in the world of nature. Limning the edge of the border area where terms (and terminologies) overlap, that exploration is a metonymic representation of the reader's necessary analysis of those points where terms separate within the poem.

Focusing on one of her two initial terms—"Immortality"—in more detail, the poem's speaker continues her own examination of a point of separation in the second stanza. That examination terminates in the realization that the guarantor of immortality is himself nothing more than a process of perpetual self-reproduction. As Cynthia Griffin Wolff notes, "Himself—Himself diversify— / In Duplicate divine" offers a spectacle that "is more than merely the mystery of the Trinity. It is the horrific proliferation of a house of mirrors." God is defined as an ultimate self-referring, a total reflexivity. But the process of mirroring that is a simultaneous separation and reproduction is itself mirrored in the process of the poem that describes it. The third stanza is a precise demonstration of that mirroring. Not only does the stanza's diction parallel the first stanza, there is also a more rigorous internal reflection, both in the syntax of its own six lines and in the complete semantic collapsing of the gap between "Eternity" and "Immortality" (by a "Miracle," no less) in the first two lines. The possible replacement of one "Term" by another is consolidated by the introduction of an abstract term, "Crescent," which, unlike the preceding "Term," far from having two potential referents, has a problematic *one*. Moreover, the reader is left to puzzle where two particular terms, the first-person "Me" of the first stanza and the third-person "Her" of the third stanza, vanish to and come from, respectively. Does one replace or supplant the other? Is "Her" a personified reference to the "Crescent"? Or is that problematic "Crescent" already the metaphorical substitute for that initial "Me"? Perhaps it is more useful to think of that movement from first to third person (significantly, from the first to the third stanza) as representing a complete restructuring of the poem's perceptive point of view. After all, perceptive rearrangement is continually demanded of the reader of the poem, for whom the interpretive enigmas seem to be of significance simply *as* enigmas. Central to the poem is its speaker's struggle to articulate a condition of undecidability, an experience of being caught *between*, in that space defined by two alternate poles. This condition seems to be the dilemma of a religious crisis, but it is also apparently an intrinsic experience *of* language and therefore a condition that the speaker cannot hope to communicate *through* language. Instead, the poem communicates the trace image of the condition itself, not through language's referential function but through language's tendency to become simultaneously self-referential. It is the interpreting reader's attempt to process the ambiguous syntax of the poem that comes to serve as an effective representation of that abstract experience of life-as-indeterminacy. Therefore, that the opaqueness of the poem eventually renders it unintelligible is its final claim to intelligibility.

These three poems discuss an experience of difference that cannot be communicated simply through the referential function of language. That experience of being different from oneself is the consequence of an attempted self-representation in a language that is itself constituted as a difference. In poem 695, Dickinson's metaphorical depiction of eternity as the perpetually incomplete revelation of the same term, a continual deferral that opens a spatial expansion of reproduced similitude, is equally plausibly an accurate representation of the workings of language:

> As if the Sea should part
> And show a further Sea—
> And that—a further—and the Three
> But a presumption be—
>
> Of Periods of Seas—
> Unvisited of Shores—
> Themselves the Verge of Seas to be—
> Eternity—is Those—

Because language is systemically dependent on differentiation and deferral, the attempt to represent an experience of self in language is inevitably compromised. The suggestive parallels between the linguistic perpetuity of the signifier, the popular immortality bestowed on the canonized artist, and the highly personal perception of the eternity promised by the Congregational Church did not just make the precise defining of the object of her faith problematic for Dickinson, they also crucially complicated her definitions of a self that could be represented only by language.

The enigma poems demonstrate how Dickinson's poetry cannot be understood apart from its results: it is a poetry in which meaning is experience. The poems are not aesthetic objects but units of force, rhetorical devices whose power is exerted on a reader in a particular direction. Power was "a familiar growth" (P. 1238) for Dickinson because her conception of poetry was as the purest manifestation of rhetorical power. What is important in these poems is not Dickinson's personal exploitation of the slippery evasions of language but the consequential effects of her poems' elusiveness on their readers.

The majority of Dickinson's poems settle for re-creating particular states of mind in the reader without the simultaneous abstract representation of the mentality. Most solicit a seductive reading experience via their sophisticated syntactic apparatus. But even those that lack a particularly detailed texture of language reproduce the sensations of indeterminacy in dilute form through a subtle shifting in, and upsetting of, narrative logic. The more easily observable shifts in the narrative of these poems help spotlight the mechanisms of a reading process that achieves its most spectacular results in syntactically complex poems. Poem 429 is an excellent example not only of how a male/female hierarchy established within a poem is often undercut, but also how the temporal reading process gradually uncovers the poem's more fundamental deconstructive difference from itself:

> The Moon is distant from the Sea—
> And yet, with Amber Hands—
> She leads Him—docile as a Boy—
> Along appointed Sands—
>
> He never misses a Degree—
> Obedient to Her Eye
> He comes just so far—toward the Town—
> Just so far—goes away—
>
> Oh Signor, Thine, the Amber Hand—
> And mine—the distant Sea—
> Obedient to the least command
> Thine eye impose on me—

There is an obvious similarity between the tone of this poem and that of Dickinson's letters to male correspondents. The narrator's voice, while apparently pleading submissiveness, manifests a subtly subversive irony that challenges any notion of a personal subservience. That irony is implicit in the third stanza, where the analogy between the moon's control of the sea and the addressee's control of the speaker is gently called into question. The disruption of the analogy is apparent in the third stanza's pronoun shift—the female moon that led a male sea is now the male addressee's leading of the female speaker. The third stanza's analogy is askew in other ways, as well: the addressee is not directly compared to the moon but to a ray ("Thine, the Amber Hand") of that moon, a significant diminution of status; the moon's "Amber Hands" (plural) become the addressee's "Amber Hand" (singular), an evident decrease in power;[20] and the first stanza's emphasis on the moon's distance from the sea becomes, in the third stanza, an emphasis simply on "the distant Sea," thereby calling into question the effectiveness of the addressee's control of a more suggestively remote speaker. These subtle changes all render doubtful the validity of the analogy, especially the actual degree of control of the addressee over the narrator. The most interesting differentiation is that while the personified sea "never misses a Degree— / Obedient to Her Eye," the speaker is "Obedient to the least command / Thine eye *impose on me*" (emphasis added). The first obedience is the acceptance of a natural authority, the second is the acquiescence to an artificial imposition. Although the shape imposed on the speaker may satisfy the addressee (who will see what he wants to see, regardless), the uncertain tone of the entire last stanza suggests that the speaker may demur and that the process of leading "docile as a Boy" actually continues. This is equally true of any control the reader (occupying the position of addressee) would wish to impose on this seductively protean poem: the controller can easily become the controlled when the object of that control proves so slippery.

Irony is an obvious means of introducing indeterminacy into any interpretation. But more interesting than the irony itself is the reader's gradual awareness of its emergence. In many Dickinson poems, the gradual infusion of doubt, an ambiguous trace suggestion that finally coalesces into a more concrete uneasiness at the end of the reading process, forces a reader to question retrospectively the intonation of the poem's voice and therefore the apparent certainty of the poem's assertions. The reader's processing of the poem is therefore intrinsically meaningful; the reading of the poem produces the disintegration of a simple, referential meaning and calls into question the validity of any meaning separate from the poem's temporal movement through the reader's mind.

However, in other poems the reading process subtly seems to reinforce and complicate rather than undercut an obvious meaning. The poem may insistently abolish simple referentiality, but the temporal reading process it demands, fragment by fragment, is meaningful in itself as the dramaturgy of its escaping theme. Poem 764 is an excellent example:

Presentiment—is that long Shadow—on the Lawn—
Indicative that Suns go down—

The Notice to the startled Grass
That Darkness—is about to pass—

This is apparently a generic Dickinson definition poem: a typical attempt to represent concretely an emotional state through analogy. But on this occasion, "Presentiment," the sense of anticipatory foreboding, is not merely embodied in the poem as its subject matter but is simultaneously an integral element of its reading, realized by a reader in the interpretive process. The reader's problems in an initial reading, both in making the connection between those two almost separately imagistic stanzas and in visualizing the metaphorical vehicle, disrupt the reading process through a subtle upsetting of anticipation. The consequent frustration produces an almost subliminal trace of linguistic discomfort, the equivalent of the sense of foreboding discussed in the poem, which can only be eased through the more comfortable rereading that retrospective hindsight permits.

The first problem for the reader is making a connection between the two stanzas, or, rather, compensating for an expectation prepared for and then frustrated. Informed in the first stanza that presentiment is like the shadow on the grass at dusk, the reader expects a further development of the analogy. In particular, experience of foreboding suggests that it requires some consciousness. Given the context of the first stanza, the reader expects that consciousness to be the property of a personification, and the reader *anticipates* the imminent arrival of an *anticipating* consciousness. As a result, "The Notice to the startled Grass" is somewhat disorienting. Retrospectively, what was anticipated was "The Notice *of* the Grass," where "Notice" would be verb instead of noun. Perhaps part of the aesthetic pleasure of the adjective "startled" is that it is precisely the state of mind of the reader at that moment. But the surprising narrative progress of the two stanzas is not quite as disorienting as the final image in the poem—"That Darkness—is about to pass." On a first reading, that phrase is strangely ambiguous to the extent that *passing* darkness is usually thought of as a fading or departure, and therefore a consequence of sunrise. And it is only after that interpretation has been considered and reluctantly rejected that the visual image of the sweep of a darkness *passing* over the grass occurs to the reader. Pushing continually against any temporarily correct reading therefore is the brooding insistence of another that is denied. That nagging awareness, activated by the two unanticipated reversals in the poem, is an almost unconscious foreboding within the poem that casts its own interpretive shadow over the reading process. As a result, the poem almost demands a more relaxed second reading that can resolve the unexpected through the reader's own foreboding anticipation of its imminence.

The effects of the poems are the result of the reader's grappling with their internal system of complex indeterminacy. That indeterminacy most often emerges where Dickinson's two separate systems of communication—the semantic (the referential function of language) and the syntactic (the temporal processing of that language by the reader)—both incomplete in themselves, are in a meaningful state of friction. The main consequence of that friction is the frustration of the comfortable possibility of singular interpretation; in fact, the frustration produced by that indeterminacy is often the *only* interpretation of those poems necessary. The emergence of indeterminacy can be located at specific points of ambiguity within the poems, and the reader's strategy of "coping" with those nodal points is itself a revelatory process. It is not just that the reader *experiences* a poetic ambiguity, a linguistic problem that can be dealt with in a reasoned, objective, critical manner; rather, the poem reproduces in that reader an ambiguous *experience* that is personally felt, a collapsing of distance that is closer to a state of mind, and with all the attendant misery that accompanies an insoluble *personal* problem.

In Dickinson's most effective/affective poems (as the effectiveness of a poem depends on its affectiveness, the two terms are here synonymous), the seductive strategy of reader involvement and compromising is honed to perfection. Alternative syntactic reconstructions of a sentence can produce fundamentally different poems according to the reader's whim. For example, poem 1069 presents its reader with an array of possible syntactic reconstructions that can significantly alter its meaning:

> Paradise is of the option.
> Whosoever will
> Own in Eden notwithstanding
> Adam and Repeal.

The significance of the first line of this impacted poem has often been underestimated. Of course, it can be interpreted as a quintessential Dickinson maxim, her aesthetic declaration that paradise is a state of mind. But the phrase itself is significantly "of the option," and the poem can be reconstructed as an evocation of the expected interpretive process of the Dickinson reader. In this case, paradise is not so much any decisive choice potentially made by the reader but the maintaining of a frame of mind where options are always available. Experience teaches us that Dickinson's poems depend on that always potentially available alternative reading that permits the reader to dwell in the paradisal state that is perpetual possibility.

It is not just the opening line that is an exercise in the optionality the poem describes. The lines that follow offer distinctly optional readings, too. In particular, the pivotal uninflected verb ("will") in the second line offers the possibility of two readings. The most obvious reading assumes that there is no break between the second and third lines of the poem and that "Whosoever will own" forms a syntactic unit. The verb is therefore conditional tense, and the sense is *"for* whosoever *wants* to own." However, if there is a significant break then "Whosoever will" forms its own syntactic unit, and it is the verb in the third line ("Own") that is uninflected. In this second reading, the verb is imperative, and the sense is "Whosoever wills." The difference between a conscious willing and a willful wanting is substantial, the latter more easily obtainable, the former demanding a significant exercise of conscious power. Similarly, the word "Repeal" presents the reader with a potentially interesting choice. It can be read as a noun and the phrase reconstructed as "despite God's Repeal of Eden for man's original sin." But the impacted syntax also allows "Repeal" to be read as an uninflected verb, of which "Whosoever" is the subject ("Whosoever will . . . Repeal"), a repealing that is consciously willed and, in defying the sentence of God, ironically parallels the original sin of Adam. As we know, the exercise of a willful *non serviam* does result in a theological option to paradise, an option only too graphically portrayed in the rhetoric of Calvinism. Thus, the choosing of *this* paradise *as* an option may be the means to the eventual denial of another. In a poem laced with syntactic ambiguity, any single interpretation denies the capacity for optional choice that the poem endorses.

Dickinson's best poems are those that are significantly "of the syntactic option." Poem 328 is a case in point:

A Bird came down the Walk—
He did not know I saw—
He bit an Angleworm in halves
And ate the fellow, raw,

And then he drank a Dew
From a convenient Grass—
And then hopped sidewise to the Wall
To let a Beetle pass—

He glanced with rapid eyes
That hurried all around—
They looked like frightened Beads, I thought—
He stirred his Velvet Head

Like one in danger, Cautious,
I offered him a Crumb
And he unrolled his feathers
And rowed him softer home—

Than oars divide the Ocean,
Too silver for a seam—
Or Butterflies, off Banks of Noon
Leap, plashless as they swim.

The poem offers a relatively straightforward narrative until the opening of the fourth stanza, where the reader must decide whether the opening phrase ("Like one in danger") completes the previous stanza or introduces the succeeding statement. Syntactic choice determines semantic choice: the clarification of the syntactic ambiguity as to whether it is the bird or the narrator who is "in danger" erases the alternate reading. The bird, with its "rapid eyes" resembling "frightened Beads," is certainly cautious. But so is a narrator who, previously cautiously concealed from the bird ("He did not know I saw") and having just playfully dissected the bird's own clinical dissection of the angleworm, is now, in a humorous sense, also at risk. Of course, the two readings are not mutually exclusive and can be reconciled by reading "Like one in danger" as a syntactic doubling that completes both phrases simultaneously, the resultant ambiguity validated by the evidence of a narrative itself suitably ambiguous.

There is a similar syntactic problem in the final stanza, where it is unclear precisely what is "too silver for a seam": is it the ocean, or is it the action of rowing upon that ocean? Once more, this can be resolved by the reader's recognition of a syntactic doubling that makes both readings simultaneously possible and *seamlessly* co-present in the poem. For if the poem's narrative argues the seamlessness of a natural world in which worm, dew, beetle, and bird coexist in dynamic equilibrium, it is also a demonstration of that seamlessness in action: the overlapping syntax that fuses the speaker and the bird she observes, and the ocean and the rowing upon it, involves the reader in a process of syntactic separation, reconnection, and eventual acceptance of indivisibility. This is a reader processing ironically paralleled by the culinary expertise of the bird, who, confronting the angleworm, neatly halves it to facilitate its consumption, but then reunifies it in the eating and as an organic whole in the digestion. In a similar way, the word "Noon" is perfectly evocative in its context both as signified and signifier; not only is midday a time where the two hands of the clock imperceptibly overlap, swallowing up the angle that the hands normally form, but the word "Noon," a tiny, impacted palindrome, is itself seamlessly stitched.

The reader's processing of a linguistic seamlessness culminates in the final stanza's frustration of the expected metaphorical expansion of the parallel between the flight of the bird and the rowing on the ocean. Instead, the reader confronts an apparently invalid dual equation—the motion of the bird's wings against the sky resembles an imperceptible rowing of oars on an ocean *that resembles in turn* the swimming motion of butterflies in the sky. This appears illogical—it is not so much that comparing birds in the sky to butterflies in the sky is redundant, but that the comparison could not be made in this particular way if it were not for the intervening clause that introduces the metaphorical association of sky and sea. The two statements on either side of the hinge word "Or" cannot therefore be read as valid alternatives: the second statement of necessity has to include its predecessor if it is to be logically comprehensible. The apparently circuitous logic of the stanza, the elaborate weaving of natural processes and syntactic clauses alike into a seamless whole, is therefore actually an appropriate conclusion to this metaphorical representation of the indivisibility of process.

Poem 742, a superbly evocative work, is a perfect example of how Dickinson's brilliant use of developing syntactic indeterminacy produces a complex series of effects in the mind of its reader, and how the creation of that state of mind is at the thematic core of the poem itself:

Four Trees—upon a solitary Acre—
Without Design
Or Order, or Apparent Action—
Maintain—

The Sun—upon a Morning meets them—
The Wind—
No nearer Neighbor—have they—
But God—

The Acre gives them—Place—
They—Him—Attention of Passer by—
Of Shadow, or of Squirrel, haply—
Or Boy—

What Deed is Theirs unto the General Nature—
What Plan
They severally—retard—or further—
Unknown—

There are two mutually supportive forms of ambiguity in this poem: the ambiguity of the individual word or phrase, and the syntactic ambiguity that envelops it.[21] For example, the phrase "Without Design" is suggestively compact enough to offer four different interpretive possibilities: that the four trees do not have a design in the sense that they fail to form a recognizable pattern for the eye; that they have, carefree, no apparent purpose in their actions; that they are positioned quite by accident, by no exterior designation; or that they are outside ("Without") a larger, existing design. Not all those meanings are incompatible, and it would be a substantial project to analyze all the possible combinations and paradoxes suggested by that one phrase. But in order to reach those knotty interpretive cruxes the reader must already have made a definitive syntactic choice: he or she has already assumed that the subject of the second line was the "Trees" ("Four Trees . . . Without Design") when it could just as easily have been the "Acre" ("solitary Acre— / Without Design"). The immediate clarification of *what* lacks design is obviously crucial before venturing an interpretation of a poem significantly centered on *another* viewer's attempted interpretation of artistic design.

Syntactic ambiguities pervade the poem. The verb "Maintain" presents an interesting syntactic problem insofar as it can serve as the conclusion of a preceding phrase for which the reader must intuitively replace the missing object (the trees maintain *themselves* despite what they apparently lack) or the verbal hinge to an object ("The Sun") in the second stanza. This is obviously an acceptable syntactic doubling: it is possible to view the trees in splendid isolation *and* as the provider of a visual frame for the sun's journey across the sky. Of course, accepting that plausible second reading does not disqualify "The Sun" from being the subject of its own sentence (the sun meets them in the morning). The same syntactic doubling is evident in the third line, where "The Wind" could be a syntactic parallel of "The Sun" ("The Wind—upon a Morning meets them") and simultaneously the inverted object of the third line ("No nearer Neighbor—have they—[than] The Wind"). In fact, this process of syntactic overspill can be carried on indefinitely—for instance, to ask the valid syntactic question of whether it is the wind or God that is the trees' neighbor assumes that the referent to "they" is the trees and not, as it could well be, the sun and the wind.

Complex syntactic questions inevitably implicate the reader in minor semantic crises. What, for example, is the precise subject for "gives" in the third stanza? Apparently, "Acre" can function simultaneously as the subject and object of the same sentence: is it that the acre gives the trees location, or, allowing for a clausal connection to the preceding stanza, that the "Acre" is given to the trees by God? This doubling effect is reinforced by the pronoun "Him"— referring potentially to both a personified acre *and* God. The third stanza is packed with such potential doublings. For example, is it the trees that provide the acre with shadow, or is it that same shade that apparently attracts the passerby? Familiarization with syntactic doubling continually opens space for potential irony. What if, for example, the pronoun "Theirs" in the final stanza referred not to the trees but back to the various species attracted to those trees in the previous stanza? And it is precisely because the syntactic ambiguities of this poem present the reader with a series of semantic options that his or her syntactic processing eventually comes to reinforce the poem's suggestive meditation on the intentionality of design.

Familiarity with the poem elides the complex temporal processing required in an initial reading, and my attempt to recapture that reading may be flawed by a premature intuition that the poem can be interpreted self-reflexively: that the significance of a poem about four trees on a solitary acre, a poem that is composed of four stanzas, each of four lines, is simply too obvious to ignore. Nonetheless, the fact that the parallel design of trees and poem is itself a symbolic doubling would suggest that the poem is not so much a meditation on its own form as a reflexive speculation on its reading effects. Reading the poem requires the completion of syntactic clauses from the options available, and that involves either looking back to a previous phrase or stanza, looking forward to a succeeding phrase or stanza, or, in a case of syntactic doubling, both movements reconciled in the interpretive process. That overall process is perfectly captured in that final reference to the trees ("What Plan / They severally—retard—or further"), which suggests just that process of retrospection ("retard"), expectation ("further"), and both ("severally") required of a reader's concretizing of the text. In such a poetic theater of randomness, any prior "Plan" of the reader, or indeed the effect on his or her "General Nature," is inevitably indeterminate, the impossibility of prediction (and predication) most certainly rendering the result "Unknown."

Similarly, the reader's temporal processing of as syntactically complex a text as poem 339 is almost certainly meaningful as *experience:*

I tend my flowers for thee—
Bright Absentee!
My Fuchsia's Coral Seams
Rip—while the Sower—dreams—

Geraniums—tint—and spot—
Low Daisies—dot—
My Cactus—splits her Beard
To show her throat—

Carnations—tip their spice—
And Bees—pick up—
A Hyacinth—I hid—
Puts out a Ruffled Head—
And odors fall
From flasks—so small—
You marvel how they held—

Globe Roses—break their satin flake—
Upon my Garden floor—
Yet—thou—not there—
I had as lief they bore
No Crimson—more—

Thy flower—be gay—
Her Lord—away!
It ill becometh me—
I'll dwell in Calyx—Gray—
How modestly—alway—
Thy Daisy—
Draped for thee!

Interpretations of this poem tend to dwell on its thematics of sexuality. The obvious sexual suggestiveness of its formal display is significantly reinforced by a syntactic processing that encourages, even demands, the reader's strenuous interactive involvement, a mutual interpenetration, a textual rubbing if you will, itself decidedly, if somewhat inexplicably, sexual in nature. Consequently, interpretations of this poem are sometimes revelatory but almost always uncomfortably self-revelatory. For that reason I hazard (and it would certainly be a hazard) no significant interpretation of this poem of my own. One can get caught up so in the web of the syntax of a poem that has the absence of depth of a mirror.

These poems inevitably stimulate in their reader a productive restlessness. The reader must continually move between two syntactic units with a residual impression of the first and an anticipation of the second. But while a second syntactic phrase may, for example, "complete" its predecessor by establishing a structurally intelligible relation with it, more often than not it also initiates further anticipatory movement toward a third syntactic phrase, which, in turn, perpetuates the process. The attempt at simplification tends to both reveal and produce complexity. The reader's aesthetic pleasure in a poem such as this (and this poem merely exemplifies the process common to all of Dickinson's poems) is therefore not so much to be found in the images obliquely signified by the language but in the actual tension of the displacing movement of the signification itself. This is a pleasure contingent on establishing, dismissing, displacing, and temporarily reestablishing various relational terms. It is the pleasure of perpetual movement and, as such, analogous to the pleasure of a desire itself defined as a pleasurable movement toward an always absent source of satisfaction. One might argue that the pleasure of a mobile and indeterminate sensuality *is* the pleasure of desire. Dickinson's perpetually restless poetry, which delights in intervalic memory and deliciously prolonged anticipation, therefore provides its reader with an object lesson in interstitial sensuality, and thus by implication in the psychodynamics of desire. To comprehend the affects of such a bifurcative and dissipative poetic would require the formulation of a powerful experiential dynamics of reading. The most thorough analysis of that experiential dynamics of reading would necessarily extend outwith the syntactic framework of the poetic text: the fact that some poems exist in variant form and that so many others have unselected variants in the fascicle manuscripts extends the possibilities of reader participation enormously and provides further evidence that Dickinson intended her texts to be experienced as process, as an ongoing, reader-implicating production at the most basic level.

Of course, contemporary reader-response critics locate the organizing principle of literature in the reader in order to emphasize the individuality of aesthetic response. For example, Stanley Fish asserts that "the formal patterns" of literature "are themselves constituted by an interpretive act"; David Bleich rejects the "objective paradigm" and argues that interpretation is a "motivated resymbolization" that expresses the unconscious motives of the reader; and

Norman Holland disputes the "biactive theory of text-reader interaction" in his argument that the "overarching principle" of interpretation is that "identity re-creates itself. . . . [A]ll of us, as we read, use the literary work to symbolize and finally to replicate ourselves."[22] In each of these cases, the form and unity of the text is a function of the reader's subjectivity; it is either a blank screen animated by the reader's fantasies or, alternatively, a structure recognizable only through the reader's membership in the larger interpretive community that validates aesthetic perception. However, in the case of Dickinson's poetic texts, I am loathe to surrender the "biactive theory of text-reader interaction." These texts clearly delimit and direct reader response: they demarcate a specific interpsy-chic field of literary experience. I would therefore agree with Marshall Alcorn's assertion that "texts are not blank screens reflecting the projections of a reader: textual signifiers *do* things to projections" and concur that while the material signifier may "not guarantee a stable referential event," it most certainly does "guarantee a stable perceptual event that plays an important role in conscious, unconscious, and narcissistic reading processes."[23] Dickinson's poetic texts re-main objective to the extent that readers are primarily concerned with percep-tion of the material signifiers and not with the interpretation of them. Interpre-tation is, in fact, an unnecessary adjunct to the processing of these texts because their particular properties do not exist as categories of referential meaning but as rhetoric pure and simple. And that rhetoric is never innocent, for, as Lacan observed, "Language is not immaterial. It is a subtle body, but body it is. Words are trapped in all the corporeal images that captivate the subject; they may make the hysteric pregnant."[24] We will return to the corporeal image of words and to the possibility of "hysteric" response in later chapters.

Chapters 5 and 6 trace "sorcery" in action as it is manifested in the critical writings of Dickinson's readers. But first, chapter 4 will examine the seductive mechanism of Dickinson's poetics in more detail. This will necessitate a return to the word "seduction" in an attempt to consolidate what I previously argued was the important *physicality* of the term.

4

The Word Made Flesh

Listen to a woman speak at a public gathering. . . . She doesn't
"speak," she throws her trembling body forward; she lets go of herself,
she flies; all of her passes into her voice, and it's with her body that she
vitally supports the "logic" of her speech. Her flesh speaks true. She lays
herself bare. In fact, she physically materializes what she's thinking; she
signifies it with her body. In a certain way she *inscribes* what she's saying.
—Cixous, "Laugh of the Medusa"

I breathed enough to take the Trick—
And now, removed from Air—
I simulate the Breath, so well—
That One, to be quite sure—

The Lungs are stirless—must descend
Among the Cunning Cells—
And touch the Pantomime—Himself,
How numb, the Bellows feels!
—Dickinson, *Poem* 272

IN THE SUMMER OF 1851, the twenty-year-old Emily Dickinson attended a performance by popular Swedish singer and antebellum media celebrity Jenny
Lind and concluded, with typical directness, that she would "rather have a Yan-
kee." However, immediately following Dickinson's musical critique is her interesting speculation on the possible reason for Lind's popular acclaim, an astute
perception that the singer's popularity was not explicable solely in terms of her
musical talent. In a letter written the following day, Dickinson observed that the
positive response of the audience (including herself) to Lind's performance was
the result of a spontaneous affection for the singer: "How we all loved Jenny
Lind, but not accustomed oft to her manner of singing did'nt fancy *that* so well
as we did *her.*" In fact, Dickinson was so struck by the appeal of the artist over
the art that she repeated her point: "*Herself,* and not her music, was what we
seemed to love—she has an air of *exile* in her mild blue eyes, and a something

sweet and touching in her native accent which charms her many friends" (L. 46). That charm, the ability to cultivate an audience's affection, was integral to Lind's appeal as an artist, and the successful exercise of that charm was, quite simply, Dickinson's definition of genius: "Genius is the ignition of affection—not intellect, as is supposed,—the exaltation of devotion, and in proportion to our capacity for that, is our experience of genius" (L. 691). In this context, Dickinson's declaration that she would "rather *be* loved than . . . called a king in earth, or a lord in Heaven" (L. 185) appears a far from sententious statement. If the "ignition of affection" and the "exaltation of devotion" in a reader were central tenets of Dickinson's impressionistic aesthetic, then her ability to cultivate that reader's love was the means of gauging her *own* genius. A similar conception of genius would actually facilitate her later reception, in the 1890s. In his review of the poems, H. R. Blackwell observes that "there is a curious fascination in the brief, obscure, and somewhat incoherent stanzas of this shy, secluded New England girl. . . . One is often in doubt what the meaning is, or whether there be any. And yet, in almost every stanza there is something that rouses curiosity and enchains attention. *The best evidence of genius is that it attracts and stimulates, and Miss Dickinson was a genius*" (emphasis added).[1]

The example of Jenny Lind provided Dickinson with a useful model for her own "performance" art. From an early age she had recognized her talent as an entertainer, informing one of her first correspondents that "I will entertain you to the best of my abilities, which you know are neither few nor small" (L. 5). She never stopped thinking of herself as a covert theatrical performer. In 1860, thanking the Norcross sisters for the gift of a coat, she was still playfully commenting on her theatrical "designs": "Do you think I am going 'upon the boards' that I wish so smart attire? Such are my designs, though. I beg you not to disclose them!" (L. 225). Integral not only to the secrecy of those designs but also to their eventual realization were the charming theatrical possibilities that stem from a personal concealment. Dickinson realized that "going out of sight in itself has a peculiar charm . . . the unknown is the largest need of the intellect" (L. 471). The perfect example of intellectual need was the unknown personified as deity: "They say that God is everywhere, and yet we always think of Him as somewhat of a recluse" (L. 551), and, to some extent, Dickinson's chosen seclusion imitated God's withdrawal from the world. Especially appealing to Dickinson, the self-conscious artist, was that paradoxical process by which the ultimate Creator, through his apparent absence, became the ultimate creation of his audience's desire. So although Dickinson's personal seclusion was at least partially determined by innate psychological need,[2] it also supported her theatrical performance; her dependence on the controlled communication of written language facilitated the creation of a series of charming personae in both her letters and her poems. Not surprisingly, especially given the mythology/ theology of the unseen, Dickinson came to think of herself in fictional terms; she observed of living in Amherst, "It is difficult not to be fictitious in so fair a place" (L. 330), and excused a temporarily lapsed correspondence with Higginson by noting, "I thought that being a Poem one's self precluded the writing Poems, but perceive the Mistake" (L. 413). In her explication of the poet's self-mythologizing, Sandra Gilbert finds an "essential reciprocity of the life/text and the literary text."[3] Gilbert argues that Dickinson's "white election" is significant because it "suggests not only that she transformed her life into art more readily than most other writers but also that, more than most, she used her 'small' life itself as an instrument of her great art: even the most ordinary materials of her life, that is, became a set of encoded gestures meant both to supply imagery for, *and* to supplement, the encoded statements of her verse."[4] This is a useful expansion of the argument first made by Gilbert and Gubar, that Dickinson's life was "a kind of novel or narrative poem," a life lived in the shadow of the Gothic romance genre, with Dickinson casting herself in the role of the female Gothic heroine.[5]

But I think the tendency of Dickinson's critical readers to explain the life in terms of the art *or* her art in terms of her life, as though the two terms were ever really separable, has been to the detriment of our total view of the poet. For one thing, it has problematized readings of her *body*. Dickinson's recognition that the artist is often of more significance to the reader than the art, combined with her awareness that there were distinct aesthetic advantages in the personal seclusion of that artist, produced an elaborate poetic compensation for her own necessary physical absence. That compensation was the attempt to *embody* herself within her poetry. Consequently, Dickinson's art is never ethereal, but aggressively physical. In her incredibly significant first letter to Higginson she asked, "Are you too deeply occupied to say if my Verse is *alive?*" Dickinson wanted this poetry to be a *living* art: "Should you think it *breathed*—and had you the leisure to tell me, I should *feel quick gratitude*" (L. 260, emphasis added). There is a powerfully implied connection here between poet and poem: if the verse breathes, then the poet feels "quick gratitude," thereby reminding her reader of that essential connection between a poet's body and a poem that ensures they breathe as one. This is a poetics of vivid presence. Dickinson's critical readers, however, usually align themselves with her friend, Samuel Bowles, who dubbed her the "Queen Recluse." The "Queen Recluse" is the great American celebrator of absence—the personal absence that was the hermetic seclusion that permitted the writing of the poetry; the eschatological absence that informs the subject matter of so much of the poetry; and, most of all, the various linguistic absences—in punctuation, in syntax, in deixis, in definitive word choice—

that so complicate that poetry's semantic interpretation. While not disputing the fact that Dickinson's is frequently a poetics of absence, I would suggest that absence ultimately serves presence in its evocation of that which is missing. Dickinson knew that "to the faithful Absence is condensed presence" (L. 587), and to "faithful" readers the absence of the poet herself could be replaced by her "condensed presence" as text.

In fact, the reason Dickinson responded to Higginson's *Atlantic Monthly* article with such enthusiasm was that she found traces of her own aesthetic interests scattered throughout it: "Have faith enough in your own individuality to keep it resolutely down for a year or two"; "do not undertake to exercise these prerogatives of royalty until you are quite sure of being crowned"; "do not indulge any fantastic preference for either Latin or Anglo-Saxon"; "do not shrink from Americanisms"; "study each phrase so carefully that the most ingenious critic cannot alter it without spoiling the whole passage for everybody but himself." Higginson's metaphors for the writing process must have been appealing, too: "Do not leave loose ends as you go on . . . but work them all in neatly, as Biddy at her bread-pan gradually kneads in all the outlying bits of dough till she has one round and comely mass." Perhaps most tellingly, Dickinson's letter to Higginson was a response to this warning: "Do not be made conceited by obscurity, any more than by notoriety. Many fine geniuses have been long neglected; but what would become of us, if all the neglected were to turn out geniuses."[6] The reclusive poet had come to need confirmation of her genius and thought Higginson, apparently a kindred spirit, was a critic fit to give it. Therefore, the sense of the living poem touching Higginson with its breath goes beyond what R. Jackson Wilson sees as Dickinson's "play" with the "metaphor of living language" that Higginson used in his article.[7] Reading Higginson's description of language "saturated with warm life" and of words that "palpitate and thrill with the mere fascination of the syllables,"[8] Dickinson perceived a writer who might share the primary tenet of her aesthetic—her sense of sentient communication—rather than a mere figure of speech that could be kneaded into a "conceit" for her own letter. After all, the notion of "living language" permeates Higginson's article in one other significant way; his editorial expectation regarding the poem—"that it should be attractive"—precisely mirrors his editorial expectation of the writer of that poem, who, knowing how "an editor's eye becomes carnal, and is easily attracted by a comely outside," should "draw near him . . . with soft approaches and mild persuasions." Writer and text were to be judged on the same seductive terms. Small wonder therefore that Higginson's aside—"How few men in all the pride of culture can emulate the easy grace of a bright woman's letter"—should produce a very bright woman's letter delivering precisely the coquettish concoction he expressed a preference for.[9]

Dickinson's initial letter of reply was not merely her acknowledgment that "by means of the poem" she, too, "enters into and in some way alters the alive percipience of other persons,"[10] it was simultaneously the practice of that art upon Higginson, an aesthetic of embodiment, of hybridization, in action. It is a measure of Higginson's obtuseness that he later actually expressed surprise at Dickinson's display of "skill such as the most experienced and worldly coquette might envy." In fact, Dickinson thought she was giving Higginson precisely what he asked for in a woman writer. What Dickinson's reply to Higginson suggests is that the representation of the "body" is of crucial importance in her poetic strategies. Of course, that "body" is not the literal one she took such care to conceal from the prying eyes of strangers: the body whose illness the family doctor was supposed to diagnose from a glimpse of its passage by an open door; the body for which her dressmaker could cut patterns only after using Lavinia Dickinson as a near model; the body only once represented by the art of photography in that early, disappointingly conventional daguerreotype. We are concerned instead with the body Dickinson preferably inscribed as language—"I am small, like the Wren, and my Hair is bold, like the Chestnut Bur—and my eyes, like the Sherry in the Glass, that the Guest leaves" (L. 268)—with the poet who genuinely believed that "a Book is only the Heart's Portrait—every Page a Pulse" (L. 794).

It is often convenient for us to forget that the breathless, ethereal Dickinson who declared "I am afraid to own a Body" also declared "I am afraid to own a Soul" (P. 1090). Admittedly, the young Dickinson disparaged the body by emphasizing her personal distaste of it: "I do not care for the body, I love the timid soul, the blushing, shrinking soul; it hides, for it is afraid, and the bold obtrusive body—Pray, marm, did you call *me?*" (L. 39); by stressing her own distance from it: "So I concluded that space & time are things of the body & have little or nothing to do with our selves";[11] and by noting its unimportance relative to the soul: "Glad to know you were better—better *physically,* but who cares for a *body* whose *tenant* is ill at ease? Give me the aching *body,* and the spirit glad and serene, for if the gem shines on, forget the mouldering casket!" (L. 54). But the Dickinson who found her vocation as poet came to consider her *poetry* as a significant representation of that self, a living, breathing entity, boldly intrusive. This is evident in her frequent recourse to the metaphor of clothing when describing the forms that inhibit the "bodily" expressiveness of language. She admitted to Higginson that her central technical problem in the writing of her poems was that "While my thought is undressed—I can make the distinction, but when I put them in the Gown—they look alike, and numb" (L. 261). Of course, this is a direct response to Higginson's comment: "When I think how slowly my poor thoughts come in, how tardily they connect themselves, what a delicious prolonged perplexity it is to cut and contrive a decent clothing of words for them, as a little girl does for her doll, —nay, how many new outfits a single sentence sometimes costs before it is presentable, till it seems at last, like our army on the Potomac, as if it never could be thoroughly clothed."[12] But years later, in a personal letter to Judge Lord, Dickinson would still return to the theme of undressed thought: "Speaking to you as I feel, Dear, without that Dress of Spirit must be worn for most, Courage is quite changed" (L. 790). What the formalities of social communication (the "Dress of Spirit") and the similar formalities of poetic convention (the "dressed thought") conceal is the sheer nakedness of language itself, an exposure of language that Dickinson associated with a naked exposure of the physical self.

The ultimate exposure of language and self (where both assume synonymity) is publication. Dickinson told Higginson that she would as soon undress in public as give her poems to the world.[13] Such fears were not peculiar to Dickinson. For any woman writer of the era, publication involved the necessary nakedness that was public exposure. While Nathaniel Hawthorne, delighted at Fanny Fern's subversive edge, observed that when women "throw off the restraints of decency, and come before the public stark naked, as it were,—then their books are sure to possess character and value," that was also precisely the problem for the woman writer. Such public writing was for Dickinson's contemporary Caroline Gilman not so much a problem of undressing as one of redressing. When she discovered that one of her poems had been secretly published in a Boston newspaper, she cried half the night and admitted to being "as alarmed as if I had been detected in man's apparel."[14] The association woman writers made between the act of writing and a public exposure of the naked self often made publication seem the equivalent of prostitution, a selling of *themselves* in the public eye. To some extent, at least, this was how men viewed it, too. Lydia Sigourney's husband observed in a letter of 1827 that his wife evinced a *"lust* of praise which like the *appetite* of the cormorant is not to be satisfied," and was guilty of an "apparently ungovernable *passion* of *displaying herself."* This prompted him to ask "who wants or would value a wife who is to be the public property of the whole community?"[15] The confusion of writing with the exposure of a body for commercial purposes (and therefore analogous to a form of prostitution) was perhaps, therefore, not peculiar to women writers.[16] Fear of male reprisal made such personal writing necessarily covert and can perhaps partially explain Dickinson's curiously ambivalent attitude toward publication.

One Dickinson poem that expresses just such an inhibited response to publication because of its dangerous exposure of the body is poem 709:

Publication—is the Auction
Of the Mind of Man—
Poverty—be justifying
For so foul a thing

Possibly—but We—would rather
From Our Garret go
White—Unto the White Creator—
Than invest—Our Snow—

Thought belong to Him who gave it—
Then—to Him Who bear
Its Corporeal illustration—Sell
The Royal Air—

In the Parcel—Be the Merchant
Of the Heavenly Grace—
But reduce no Human Spirit
To Disgrace of Price—

This poem has often been interpreted as though it communicated to the reader something about Dickinson's personal attitude toward the publication of her poetry. Of course, Dickinson's habitual reference to her poetry as "Snow" would seem to reinforce this reading. Moreover, the research of Karen Dandurand and Joanne Dobson, among others, has suggested that Dickinson *chose* not to publish.[17] Indeed, the fact that she did publish a number of poems is now frequently used to support the argument that she could have had many more in print if that had been her desire. Dickinson's apparent skepticism about the value of publication would therefore seem to confirm the plausible reading that the complaint in this poem is a personal one. However, even aside from the fact that Dickinson, at various times in her poetic "career," expressed a more acutely ambiguous response to the idea of publication, it is extremely dangerous for the critic to assume that in this poem he or she hears the voice of *the* poet as opposed to the voice of *a* poet. The fact that the narrator of this particular poem at one point identifies with the instantly recognizable starving artist in the obligatory "Garret" would make her only problematically Dickinson herself. In fact, reading the poem as the ingenuous complaint, or rather marvelous rationalization, of an unpublished poet may give the poem a neatly ironic, cutting edge. However, if we do assume that the statement made by this poet has Dickinson's unequivocal sympathy, it is worth examining in more than passing detail the nature of her objection to publication.

The most serious objection to publication raised by this particular poet-narrator is that her art would be substantially devalued by its contamination with a commercial instinct ("Disgrace of Price"). But it is interesting that the depth of that contamination goes considerably beyond the mere commercialization of the text. The crucial question raised by the ambiguous syntax of the third stanza is, To whom does the thought that energizes a poem properly belong? Who precisely is the "Him who gave it"? The second stanza suggests that the referent to "Him" might be the "White Creator," who might, in turn, be God. If so, then thought belongs initially to God, and, as he "gave it," such thought now presumably belongs to everyone created in his image. Therefore, it is the bodies of human beings that are literal "Corporeal illustrations" of that thought insofar as the human body can be thought of as the most singular representation of God's creative imagination. There is, however, clearly an alternative, and more fascinating, reconstruction of the poem's syntax that would assume a clear division between the second and third stanzas. In this case, "Him who gave it" would be identified as the writer, while "Him Who bear / Its Corporeal illustration" would be the reader who appropriates the communicated thought. The reader's bearing a "Corporeal illustration" would refer to the reader's bearing the body of the text in the sense of *carrying* the published package or book on his or her person. Alternatively, the more interesting interpretation is that the reader bears the "Corporeal illustration" of that thought in the sense of re-creating the image of the author inscribed in the text. In this reading, the author's assumption is that her text and herself are so blurred together in the writing for effective presentation to a reader that, in any subsequent transaction, the selling of that text would be the selling of the "Corporeal illustration" of herself. In other words, it would indeed be the equivalent of selling her physical body, a prostitution of sorts.

The persistence of the physical body as text is a subject frequently explored in Dickinson's poetry. Indeed, many of her best poems are ironic meditations on the failure to escape a body continually reinscribed by the language that seeks to move beyond it. The poet's most exotic psychic voyaging to the conceivable limits of her poetic imagination, those voyages that permit her to take care of the "business" that is her exploration of "Circumference," are often a studious limning of the border area between life and death, and therefore between bodiliness and bodilessness. Such poems suggest that only in the transient, indeterminate moment that is the recognition of personal mortality will the self, confronting the reality of its physical annihilation, be motivated to make the imaginative leap toward a conception of that which could be outside of, or apart from, the physical body. But these poems also demonstrate that even the motivation of mortality is ultimately insufficient when the failure to conceive the soul in linguistic terms is inevitable. After all, how can one physically define an entity only conceivable as precisely the negative of everything physical? The problem to which Dickinson continually returns is the linguistically inconceivable nature of the spirit's bodiless survival, the fact that "The Spirit lasts—but in what mode— / Below, the Body speaks, / But as the Spirit furnishes— / Apart it never talks" (P. 1576). So while the desire to "burst the fleshly Gate" (P. 277) is the ever-present motivation of her narrator's poetic questing, Dickinson's intensely corporeal conception of identity continually dooms the imaginable realization of that quest. Invariably, the collapse of that quest occurs whenever the speaker gropes for a language that would transcend the limitations of its grounding in mortality in order to represent a spiritual dimension beyond.

For example, in poem 351 the personal exploration of a posthumous existence can only occur within the limits of a vocabulary that inevitably evokes physicality. It becomes increasingly obvious to the poem's narrator that it is impossible for her to separate herself from the corporeal terms in which a previous existence had been so vividly experienced and categorized. However, on this particular occasion that inescapable fusion is to her advantage. The persistence of language is a comfort to the narrator precisely because it permits her to reconstruct a recognizable sense of physical identity within her initially unrecognizable new spiritual state:

I felt my life with both my hands
To see if it was there—
I held my spirit to the Glass,
To prove it possibler—

I turned my Being round and round
And paused at every pound
To ask the Owner's name—
For doubt, that I should know the Sound—

I judged my features—jarred my hair—
I pushed my dimples by, and waited—
If they—twinkled back—
Conviction might, of me—

I told myself, "Take Courage, Friend—
That—was a former time—
But we might learn to like the Heaven,
As well as our Old Home!"

The irony of the first image is acute. The attempt to feel her "life" with her hands to see if that life is there can only make the speaker eventually aware that what is missing are precisely those necessary hands. As the strongest evidence of self previously known to the narrator was the awareness of her own body, the absence of the sheer physicality of "hands," "features," and "hair," is inevitably distressing to her, particularly because the habitual recourse to her five senses—each, in turn, explored and dismissed with increasing frustration—can bring no "Conviction" of her own identity, that is, an identity that has been previously predicated on specular recognition ("held my spirit to the Glass"). Of course, Lacanian psychoanalysis defines identity precisely in terms of initial specular recognition, so it is tempting to read the narrator's situation as a posthumous revisiting of the "mirror" stage. What the archetypal Lacanian child finds (or actually misrecognizes) in the mirror is a gratifyingly unified image of itself, a pleasing "imaginary" unity that it does not experience in its own body. The discovery of that imaginary unity is the first step the child takes on its way to the construction of the ego. But for the narrator of the poem there is initially no means of constructing a new center of self in a new spiritual dimension because there cannot even be the possibility of misrecognition when there is no reflection at all to be found in the mirror.

What makes the narrator's adaptation to her situation so fascinating is her use of language to construct an "imaginary" of her own. Ironically, in the heavenly realm of images the only available imaginary is the memory of the retrospectively pleasing unity that was her own body. It is that body that the narrator's language reinscribes as her initial failure to achieve the necessary self-recognition becomes the stimulus to the search for an alternative that she ultimately finds in the very discursive track that the search for presence has left. In short, the physical body persists as a trace simply through the fact of its reappearance in the language that searches for it. Just as the body may retain the nervous "feeling" of an amputated limb, so the soul retains through linguistic reinscription the "sense" of the amputated body. The central irony of the poem is precisely this: the speaker's discursive responsiveness to her increasing recognition of the actual absence of the body eventually becomes for her the ingenious solution to the problem that absence presents. Her persistence in using language to search for that absent body reinscribes the figure of that body—the body-as-poem—within the territory of her new spiritual dispensation. The soul's identification with that textual body, or rather the soul's sense of difference from that textual body, then becomes the means of forging a new sense of unitary selfhood.

The language of the poem reinscribes presence by offering to the narrator the possibility of her own grammatical doubling. That narrator has previously become habituated to the duality of being—that dyad Dickinson elsewhere describes as a "Profound—precarious Property— / Possession, not optional— /

Double Estate" (P. 1090). Therefore, experiencing her new singularity as a necessary lack of self, the narrator's adaptation to her new environment involves the creative reconstitution of the soul/body duality within her new immortal dispensation. Unsure of what to call her singular immortal state—and dismissing inadequate terms such as "life," "Being," and "features"—she returns to the more comfortable soul/body relationship by conceiving her sole/soul self in relation to the body she perpetually reinscribes in language. That linguistically conceived body becomes a "Friend" that can be directly addressed, while the soul becomes newly recognizable as the "I" that can do the addressing. Ultimately, the narrator can only come to "terms" with her own new identity, indeed can only recognize it *as* an identity, by the doubling of herself and the establishment of a relationship between the two poles. Thus, the apparent *division* of her own identity in fact *constitutes* that identity. Moreover, that identity, comprised of a subject of the enunciation and a subject of the enunciating, is once more the property of the speech act. Of course, this necessary separation—one literalized by the quotation marks of the final stanza—is the means of coping with a new immortal situation that has never in all of Dickinson's canon looked a bleaker prospect. Indeed, can the final resignation to an eternity of talking to oneself really be considered an adequate coping mechanism? Crucially, it should be noted that this important poem is not merely concerned with the persistence of the body in language; it also demonstrates the irony of how language, when used to protest the absence of the body, deconstructs itself by virtue of the simultaneity of its reinscription of that same absent body.

The ironic reinscription of the body by a writing that deliberately seeks to exclude it from a larger argument is evident in poem 1492. This is a particularly problematic poem, initially problematic because it may not actually be a poem. It was written by Dickinson in 1880 and included as part of a letter sent to Perez Dickinson Cowan. Cowan, the pastor of the Congregational Church in Wellesley, was by then well accustomed to being engaged by his cousin in an epistolary discussion of religious subjects of particular concern to her. Most frequently, such discussions concerned the Dickinson "flood" subject of immortality. This poem might therefore be considered part of Dickinson's larger ongoing dialogue with scriptural authority (and, more immediately, with men she considered scriptural *authorities*) on that subject. On this occasion, it is Dickinson's meditation on 1 Corinthians 15:35—"But some will say, How are the dead raised up? and with what body do they come?" This passage was perhaps particularly relevant to the context of the letter because of the recent death of Cowan's daughter. He had previously sent Dickinson a memorial account of the girl's brief life, and Dickinson's letter was her consolatory reply:

nates—by rendering unnecessary—faith, the passage calls into question the very basis of knowledge. Momentarily, it is knowledge itself that is unknowable.

This challenge to the assumption that any scriptural knowledge is easily accessible is complicated even further by the syntactic and semantic minefield that is the poem's conclusion. As readers we must there confront the problem of whether the two lines are separate syntactic units or have a semantic connection that might make them one phrase. Specifically, what was it that "passed through Bethlehem"? The syntax permits three possible reconstructions: it was either "Paul," "the Man" (Christ) that Paul "knew," or "the News" that "the Man" "knew." The reconstructive choice made in a particular reading might very well demonstrate a reader's proclivity for basing knowledge on either faith or evidence. Since the syntax of the narrator's own text ensures that it offers only the most difficult knowledge to its reader, her expression of the implicit belief that knowledge is easily accessible is continually contradicted. That belief is perpetually challenged by a grammar that frustrates the reader's appropriation of the knowledge the narrator assumes to be so easily textually communicable. Of course, the question of the authority of the knowledge available in a written text is one specifically raised by the poem's conclusion. The apparently positive assertiveness of those lines as regards knowledge—the fact that "Paul knew"—is somewhat undercut by the reader's *knowledge* that the most successful missionary of the Christian gospel had himself only secondhand knowledge of the physical resurrection of Christ. Christ appeared to Paul only as the disembodied voice that accosted (and blinded) him on the road to Damascus. The entropic dissipation of those last lines—"Paul knew the Man that knew the News"—stresses to what degree the latter-day apostle's own knowledge was distant from the immediacy of the good "News" to humanity that was Christ's Resurrection. This serves to remind us of the degree to which the narrator's own knowledge of the Resurrection is a matter of *textual* faith, too; Christ's "body," accessible only as *embodied* in Scripture (the Word as word) or in the symbolic bread of the Sacrament, is available only at a remove, through its textual figuration. The problem with textual figuration is evident in the narrator's own text, for there the repetition of similar signifiers ("knew . . . knew . . . News") serves only to emphasize the potential incompatibility of the effective spread of the gospel message ("News") and true knowledge (those duplicated "knew[s]") when language can evidently produce such double signification and therefore potential for misinterpretation.

The problems evident in the narrator's textual reading serve to raise a series of other, more difficult, questions for the reader of the narrator's text. For that reader, the recognition of the limitations of the narrator's reading method and the necessary declaration of autonomy from her assumed position involve addressing the initial rhetorical question more literally as a query concerning the limitations of personal knowledge. Eventually, that question can be seen to provoke more than the unanswerable eschatological questions of what body the resurrected would assume and how we could know that it is them. More interestingly, it raises the question of how, since so much knowledge is predicated on presence, we can as readers assume the veracity of *any* written text. After all, it is this question of presence that makes the irony of the narrator's position so acute. The narrator's "knowledge" of the Resurrection (which might be defined as the return of presence) depends on her faith in the reliability of a written text (the Bible), but what ultimately makes any written text unreliable (the most immediate example being her own "scripturally inspired" text) is precisely the fact that it, too, necessarily defers the presence (her own) that could validate the fact that a reader's interpretation was authoritative. The most crucial question is therefore precisely the one that the narrator refuses to address—"with what body do they come?"—for her own faith in the return of "presence" is predicated on a written text that appears to be a celebration of absence. The poem's central irony is the fact that the narrator's ignoring of the question of *what* body ultimately provides an answer to it: the assumption of that body's "formal" unimportance is everywhere challenged by the ubiquitously interfering body evoked by the rhetorical structure of her argument. This is evident, for example, in the third line of the first stanza, where the narrator's excited celebration of the dead's resurrection is necessarily qualified by the fact that the expression of that rejoicing will require location and that the location of the body's second coming is conceivable only within the confines of space ("What Door") and time ("What Hour") that already structure her physical awareness. So while the narrator avoids addressing the initial question *as* a question by reading it figuratively as opposed to literally, and by assuming that the purely rhetorical nature of that question ensures that she does not have to consider the specific detail of *what* body it is that rises from the dead, it is her failure to take that literal question into account that troubles the logic of an argument whose rhetorical presentation signals the inevitable return (or resurrection) of those questions of bodily identity that are initially excluded.

The fact that the narrator can only imaginatively conceptualize bodily resurrection in terms dictated by her experience of physical location, and how the recourse to such imaginative conceptions comes to problematize her argument, is apparent in her invocation "Run—run—My Soul!" The urging of her own soul to "run" only emphasizes her need to personify a spiritual state in order to grasp it imaginatively; not only does she need to impose a visible physical motion on the soul, thereby enabling herself to visualize it moving through space, but the repetition of that urging, with its suggestion of repeated movement, reinforced by the decapitalization of the second "run" that emphasizes the difference ("Run—run") in repetition, creates the spacing that is a differentiation in time. It scarcely matters that the terms of her discussion shift from a more general concern with the form the resurrected might assume to a more specific concern with the physical form her own resurrected soul might assume. In either case, the "Soul" can be discussed by the narrator only within the frame of a rhetoric whose reference continually evokes that soul's relational presence to a physical body. This is apparent in the narrator's second command to her soul—"Illuminate the House!" This commanding of the soul, which raises the question of who or what is doing the commanding, assumes a master/slave relationship that is clearly an attempt to define the soul in terms of some hierarchical relation to the body. That hierarchically conceived spatial reconstruction of the soul imagines it as the architectural interior that illuminates a structure from within. The only "House" presumably illuminable by that soul is the structure of the body that contains it, the architecture of that structure forming the temple of the Holy Ghost.[18] Thus, it is not so much the case that the soul is inconceivable to the narrator, but rather that such an entity is inconceivable until it is considered in differential relation to the physical body. Therefore, just as the certainty of the narrator's faith in the Resurrection eventually came to revitalize the awkwardly avoided question of the nature of the bodily form the resurrected assume, so her reliance on a bodily trope to represent her personal conception of the soul necessarily leads to the eventual linguistic reinscription of that neglected body.

Indeed, the formal arrangement of the poem can itself be seen to reinscribe the body. The narrator's plea that her soul "Illuminate the House!" could also be considered a request for help: specifically, that her soul shed light on the nature of the body and therefore provide the "enlightenment" that would permit escape from the discursive impasse reached at the end of the first stanza. Clearly, that rhetorical exclamation proves to be *itself* the solution. The narrator's suddenly new perception of a body and a house as metaphorical equivalents provides the means of exit from that impasse, facilitating the transition between the two stanzas of the poem, in which the final word of one ("House!") leads to its metaphorical equivalent ("Body!") in the other. Indeed, the fact that the word "body" is newly capitalized and exclamatory serves to emphasize the importance of its readmittance into the argumentative structure of the poem. The question of the importance of the body, a question originally dismissed by the narrator in the first stanza as of relative unimportance, has reemerged as the focus of her discussion in the second stanza. Of course, it is not just that the question of the form the risen body might take has been resurrected in the second stanza: the body itself has been resurrected *as* that stanza. That poem is itself the architectural replica of body/house that formally duplicates the terms of its argument. The first stanza is concerned primarily with the nature of a soul only conceivable as a difference from the physical body; the second stanza sets about reinscribing that body as linguistic difference, that difference emerging from that complexly impacted syntax examined earlier.

Thomas Johnson's note on this poem indicates that it was "incorporated" within the text of a letter.[19] But the fact that the poem was "incorporated" within prose is only the first of a number of textual incorporations. A poem that initially asks "with what body do they come?" obviously has incorporation as its subject matter, especially when that poem is at the same time a text that questions a text (Corinthians) that questions a text (the Gospels). The poem constructs its initial argument by decontextualizing a rhetorical question from within a letter (Paul's letter to the Corinthians) and then recontextualizing that question within another letter (Dickinson's letter to Perez Cowan). Thus, the poem that is extractable from within Dickinson's letter contains within its body an extract from another letter. Clearly this is a poem about the "incorporation" that is the product of intertextuality. However, the poem is concerned not merely with the "incorporation" that language permits between texts but also with a potentially similar kind of "incorporation" that language might permit within texts. The fact that Dickinson's narrator continually formally "resurrects" *in* language a body whose resurrected form her argument—made *through* the communicative medium of that same language—dismisses as unimportant shows how the rhetorical slipperiness of language can not only reinscribe the body but also provide the key to a blasphemously personal *aesthetic* resurrection.

Dickinson's meditation on the text of 1 Corinthians 15 is highly suggestive in its wider relevance to her poetic project. In Paul's interpretation of the Resurrection, developed in his letter to the Corinthians, he crucially asserts that both the body *and* the spirit have an existence beyond the grave. Dickinson is particularly interested in that affirmation of the body that is the Pauline resurrection. As Christopher Benfey has observed, "She is concerned, in many poems, with the peculiar expressiveness of the body *after death*, as though its resurrection consisted in this expressiveness. The mystery for her is not that the spirit should remain expressive, but that the body should."[20] That concern with the particular expressiveness of a resurrected *body* is also evidence of Dickinson's more general concern with the possibility of an embodiment in expressive language that could duplicate that resurrection through its conferring of an artistic immortality. Central to this project of embodiment so vital to Dickinson's aesthetic is her interpretation of the Christian Incarnation as having a parallel applicability to her own poetry. The Word could be transmuted into the word.

Dickinson's interest in an equivalent poetic incarnation is evident in what might well be her most crucial prose fragment:

> The import of that Paragraph "the Word made Flesh"
> Had he the faintest intimation Who broached it Yesterday!
> "Made Flesh, and dwelt among us."
>   (P. 4)

She later developed this fragment into one of the most significant poems in her canon:

> A Word made Flesh is seldom
> And tremblingly partook
> Nor then perhaps reported
> But have I not mistook
> Each one of us has tasted
> With ecstasies of stealth
> The very food debated
> To our specific strength—
> A Word that breathes distinctly
> Has not the power to die
> Cohesive as the Spirit
> It may expire if He—
> "Made Flesh and dwelt among us"
> Could condescension be
> Like this consent of Language
> This loved Philology.
>   (P. 1651)

This astonishing aesthetic statement unquestionably appropriates theology as the basis of an alternative poetics. The implication of the poem is that language is the perfect surrogate for, or perhaps alternative to, the absent Logos.[21] But what is the precise connection between the Christian Incarnation and the everyday poetic incarnation? How does Dickinson's strategy resemble the manifestations of the word? I think, quite simply, we need to take her at her *word.* For Dickinson the Word made flesh is the basic principle of perfect representational practice, where the word is a symbol fully invested with the presence that it represents. The principle of incarnation is the unitary presence of meaning in which the spectacular body functions both as symbol and as essence. So, like Christ, the blasphemous "Queen of Calvary" is simultaneously the author of and *incarnate* in the word. There is, therefore, a plausible explanation of the implied message of the poem—an explanation, moreover, for which there is ample evidence elsewhere. If God was the Creator who made himself incarnate in his surrogate, Christ (the Word), through a process that infused a spirit into human flesh, then Dickinson is the creator incarnate in *her* surrogate, poetry (the word), through a reader's processing of a language that evokes the physical presence of the writer. Confirmation for Dickinson that her language breathed was important because she crucially thought of herself as somehow embodied in the shape of her own words. Understanding the significance of that embodiment is the key to comprehending Dickinson's reader-oriented poetic strategy. There can be no doubt that this is a reader-oriented strategy. After all, the process of transforming word into flesh is also preliminary to the transforming of that flesh and blood into bread and wine. Incarnation is the prerequisite of the Eucharist (although Dickinson would undoubtedly prefer the Congregationalist "Communion" to the Catholic term). In this case, of course, communion is not with God. The poems are access to a communion with a reader, and therefore Dickinson's words are themselves blasphemous sacraments; specifically, sacraments designed to effect a transformation of that reader. In so doing, not only does Dickinson usurp the Logos as a male prerogative, she enacts a miracle that parallels those of Christ. Not satisfied with merely developing the aesthetic secular equivalent of religious communion, she must also find the method of resurrecting her body (always, after all, Dickinson's primary concern). That aesthetic resurrection, one that perhaps makes Dickinson the first Lady Lazarus, is her ultimate female blasphemy. In effect, she answered Paul's question "Who shall deliver me from the body of this death?" (Romans 7:24) by rephrasing the question as "*What* shall deliver me from the body of this death." The answer was, poetry.

My suggestion that Dickinson sought to embody herself within her poetry is, to say the least, theoretically problematic. The recently influential critical/philosophical project of Jacques Derrida has been a sustained questioning of the phonocentric metaphysics of presence. Derrida's emphasis on the impossibility of full and literal representation, on the fact that a literal body cannot be constituted out of mere language, signifies the death in writing of the subject. When Derrida states that no language has the primacy of presence, he assumes an absolute space between presence and representation in discourse. Language and presence are mutually exclusive because one is the replacement for the other: language stands in lieu of presence, filling the space hollowed out by its departure. Letter and being are thus as distinct and irreconcilable in space and time as signifier and signified: *possession* of the desired object and its *representation* in words are absolutely opposed activities. In fact, representation is the art of *dispossession* and, as such, often nothing more than an elaborately *unsatisfying* compensation for a presence deferred in the movement of language. Presence is continually undone by what Derrida calls *differance*, language's simultaneous spatial movement of differing and temporal movement of deferring: "Differance is what makes the movement of signification possible only if each element that is said to be 'present,' appearing on the stage of presence, is related to something other than itself but retains the mark of a past element and already lets itself be hollowed out by the mark of its relation to a future element."[22] But while presence may well only be a metaphysical myth, the desire for presence is at the heart of language, and that desire for presence is, significantly, as much present in the process of reading as in the process of writing. To read a poem is to experience the loss of presence, most specifically the presence of a writing subject. But the trace of that presence is felt in its loss. There remains a sense of correspondence between the removed object and the trace that replaces it, for example between the poet and the language that fails to cover completely the track of her escape. Although as readers we cannot immediately recover the lost presence, we can still sense its lingering trace, there, at a remove, distanced by space and time. Presence tantalizes through the seductive suggestion of its possible recovery. Of course, ultimately presence cannot be detected by its trace, because that trace is merely another absence, another sign that can designate presence only by virtue of its differing *from* that presence. As such, presence can never be recovered. But the *illusion* that it actually can be recovered is the perpetual motor of our reading desire, a desire for the complete possession that could heal the more fundamental difference within, what Dickinson would have characterized as "internal difference, / Where the Meanings, are" (P. 258). This is why it is so crucial to the eventual success of Dickinson's lyric poems that they make significant demands on the reading process, why they are, first and foremost, linguistic devices that a reader must concretize sequentially and process temporally. Sharon Cameron observes in *Lyric Time* that "temporality must have illusion at its heart, and must be prompted by the desire to transform the 'trace' of presence . . . into the lost presence itself, to retain in the insistence of the symbolic gesture that which no longer is."[23] The necessity of a slow temporal processing of the poems by the reader becomes the catalyst of that reader's desire. Since the most important manifestation of that desire is the desire for presence, the Dickinson reader's most blissful illusion is represented by the gesture toward the reconstitution of Dickinson herself as a corporeal form.

Of course, the major and sometimes controversial goal of some schools of contemporary feminist criticism has been to demand the reinscription of the female body in the text as critical practice. Adrienne Rich demands of her fellow women writers that they "touch the unity and resonance of [their] physicality, the corporeal ground of [their] intelligence."[24] It has become a commonplace of

French feminist criticism that writing the body is the solution to overturning the structures of phallogocentrism: Chantal Chawaf has asked, "Isn't the final goal of writing to articulate the body?" and Helene Cixous has famously declared, "More body, hence more writing."[25] The French feminist emphasis on the possibility of *ecriture feminine* has been treated with justifiable suspicion by American feminist critics because of its reliance on the edifices of male psychoanalytic giants Lacan and Freud and its apparent rephrasing, in hardly more palatable terms, of the Freudian notion that anatomy is destiny. But it is perhaps too easy to dismiss the formulations of French feminism as simply an unfortunate return to the essentialism of biological determinism. A more valid attack on *ecriture feminine*'s formulation of anatomy as textuality is that it is merely a utopian possibility and nowhere evident as literary practice. It is this that I would dispute by arguing that the poetry of Emily Dickinson clearly derives from the antebellum period's own version of *ecriture feminine*. Some feminist critics have in fact already speculated on the applicability of the formulations of *ecriture feminine* to Dickinson's poetic strategy.[26] As we saw evidenced by Dickinson's correspondence, her poetic project foregrounds the friction caused by the dual functions of language as communication and signification. At least in spirit, therefore, that project evokes the genotextual subversions posited by Kristeva. Dickinson's emphasis on the semiotic components of language inevitably makes her poetic, in a sense, a poetic of *bodily inscription*. Indeed, when we read the responses to her poetry by the first-edition reviewers, for example the *Catholic World* reviewer, we cannot help but think of Kristeva's theory of the semiotic interference with the symbolic in the poetic text. The reviewer senses an uneasy juxtaposition within the poetry, but finds it difficult to characterize the discordant note he hears: "It recurs again and again, faint, strange, remote, like a phrase half-remembered from some angelic melody, but beaten back and *made dissonant by perverse limits*. . . . It strikes into the true melody from below, and makes a discord, but one *strangely powerful in seductive charm*" (emphasis added).[27] Would it be going too far to suggest that the "perverse limits" and "seductive charm" are the subtly implicit manifestations of what might be characterized as a poetically inscribed female body? We may presume that if words can acquire the material attributes of the world through their referential transparency out to that world, then the body can in a sense be "lifted" into a language that aspires to the mimesis of materiality.[28] Elaine Scarry, assuming that a writer can "affirm the individual's authorization over the space of passage between the physical and the verbal," uses the term "hybridization" to describe the endpoint of the process—"the fusion of body with cloth, page."[29] What is so intriguing about Dickinson's particular "hybridization" project, her poetic fusion of body and text, is that with minimal fuss it anticipates in practice one of the major theoretical goals of an *ecriture feminine*.

It was not just the influence of the incarnational tendency of the Christian imagination—though that should never be underestimated—that influenced Dickinson's highly individualized technique of hybridization, her mimesis of material presence. Various rhetorical forces present in antebellum and Victorian fiction were also centering on the problem of textually representing the body. An obsession with corporeal identity is evident in many canonical texts of the antebellum period. Sharon Cameron points out that American fictions of this period are concerned not simply with defining the self but "seem preoccupied with questions of identity conceived in corporeal terms" and "predicated in terms of the body."[30] Of course, problems of human identity considered in terms of the body are not peculiarly American, and there is a more general tradition of the body in literature as being less a palpable object and more a figure or image. But the representation of a corporeal self may be a characteristic form of expression in a country particularly concerned with analogical definitions of personal and national space and expansiveness. The expansion of national boundaries may come to have an analogic relation with the limits and extent of a personal identity. To some extent, therefore, Cameron suggests that "the impulse to define the body and its palpable boundaries"[31] takes a specifically American form and is a philosophical and psychological subject rather than an explicitly literary one. Even more interestingly, she traces in the works of Hawthorne and Melville (while suggesting that it has larger applicability) the creation of a third entity that "neither body nor soul, neither one self nor another, knits the respective entities together. The third entity, moreover, while not being material—while transcending the corporeality to include the spirit that is 'outside' or 'within' it—is nonetheless bodily, sometimes manifesting itself as an actual 'third' person. Thus, the body of flesh and blood is complemented by a markedly different corporeality that both encompasses and transcends it."[32] In the case of Dickinson, the creation of this "different corporeality" is the inevitable product of a hybridization that fuses body and language together in a new linguistic representation of corporeality.

The project of hybridization undertaken by Dickinson was of course a far from solitary one. Most obviously, the insistence on a transformative equation between "body" and "text" is equally fundamental to the poetic project of Walt Whitman. But perhaps more interestingly, the attempt to inscribe the specifically female body within a literary text was also characteristic of the Victorian novel and evident in the poetry of Dickinson's most eminent precursor, Elizabeth Barrett Browning. In her study of Victorian fiction, *The Flesh Made Word*,

Helena Michie notes the absence of the female body, of female corporeality, in the typical Victorian text, and notes that the methodology of Victorian representation actively obstructed the reader's (or, in the case of visual art, the viewer's) clear perception of that body. The representation of women as fictional characters enforced the seductive absence of the specificity of the female body by displacing the sexuality of that body onto a figure. The denial of the body, and therefore of sexuality, reduced the central heroine of such a text to nothing more than a cipher of male lust, a blank page on which male characters could inscribe their own narratives. Thus, the heroine became little more than the reflection of the desires of others. Yet at the same time, "mainstream Victorian feminism was entirely defined by the body and shaped by its contours."[33] The body was the essential component of an ongoing protofeminist debate. Simply in the interests of topicality, this meant that writers of the period, both female and male, had to adopt methods of carefully reinscribing the body; they had to reconstruct and rebuild the palpability of the female body from within given artistic structures that were essentially patriarchally predetermined. This they attempted to do, not unexpectedly, through the medium of rhetoric: "With their uses of traditional metaphoric devices, Victorian authors opened secret passages for the reintroduction of women's bodies into texts that had, on the surface, cleansed themselves of such presences. In the face of taboo and absence, Victorian writers of all sorts of texts created a presence that was all the stronger for appearing not to exist."[34] Subversively, and with no little subtlety, the writers reinscribed the body by inverting the original displacement of sexuality as a motion between body and figure back onto the body. However, sexuality could only be reinscribed back onto the body with the complicity of the reader and through the reader's participation in constructing the text as his or her desire mirrored in the rhetoric. It is in the rhetoric of Victorian fiction, in the textual interstices, that the female body makes what could be characterized as a "guessed" appearance. Thus, Michie observes that the heroine's body is not "captured" in language but "appears and disappears from the texts that are its stages in an intricate choreography of tropes, a dance that itself bespeaks physicality."[35] The reader of Victorian fiction learned to look for the inscription of the female body in the strangest and most unlikely places. Michie finds the reinscription at times vividly palpable. For example, she views the texts' focus on the dietary intake of the central character as the encoding of an anorexic body: "The anorexia at the center of many Victorian texts turns the act of reading into a diagnosis, the text itself into a symptomology. The novel in particular confronts us with a variety of 'symptoms,' those gaps in realism that are themselves signs of dis-ease. Paradoxically, then, the seemingly bodiless text turns before our eyes into the semblance of a Victorian woman's body to be constantly, almost obsessively, watched and charted in much the same way that 'real' female bodies were treated by Victorian physicians."[36]

This conscious inscription of the female body extends beyond the Victorian novel. Elizabeth Barrett Browning's narrative poem *Aurora Leigh* is a massive attempt, and a highly conscious one, to inscribe the female body in language. Throughout the poem, the body is nothing less than a metaphor for writing itself. Cora Kaplan, in her introduction to the Women's Press edition, vividly captures the sheer physicality of *Aurora Leigh* as text (the fact that Aurora Leigh is both the name of the central character and of the text is obviously of particular importance), noting how "approved and taboo subjects are slyly intertwined so that menstruation, childbirth, suckling, child-rearing, rape and prostitution, are all braided together in metaphorical language," and how the sexuality of Aurora, the character/narrator, is "displaced into her poetry, projected onto landscapes, the Age, art, through the 'woman's figure.' "[37] Kaplan's valid observation that a passage such as "Spring's delicious trouble in the ground, / Tormented by the quickened blood of roots, / And softly pricked by golden crocus sheaves" has a subtle erotic detail worthy of Browning's contemporary Walt Whitman and anticipates the textual erotics of a Dylan Thomas is equally applicable to any number of other passages in the poem. It therefore becomes increasingly clear why *Aurora Leigh* became such a significant text for Emily Dickinson and why it was a poem she viewed as *transformative*: it was perhaps the most successful example to date of an author inscribing the female body as text.

But Dickinson's poetic project of hybridization was primarily determined by the specific historical circumstances of the sentimental culture within which her body was already inscribed. It has often been observed of antebellum society that the codes of sentimentalism were so generally pervasive as to ensure that middle-class American women eventually came to model their lives in relation to the linguistic and narrative conventions of the sentimental novel. Rather than art imitating life, the mimesis was the patterning of everyday life on the fictional codes of sentimentalism. The basic conventions of sentimentalism emphasized a moral, emotional, and spiritual code whose focus on the immortality of the soul necessarily devalued the experience of the body. As woman's increased moral status also effected her effacement from political and social concerns, the distinction between body and soul ultimately served to increase social control over a physical body defined by the limit of domesticity. The Christian and sentimental traditions worked hand in glove in their offering the female subject only a distinctly noncorporeal freedom. Nineteenth-century "feminists" were only too aware of the obstacles they had to confront in order to reassert the corporeality of identity by reforging the links between a woman's person and her body. An 1856 letter from Lucy Stone to Susan B. Anthony questioning whether it was the time to address sexual rights, specifically the ownership of the body, reveals the extent to which this was an off-agenda agenda of the women's movement: "No two of us think alike about it, and yet it is clear to me that question underlies the whole movement, and all our little skirmishing for better laws and the right to vote, will yet be swallowed up by the real question viz: Has woman a right to herself? It is very little to me to have the right to vote, to own property, etc., if I may not keep my body, and its uses, in my absolute right. Not one wife in a thousand can do that now."[38] The reforging of that link between body and personhood was a crucial subtextual component of that same sentimental fiction. As Karen Sanchez-Eppler has pointed out, sentimental fiction has its own bodily grammar, in which "bodily signs are adamantly and repeatedly presented as the preferred and most potent mechanisms both for communicating meaning and for marking the fact of its transmission," which, in turn, suggests that, "with its reliance on the body as the privileged structure for communicating meaning, sentimental fiction thus constantly reinscribes the troubling relation between personhood and corporeality that underlies the project of feminism."[39] Dickinson's poetics, like the sentimental fiction whose rhetorical strategies it adopts and pungently rewrites, constantly attempts to reinscribe that troubling relation within the tense linguistic perimeters of a poem. Sentimental value is assessed in proportion to emotional intensity, to vibrant responsiveness to the slightest emotional stimulus. Dickinson's typical response to poetry, remember, was measured precisely in terms of the emotional intensity of sentimental excess: "If I read a book [and] it makes my whole body so cold no fire ever can warm me I know *that* is poetry. If I feel physically as if the top of my head were taken off, I know *that* is poetry. These are the only way I know it. Is there any other way?" (L. 342a). The bodily grounding of Dickinson's definition of poetry makes it ultimately explicable as an aesthetic of sensibility.[40] Sentimental fiction is an intensely bodily genre because sentiment and feeling are actively inscribed in the reading process. Indeed, reading such fiction is of necessity an empathetic *bodily act*, for the success of a story is to be gauged by its ability to transform words into a personal, physical reaction, into the rhythm of the pulse and the opening of the tear ducts. The sheer physicality of the sentimental reading experience collapses the objective distance between the events narrated and the act of reading. The sentiment implicit in the story is physically inscribed in the flesh of the reader because tears limn the area where character and reader merge—the tears of one consequentially provoke the tears of the other, and in a successful sentimental text both would flow together in lachrymose sympathy.[41] Dickinson's attempt at textual hybridization is ultimately part of a larger aesthetic of sensibility that owes more to a contemporary reading of Ik Marvel than to the classical influence of Longinus.[42] That aesthetic of sensibility may have had its limitations, but, energized by Dickinson's vividly incarnational imagination and her demanding affective stylistics, it helped produce the "body of writing" that ensured that an antebellum "writing of the body" was substantially more than a mere theoretical speculation.

In this chapter I have emphasized Dickinson's particular interest in the possibilities and consequences of inscribing the body in/as language. The incarnational tendency of her peculiarly heterodox Christian imagination predetermined a disposition toward textual embodiment; the aesthetics of sentiment pervasive in antebellum culture served to reinforce the secular possibilities of textual embodiment; the example of a number of her significant contemporaries, not least Elizabeth Barrett Browning, demonstrated the possibility of a poetic experimentation with the theme of textual embodiment; and the example of the fascination of celebrity evident in the Jenny Lind cult emphasized the obvious potential advantages of textual embodiment, particularly for an artist whose poetics was primarily affective insofar as it was concerned with the ignition of her audience's affection. In the next chapter, we will find evidence that Dickinson succeeded in making the word flesh to the extent that her poetic text habitually evokes the presence of the body in the writings of critical readers implicated as rhetorical *seducers* of the text. In other words, it appears that the rhetorical seduction *in* the poetic text may become, in due course, the rhetorical seduction *of* the poetic text. In this chapter we will see that Dickinson's poetic text is transactional to the extent that it functions as a form of persuasion whereby text and reader are implicated as *desiring bodies:* the reader works on the text and the text on its reader in a complex double dialectic of two bodies inscribed in language. Further, the hermeneutic frustration typically elicited by the poems, under the rubric of rhetorical seduction, facilitates a drive toward the corporeal reconstitution of the poems on the part of readers whose emotional responses to the formal agitations of the poems translates those poems into true figures of desire and the Dickinson poetic corpus into an abstract somatic scenography.[43] The evidence of that corporeal reconstitution also demonstrates the extent to which Dickinson's reconnection of the text with the body and pleasure did not result so much in a disintellectualized writing as in a later, disintellectualized critical reading whose habitual strategy is to transform the poet into one of "those wonderful hysterics . . . with their carnal, passionate body words."[44]

5

Reading Seductions (1)

I was at last obliged to recognize that these scenes of seduction had
never taken place, and that they were only phantasies which my
patients had made up or which I myself had perhaps forced on them.
—Freud, "An Autobiographical Study" (1925)

I am glad if Theodore balked the Professors—Most such are Mani-kins,
and a warm blow from a brave Anatomy, hurls them into Where-fores—
—Dickinson to Mrs. Holland, June 1884

IN PREVIOUS CHAPTERS I examined Dickinson's negotiation with and personal rhetorical adaptation of a specific antebellum discourse of seduction. In this chapter I will begin to trace some connections between the particular discourse of seduction that is Dickinson's poetics and the more contemporary discourse of seduction that is psychoanalysis. It is not my intention to engage Dickinson's poetry by reading it through the lens conveniently provided by psychoanalytic criticism, but to show how Dickinson's reader-oriented poetic method has a startling affinity to psychoanalysis, both in its initial historical formulation and in its textual practice. Throughout this chapter, therefore, I am not so much interested in the application of psychoanalysis *to* Dickinson's text as in the mutual *interimplication* of the psychoanalytic and literary texts.

If in recent years the term "seduction" has become a convenient metaphor for deconstructive practice, it is a consequence of the prevailing investment of psychoanalysis—sometimes Freudian, but more usually its Lacanian derivative—in contemporary postmodern theoretical discourse.[1] Psychoanalysis has been from its inception a discourse concerned with an act of seduction: initially a discourse *about* seduction, it was later revised by Freud into a discourse *of* seduction. The initial trauma theory of hysteria, which was based on Freud's original case studies, is in fact now known as the "seduction theory." This is because Freud at first suspected that the hysterical symptoms of his predominantly female patients were caused by their early childhood abuse; in other words, that the "seduction" in question was the blatant sexual abuse of the child by an adult family member. Originally, therefore, "seduction" served as a protective euphemism; it was Freud's discreet metaphor for the issue of incest, an issue that he was—perhaps understandably, given the historical and political context of his original Viennese case studies—unwilling to confront directly.

Freud would reconsider that initial seduction theory (and the possible repression involved in that rethinking has come to be a significant scene of contention in psychoanalysis)[2] in order to formulate the theory of the Oedipus complex, which was to be the foundation of his psychoanalytic method. The genesis of Freud's Oedipal theory was his new assumption that the "seductions" reported by his patients were, in fact, not real. Instead, the hysteric's "seduction" was now regarded as a constructed fantasy or screen that actually represented repressed childhood desires. That fantasy was itself in need of interpretation. This revision of Freud's initial seduction theory is important in its deflection of both the significance of seduction and the identity of the seducer. The original seduction theory acknowledged an actual historical incident of seduction and the patient's resistance to it; the revised Oedipal theory assumed that no seduction occurred and that the patient's hysteria concealed the memory of her own desire to seduce the person to whom she would later attribute the act of seduction. In this way, Freud's Oedipal theory inverts the supposition of his initial seduction theory: the "hysteric" in the revised theory is no longer the seduced but the potential seducer.

In particular, the hysteric patient is the potential seducer of her analyst. Because the hysteric's fantasies of seduction were developed by her for the benefit of an analyst who to some degree shared those same fantasies, Freud concluded that the analyst had a crucial role to play in their construction. Indeed, if those fantasies were essentially a production of the embodied relationship between analyst and analysand, then there was always the possibility that either the analyst could impose the fantasy on the patient or, alternatively, the patient could successfully actualize the fantasy in her relationship with the analyst. In this way, "seduction" was to remain theoretically crucial to Freudian psychoanalysis. The reconsideration of the original seduction theory, far from diminishing the importance of "seduction" to psychoanalysis, actually increased the significance (in every sense of the word) of the act as a key rhetorical strategy. Psychoanalysis itself became a self-reflexive meditation on how the actual interlocutions of the psychoanalytic encounter—of how the analyst and the analysand interact in the dialectic relationship that is the talking cure—imply or actualize a *verbal* seduction of sorts. Freudian psychoanalysis was now essentially the study of how a rhetorical seduction could be conducted by means of interpretation, and the "scene of reading" of that specific psychoanalytic seduction was more usually called "transference."

The poetics of Emily Dickinson also evolved from her personal adaptation of an existing discourse *about* seduction. And we have seen how that antebellum discourse concerning seduction—a discourse produced by a very real and ongoing social debate concerning the gendered power dynamics of nineteenth-century culture—was reconstituted by her into a discourse *of* seduction, the most obvious manifestation of which is her affective, reader-implicating poetics. The relationship of Freudian psychoanalysis to Dickinson's poetry, given their parallel mode of seductive development, is, we must presume, mutually informative. The question critical readers need to ask, therefore, is not what psychoanalysis can teach us about the poet but what the poet can teach us about the workings of psychoanalysis.

Typically, however, literary critics apply psychoanalysis to Dickinson.[3] And in many ways she seems the perfect subject for psychoanalytical biography and criticism. As the author of the definitive Dickinson psychobiography, John Cody, has pointed out, the poet's relationship with her dominating father; her failure to communicate with an essentially absent, valedictorian mother; her later retreat into self-imposed reclusion; her often ambiguous sexuality; and, most of all, the articulate capacity for fantasy evident in her poetry combine to make her "the psychoanalysand par excellence."[4] In his problematic study, *After Great Pain,* Cody succinctly demonstrates how Dickinson, the analysand, provides a wealth of material for her critical analyst. But Cody's basic Freudianism is reductive. His application of a psychoanalytic schema to Dickinson's life, and his consequent analysis of her as a case study, exemplifies the type of distortions that the Freudian psychoanalytic method produces when applied indiscriminately (and determinedly) to an individual writer. Cody's psychoanalytic reading of Dickinson first necessitates his manipulation of her into the position of psychoanalytical analysand. Thus, Dickinson's lyric poetry is read by Cody as confessional, as a discourse marked by autobiographical disclosure, despite her famous protestation of the fact that the speaker of the poems was a "supposed person." What Cody's psychoanalytic biography continually denies, therefore, is the power of Dickinson's literary imagination. Indeed, the poet's imaginative power is precisely what *cannot* be addressed, because that might well deny Cody the mastery of the poems that comes from considering them solely as psychological documents to which he, as a practicing analyst, has privileged access. In fact, the one characteristic of Dickinson's poetry that most of her critics could agree on is its refusal of just the kind of critical mastery Cody assumes possible.

But that is not to say that Cody's attempt to make Dickinson the analysand in a psychoanalytic dialectic is completely invalid. On the contrary, I would certainly concur with his assertion that she is the analysand par excellence, at least insofar as the Freudian analysand par excellence is a female "patient" displaying a symptomatically hysterical discourse. Just as Freudian psychoanalytic theory was initially shaped as a response to hysterical discourse, so too have many of the critical theories formulated in response to Dickinson's poetic text. For example, Cody considers Dickinson a "hysteric" individual, and there may well be some validity in that diagnosis. More interesting, however, are less speculatively personal theories, those critical analyses that characterize Dickinson's language strategy as itself "hysteric." This is how Dickinson's language is described by David Porter, whose opinion, as one of the best critical readers of Dickinson's linguistic techniques, is not easily dismissed. Porter follows the example of T. W. Higginson, the first critic to assign the term "deviant" to Dickinson's poetry, when he describes Dickinson as a "deviating poet" whose "highly deviant language" uses "deviant constructions."[5] But Porter also specifies the particular nature of that language deviance by asserting that Dickinson's is a "language . . . covering hysteria"; that poem 753 has a "hyperbole that threatens to erupt in hysteria"; that the language of poem 135 "seems to be the surface display of a latent hysteria"; and that poem 1072 "has no knowledge at all, only hysteria."[6] Porter's powerful analysis of Dickinson's poetics of "the aftermath" can thus be seen to derive from the Freudian assumptions that "hysterics suffer mainly from reminiscences" and that "the mechanism of poetry [creative writing] is the same as that of hysterical phantasies."[7]

Although Porter does observe of Dickinson's language strategies that "these defects are the nodes of meaning where her personal identity is most intense," he does not, unlike Cody, characterize Dickinson herself as being in any way personally or psychologically deviant.[8] This is an important distinction: it is not Dickinson who is "hysteric," but her language. Dickinson's poetry is a hysterical discourse. This characterization has a certain analytic precision. I have already observed three ways in which Dickinson's poetic discourse can be considered symptomatically "hysterical." First, she habitually utilizes the lyric as an apparently confessional mode and invariably tells stories through the grammar of a textual body by means of the self-reflexivity of an intrusive "I." Second, the stories she tells frequently display, in terms of their subject matter, either an interest *in* the possible ramifications of seduction or the scarcely concealed presence *of* a potential male seducer. Third, and most important, in telling those apparently personal stories of seduction, her poetic discourse is oriented toward her analyst in such a way that her language can itself be the means to his or her rhetorical seduction.

Critics' tendency to describe Dickinson's language in terms of hysteria may therefore be a gauge of her analytic sophistication. In emphasizing how the discourse of the hysteric and the discourse of the analyst can never be decisively distinguished one from another in the analytic situation, Lacan characterizes psychoanalysis itself as a "hystericization" of discourse. Because the dialectic of the talking cure is transferential *and* countertransferential, a "hysterical" discourse is always liable to reproduce its effect in the mutually implicated discourse of its analytic "reader." Therefore, since critical readers have identified Dickinson's poetry as a hysterical discourse (and therefore, by implication, an analytic one) we need to examine the response of analytic readers to it. Rather than asking the hackneyed psychoanalytic question of whether Dickinson is in any way personally pathological, it is more useful to ask what makes her art an object of desire *for* readers or, more precisely, to examine the power of her art *over* readers. No longer regarding the poet as a suitable analysand, as a prime candidate for psychoanalytical study, I therefore want now to reconsider her as an exemplary psychoanalyst, as the Freudian blank screen that gathers the transference of her readers. To that end, I will necessarily focus on the written responses of Dickinson's readers to her poetic texts. For while it has often been speculated that when Dickinson consulted Henry Williams, M.D., a Boston oculist, she was suffering from a hypersensitivity to light induced by psychological causes, a form of "hysterical blindness," I suspect the more significant "hysterical blindness" to be that which her poetry has induced in its critical readers.

This reading *of* reading assumes a further validity when we consider that Dickinson was herself very interested in the response of an audience to an artist's performance. When she saw Jenny Lind perform in Northampton, her memorable observations were these: "How we all loved Jenny Lind, but not accustomed oft to her manner of singing did'nt fancy *that* so well as we did *her*," and "*Herself*, and not her music, was what we seemed to love." In the previous chapter I observed that these comments are evidence of the young poet's early fascination with the power of the artist over the art. But Dickinson's consistent use of the collective pronoun in this letter is equally a testament to her close observation of the response of Lind's immediate audience. Indeed, she goes on to catalog, with hyperbolic amusement, her father's specific reactions to the "show": "Father sat all the evening looking *mad*, and *silly*, and yet so much amused you would have *died* a laughing—when the performers bowed, he said "Good evening Sir"—and when they retired, "very well—that will do," it was'nt *sarcasm* exactly, nor it was'nt *disdain*, it was infinitely funnier than either of those virtues, as if old Abraham had come to see the show, and thought it was all very well, but a little excess of *Monkey!*" That Dickinson should express a special interest in the response of the audience to the "show" is hardly surprising. Not only does she express in her poetry an absorbing interest in the capacity of a poem to render its effects on a reader, but the Dickinson philosophy of controlled reader response is perhaps most perfectly expressed in poem 1206:

> The Show is not the Show
> But they that go—
> Menagerie to me
> My Neighbor be—
> Fair Play—
> Both went to see—

The speaker is not so much viewer as she is *voyeur.* Uninterested in the performance itself, her primary fascination is with the reactions of the audience to that performance. Indeed, for her, the peripheral "Show" put on by the viewers supersedes anything the actual "Show" can produce. The better entertainment is the viewing of the uninhibited and therefore genuine reaction of one's "Neighbor." That original "Show" is of interest only as the catalyst for another. Importantly, the uninhibited response of the audience, that more significant "Show," is a consequence of its ignorance: these are observers who, little suspecting that they are simultaneously observed, are momentarily exposed by the very fact of their viewing. "The Show is not the Show" can be considered a neat summation of that Dickinson aesthetic of reception, which assumes that what is of interest is not the response, but the attitude assumed by the responders, and that the reading is less valuable than the subsequent exposure of the readers in the course of their analysis. As such, it can serve as useful textual confirmation of my suggestion that insight into Dickinson's poetry comes not only through penetrating analysis and explication of the poetry itself, but also through an analysis of the wild, strange "menagerie" of responses to that poetry, and that the examination of Dickinson's poetic necessitates a parallel study of its various *affects* as those affects are manifested in critical readers.

The possible affective manipulation of the reader by the poem is facilitated by the poem's exaggerated offering to the reader of the possibility of its *own* manipulation. For example, poem 738 is a poetic offering insofar as it is possible to imagine that the voice is that of the poem as it directly interpellates its reader:

> You said that I "was Great"—one Day—
> Then "Great" it be—if that please Thee—
> Or Small—or any size at all—
> Nay—I'm the size suit Thee—
>
> Tall—like the Stag—would that?
> Or lower—like the Wren—
> Or other heights of Other Ones
> I've seen?

Tell which—it's dull to guess—
And I must be Rhinoceros
Or Mouse
At once—for Thee—

So say—if Queen it be—
Or Page—please Thee—
I'm that—or nought—
Or other thing—if other thing there be—
With just this Stipulus—
I suit Thee—

The poem assumes that it will be what its reader chooses to make it, responsive to every whim. This is generally true of Dickinson's canon: her poems can suit the desire of their readers perfectly. In this case, whether that reader interprets this poem as representing the voice of Dickinson discussing her varied personae ("if Queen it be") or, my own pun-determined choice, a representation of language speaking itself ("Or Page—please Thee"), or anything else at all ("Or other thing—if other thing there be") is ultimately all the same. The fact that the speaker/poem offers the possibility that she/it can be made absolutely malleable to the desire of its addressee/reader is all that matters. My own refashioning of the poem—the interpretation of it as a self-reflexive poetic allegory—is simply a "suitable" example of how the speaker's "Stipulus" ensures her poem's successful initial engagement with a reader's interpretive desire. I also assume that the stunning conclusion to poem 505 is an accurate representation of Dickinson's aesthetic stance:

Nor would I be a Poet—
It's finer—own the Ear—
Enamored—impotent—content—
The License to revere,
A privilege so awful
What would the Dower be,
Had I the Art to stun myself
With Bolts of Melody!

The rendering "Enamored—impotent—content" precisely demarcates the specific affects of a Dickinson poem on its reader. Of course, syntactic ambiguity is often the cause of an initial reader enamoration, and this poem is no exception to its own rule: the phrase "It's finer—own the Ear" is a finely tuned ambiguity. Is it better to be the reader (who owns that receptive ear) of the poem? Or it is better to be the author (who owns and therefore controls the receptive ear *of another*) of that poem? The ear that is most frequently "owned" by the Dickinson poem is that of its critical reader. And if we can imagine the speaker of poem

1496 as the poem itself, then we listen to the voice of a language aware of its being regarded as an object of a specifically male critical desire:

All that I do
Is in review
To his enamored mind
I know his eye
Where e'er I ply
Is pushing close behind

Crucial to the Dickinson strategy of enamoration is one of the most common themes of her poetry: her notion that the best pleasure is an experience of loss. For Dickinson, that pleasure is usually defined as the awareness of a distance between desire and its goal; the act of desiring is, in itself, unsurpassable, and infinitely more delightful than the consummation that can accommodate it. The phraseology may change from poem to poem, but the implication is always the same: that "Delight is as the flight" (P. 257); that " 'Heaven'—is what I cannot reach!" (P. 239); that "Spices fly / In the Receipt—It was the Distance— / Was Savory" (P. 439); that "Impossibility, like Wine / Exhilarates the Man / Who tastes it; Possibility / Is flavorless" (P. 838); that "Who never lost, are unprepared / A Coronet to find!" (P. 73); that "Not of detention is Fruition— / Shudder to attain" (P. 1315). As "Within its reach, though yet ungrasped" is "Desire's perfect Goal" (P. 1430), the poems' narrators revel in the "sumptuous Destitution" (P. 1382) that is an "ecstatic limit / Of unobtained Delight" (P. 1209). Frequently, the poems are miniature studies of this pleasure paradox, vignettes of joyous deprivation. An example of this is poem 67, that famously successful poem[9] about the nature of success, the first stanza of which reads

Success is counted sweetest
By those who ne'er succeed.
To comprehend a nectar
Requires sorest need.

and poem 1036's definition of satisfaction (which is ultimately, given the logic of the poem, dissatisfaction!):

Satisfaction—is the Agent
Of Satiety—
Want—a quiet Commissary
For Infinity.

To possess, is past the instant
We achieve the Joy—
Immortality contented
Were Anomaly.

The philosophical argument for the necessity of *dispossession* is perhaps most perfectly encapsulated in poem 807:

Expectation—is Contentment—
Gain—Satiety—
But Satiety—Conviction
Of Necessity

Of an Austere trait in Pleasure—
Good, without alarm
Is a too established Fortune—
Danger—deepens Sum—

That the fragility that is momentary possession is a value in itself, that "Danger—deepens Sum," is the repeated refrain of the poetry. While it might be rephrased as "Uncertain lease—develops lustre / On Time / Uncertain Grasp, appreciation / Of Sum" (P. 857); or "Peril as a Possession / 'Tis Good to bear / Danger disintegrates Satiety" (P. 1678); or "In insecurity to lie / Is Joy's insuring quality" (P. 1434), the same basic philosophy is consistently expressed. Desire defines pleasure, and, since desire is always process, whether one strives to possess or suffers the insecurity of temporary possession, true pleasure can never be stasis. Pleasure must assume the dynamism of the desire that constitutes it. Central to Dickinson's poetics, therefore, is a psychodynamics of desire in which desire is cultivated as an end in itself, in which the ultimate aesthetic pleasure is realized through the frictive frustration that dilates the interval of desire that precedes interpretation. The intensity of desire is sufficient to render any eventual satisfaction a virtual anticlimax, for, while the satisfaction of attainment is finite, the motor of desire is infinite, involving *process*. The postponement of satisfaction and the distance of the object of desire are therefore the prerequisites for the eventual realization of an intensely exquisite longing, the state of perpetual deferral that is *being a desiring subject*. The consequence of the absolute centrality of this process of desire is that the poetry, the continual exploration and mapping of the psychic space of frustration that opens between desire and an unattainable goal, is equally the most continually restless of pleasures for the subject who reads.

The most detailed discussion of this paradoxical poetics of desire is Richard Wilbur's brilliant essay "Sumptuous Destitution." Wilbur chooses to discuss Dickinson's "economy of desire" solely as the expression of her aesthetic philosophy. And that philosophy interests Wilbur, himself a poet, as being a truth of art of possibly universal application and therefore far from peculiar to his precursor. Wilbur considers Dickinson's not a personal philosophy per se— what she *discovered* was "that the soul has an infinite hunger, a hunger to possess all things. . . . The creature of appetite . . . pursues satisfaction, and strives to possess the object in itself; it cannot imagine the vaster economy of desire, in which the pain of abstinence is justified by moments of infinite joy."[10] This reduction of Dickinson's poetics through generalization is misleading precisely because the calculated postponement of satisfaction has ramifications beyond the poet's philosophic theorizing. It is also implicit in the writing of her poetic text, in her strategic approach to a reader. "Sumptuous destitution" is the *practice* of the poetry to the extent that the poems are the exemplification of Dickinson's aesthetic philosophy *in action*. The central tenet of this philosophy is that interpretive frustration, and a consequently provoked desire for meaning, is preferable to an easy hermeneutic possession, and that frustration of the reader's desire—both the narrative desire to reach an ending and the hermeneutic desire to penetrate a meaning—is simultaneously the pleasurable stimulus of it. In other words, to understand the full implications of Dickinson's aesthetic philosophy we need to take into consideration the effects of her "frustrating" poetry on its reader. If "True Poems flee" (P. 1472), then what does that mean for a reader who is a "creature of appetite" seeking "satisfaction" and "possession"? If "consummation" is "the hurry of fools" (L. 922), then what if the purpose of Dickinson's poetry is to educate the reader in the "vaster economy of desire" that is nonconsummation, a lesson taught through a sophisticated syntactic playing on the reader's "hunger"? And what if that "hunger" extends beyond the appetite for knowledge? In other words, what if Dickinson's poems are, most importantly, vivid explorations of the psychodynamics of their readers' desires?

The psychodynamics of desire is, of course, the primary study of contemporary psychoanalysis. And since the business of both psychoanalysis and literary criticism is the interpretation that deals with a crisis in signification, the most valuable analogy between them concerns the nature of reading. Shoshana Felman's discussion of the significance of the Lacanian reading of Freud for textual interpretation is valuable here.[11] In his 1951 article, "Intervention in Transference," Lacan describes the relationship between transference and countertransference as a dialectical process in which both patient and analyst are implicated. The transference is always a response to the analyst's countertransference:

> What needs to be understood regarding psychoanalytic experience is that it proceeds entirely in a relationship of subject to subject—which means that it preserves a dimension irreducible to all psychology considered as the objectification of certain properties of the individual. . . . What happens in an analysis is that the subject is, strictly speaking, constituted

through a discourse, to which the mere presence of the psychoanalyst brings, before any intervention, the dimension of dialogue.[12]

Freud invented psychoanalysis on the basis of his clinical experience with hysterical patients *and* of the self-analysis he performed to cure his own hysterical symptoms. It was while listening to hysteric discourse that Freud "read" that there was an unconscious, for he was implicated in the hysterics' discourse, directly affected by hysterical narrative. As Felman puts it, "Freud's discovery of the unconscious is the outcome of his reading in the hysterical discourse of the Other his own unconscious."[13] This has significant implications for the psychoanalytic critic of literature because it suggests the following:

> The activity of reading is not just the analyst's, it is also the analysand's: interpreting is what takes place *on both sides* of the analytic situation. The unconscious, in Lacan's eyes, is not simply the object of psychoanalytical investigation, but its subject. The unconscious, in other words, is not simply *that which must be read* but also, and perhaps primarily, *that which reads.* The unconscious is a reader. What this implies most radically is that whoever reads, interprets out of his own unconscious, is an analysand, even when the interpreting is done from the position of the analyst.[14]

For Felman, the psychoanalytic approach to literature would be far more useful textually than biographically. The reading situation can still be assimilated to the psychoanalytic dialectic, but the poet will now be far more than simply the analysand on the couch. In fact, the status of the poet is not simply that of the patient but also that of the analyst, for if "unconscious desire proceeds by interpretation" then the converse is equally true—that "interpretation proceeds by unconscious desire." As Felman observes, Lacan's foregrounding of the analytic dialectic—the fact that since interpretation always takes place within a transferential situation of reading, the interpreter is both analyst and analysand—has tremendous implications for a literary critic who is in the place of the psychoanalyst in the "relation of interpretation" but equally in the place of the patient in the "relation of transference."

Readers of Dickinson's poetry are, I believe, especially susceptible to becoming patients in the "relation of transference." I have already observed that Dickinson's poetic discourse does not merely discuss but is also predicated on a condition of deferral ("sumptuous Destitution") where gratification continually recedes before attainable grasp. That poetic discourse not only sustains its reader in the often uncomfortable state of *being* a desiring subject, but, as a result of its notorious linguistic opacities, its oscillation between ambiguities and indeterminacies, it eventually forces a confrontation with the process of reading that, I would suggest, is not unlike making sense out of unconscious material.

Indeed, as we shall see, not only is there considerable evidence that the syntax of Dickinson's poetic texts introduces disruptions into the habitual process of reading poetry, thus producing and revealing feelings of inadequacy and vulnerability in her readers, but it may well be that those syntactically impacted poems put their readers through an experience of reading analogous to psychoanalysis. Consequently, it does not matter whether the reader comes to Dickinson's poetry with a preconceived psychoanalytic critical grid or not; in the actual process of reading as a critical analyst, he or she inevitably assumes the position of a psychoanalytic analyst within an actualized parataxic field of interpretation.

Psychoanalysis might be defined as the study of how a rhetorical seduction may be conducted by means of interpretation. I think it hardly coincidental that critical analysts of Dickinson's texts have notoriously attempted to interpret them in terms of "scenes of seduction," either factual, fictional, or rhetorical: William Shurr has recently given more credence to the theory that Dickinson's "relationship" with Rev. Charles Wadsworth resulted in her being "seduced and abandoned, and that such an event had something to do with the poetry"; Cynthia Griffin Wolff has suggested that the poetry "might best be read against a purely literary model, the novel of seduction"; Suzanne Juhasz has argued that the poet's letters effect a strategic "rhetorical seduction" of their reader; and Karl Keller has found in the personae of the poetry both the bold assertiveness of a "crude seductress" *and* a "daring virgin inviting seduction, foreplay and penetration."[15] We have already seen how Dickinson's use of the lyric as an apparently confessional mode has led John Cody to diagnose her as the quintessential hysteric, and how that diagnosis has been disputed by David Porter's assertion that it is Dickinson's poetic discourse that is symptomatically hysterical. This prevalent critical desire to identify and validate a scene of seduction in relation to Dickinson's poetry, or to attempt to manipulate the poet (and/or her discourse) into an analytic situation of seduction is itself symptomatic: it is the ostensible figure of the seduction of the critical analyst as desiring subject by the grammar of Dickinson's textual body.

Lacan cryptically (as always) observed that "as soon as the subject who is supposed to know exists somewhere . . . there is transference."[16] It is the belief that a subject possesses knowledge, whether that subject be a text or a person, that initially produces transferential effects. Dickinson's poetic texts, regarded by their critical analysts as sites of knowledge open to an interpretive archaeology, may therefore facilitate, through their syntactic deferral of meaning and consequent perpetuation of unconscious desire, the analytic seduction that is transference. However, if Dickinson's poetics of seduction functions as a transferential model analogous to the Lacanian psychoanalytic dialectic—the text filling the position of analyst and the reader the position of analysand in a situation where both subject positions are fluid—then the study of the *affects* of that transference on readers is perhaps the only interpretation of the poetry necessary. And since it is Dickinson's *text* (and not the biography of her personal neuroses) that is the true analytical *case* in the history of literary criticism, the construction of a *critical case history* for the poet, a history that can duly serve as a more convenient analytical object, is thus a valuable project in and of itself.

Assuming that the critical responses to Dickinson's poetry are the valid locus of psychoanalytic interpretation,[17] it follows that contradictions within the compiled critical case history should be significant. As we will see, the variation in the degree of transferential affects from reader to reader seems at least partly explicable in terms of gender. This is not surprising when we consider that transference is a situation of seduction precisely insofar as erotics are encoded in an act of reading that demands the crossing of the limits of subject/object positions. It would be strange indeed if the poet's rhetorical seduction of male and female critical readers proved to have consequences of identical magnitude. In this chapter I want to focus solely on Dickinson's male readers, for two reasons. First, the Freudian romance—the male analyst reading (and being read by) a female analysand—can, obviously, more precisely demarcate the critical scene of reading established between Dickinson's poetic text and a specifically male reader. Second, as Dickinson discovered while observing her father's response to the Jenny Lind "show," there is often substantial entertainment in viewing the uninhibited response of a male critic to a female "performer," especially when the success of her performance is inextricably linked to her personal appeal. But before I begin my examination of the uncanny effects contingent on male critical readings of the "body" of Dickinson's poetry, I want to emphasize that the analysis of the rhetorical seduction of male critics by that poetry is not simply a study of the sexism implicit in so many critical readings of the poet. The extent of overtly sexist Dickinson criticism has been ably documented by others.[18] I believe the extensive sexism in Dickinson studies is merely reflective of a larger gender dynamic that occurs in the hermeneutic space between the male reader and the poems in the act of interpretation. What we find in male critical readings of Dickinson's poetic text is something more revelatory than a tacky chauvinism.

Since the discourse of the analyst and the discourse of the "hysteric" can never be decisively distinguished from one another in the analytic situation, "hysteria" might be characterized as precisely the disorder that puts in question objective knowledge. The particular objective knowledge that hysteria places in question, however, is that of the male analyst. Freud's archetypal analyst is male and his archetypal analysand, the hysteric, female. This may be in itself a fantasy situation—the figuration of the desired relationship between the male authority figure and the female patient. Martha Noel Evans has noted the extent to which some of the basic gender premises of psychoanalysis remain unexamined. In particular, she observes that many contemporary French analysts still automatically assume, when writing about hysteria, that the position of the analyst as interpreter is male and that the position of the analysand as interpreted is female. Consequently, and with minimal reflexive irony, the "hysterics" are duly characterized as "difficult patients who elicit reactions of hostility, impatience, anger, exasperation, and sometimes love," while the harried analyst, "whether yielding to anger or to desire . . . playing the male role in this romance, appears to feel undone by the hysteric, who perpetually attempts to dislodge him from his place as an authority." Evans amusingly describes what occurs when the analyst is confronted by the hysteric's false seductiveness, false in that she does not follow through on her original offer of love to him—in short, that she is a tease:

> This sequence of seductiveness and withdrawal seems to be particularly enraging to male analysts. Desire is first aroused according to the normal procedures of female seduction by a woman posing herself as an object; but then desire is left unsatisfied by the hysteric's insistence on her status as a subject. . . . In these circumstances, analysts say they feel undone, impotent or castrated, and their response is to master their anger and humiliation by returning the hysteric to object status as an item in textual theory. The act of theorizing therefore becomes the equivalent of phallic display.[19]

Since Dickinson so actively invites her own—or, more precisely, her poetry's—diagnosis as "hysteric," it is equally possible to trace the phenomenon examined by Evans as it pertains to *her* male critical analysts. Whether each critical text that takes Dickinson as its subject matter is, in its own unique way, a phallic display for the analyst's male colleagues is beyond the scope of this discussion, at least insofar as it might bring the discussion too close to home. But certainly, in the pages that follow, Evans's description of the male analysts being "undone" or left feeling "impotent" or responding with "anger" or "exasperation" or even "love" cannot help but acquire a certain resonance, for these types of response are precisely those evoked in Dickinson's male analysts over a considerable expanse of critical history. To study male readers of Dickinson's poetry is to be inevitably reminded of the Freud of "Observations on transference-love":

> When a woman sues for love, to reject and refuse it is a distressing part for a man to play; and, in spite of neurosis and resistance, an incomparable magic emanates from a woman of high principles who confesses her pas-

sion. It is not a patient's crudely sensual desires which constitute the temptation. These are more likely to repel, and it will call for all the doctor's tolerance if he is to regard them as a natural phenomenon. It is rather, perhaps, a woman's subtler and aim-inhibited wishes which bring with them the danger of making a man forget his technique and his medical task for the sake of a fine experience.[20]

As we will see, the examination of Dickinson's critical readers uncovers covert and overt expressions of love and hate, of attraction and repulsion, of tolerance and intolerance, and identifies a vast proliferation of technical lapses "for the sake of a fine experience" that stretches from the New Criticism to the critical fictions of our own postmodern moment.

Of course, while the study of specific male critical analyses of Dickinson's poetry, from the 1890s to today, can provide the empirical evidence of the existence and success of her rhetorical seduction of the reader, perhaps the most compelling proof is simply the fact of her continued functioning as a "strange attractor" in the field of literary criticism; for the literary critic's strange attraction to Dickinson, itself the subject of this analysis, is the consequence of her particular susceptibility to an easy critical appropriation, an appropriation that is directly related to her gender. Perhaps the most prophetic statement ever made by a Dickinson reader was A. C. Ward's observation of 1932 that "the supposed enigmatic personality of Emily Dickinson will no doubt make her the victim of literary body-snatchers throughout successive generations."[21] Successive generations of readers have indeed proven to be particularly adept body-snatchers, seizing the "body" of her poems (the *corpus*, if you will) for their own, often dubious, critical purposes. Indeed, Dickinson's critical fashionability since the 1970s, her persistent academic popularity, is a direct consequence of the capacity of her poems to be continually made over, or fashioned, into a new, more contemporary image reflective of the recent critical theory that seeks to analyze them.[22] And if there has been one staple of that criticism, it has been the confusion of the "body" of poetry with the physical "body" of the poet. A critical reading of an individual poem is always liable to slip into a critical analysis of the poet's life: as a frustrated woman; as a woman crippled by dysfunctional family relationships; as a woman trapped within her self-made signifying system; as a woman uncovering new sources of power within the margins of a powerless deprivation.[23] Thus, the posthumous life of Dickinson's art has always proven inseparable from the posthumous art of her life. The movement from poetry to poet, and the inability of readers to differentiate between the textual and the physical body, might, however, be considered not so much evidence of a critical failure as of a significant artistic success. That the desire for the substance, or body, of Dickinson should be the transformation of the desire for a sexual body, and that her readers should experience that specific confusion, was the specific intention of the rhetorical fusion of textuality, sexuality, and eschatology through which she sought to make her word flesh, by means of which she could make palpable the figure behind the figure.

The "sexist" critique of Dickinson's hybridized body/text is most evident in New Critical and psychoanalytic readings of her poetry. Unlike the psychoanalytic approach to literature, where Freudian or Lacanian sexism is often implicit, there is nothing intrinsically sexist in the reading method of the New Criticism. The New Critical protestation of scientific objectivity, and the emphasis on textual form, would seem to mitigate against an overt sexism. Since blatant sexism *is*, however, evident in the New Critics' readings of Dickinson, we must assume that the criticism of an earlier era, less sensitive to issues of gender, was simply more careless in its subjective expressiveness. Rereading that criticism should not make the contemporary critic more complacent in his self-congratulatory righteousness; the sexism of the postmodernist age, like all its other manifestations of subjectivity, is merely more self-aware, and therefore more covertly and carefully expressed. The male New Critics therefore present us with a more honest portrait of Dickinson's male reader than do their circumspect successors.

The typical portrait of that New Critical reader is of a man who regards a female poet as fundamentally *other*. This is evident, for example, in the commentary of R. P. Blackmur, who apparently found it difficult to think of Dickinson in human terms. At first she is feline—"it sometimes seems as if in her work a cat came at us speaking English." Later, Blackmur decides that if Dickinson is a cat she is certainly not a full-grown one, her work revealing "the playful ambiguity of a kitten being a tiger." But if at times she is nothing more than a paper tiger, on other occasions Dickinson has a more significant bite: "It is as if she got . . . the sense of vampirage which is usually only a possible accompaniment of relation."[24] Blackmur's discussion of Dickinson is often only barely contained within the framework of the human: whenever he has recourse to metaphor, the subject of his analysis invariably evokes an extrahuman analogy. The emphasis on Dickinson's otherness in Blackmur's criticism is at least partly because of his heightened awareness of her as a woman. Of course, that sense of otherness is not merely a consequence of the dearth of woman poets in the critic's experience (although that is possible explanation enough), but also evidence of a poetic strategy whose single most important component is a subtle emphasis on the writer's gender, and consequently on her otherness in relation to a male reader. And while individual New Critics disagreed on the value of Dickinson's poetry, there was a consensus on the personality of the poet. Allen

Tate found in Dickinson's poetry a power emanating from the frustrations of a deprived woman, or, more precisely, "a dominating spinster whose every sweetness must have been formidable."[25] The nature of Dickinson's frustration is more explicitly examined by others: John Crowe Ransom remarked that Dickinson did not have "her own romance, enabling her to fulfill herself like any other woman," and David Higgins chronicled the aesthetic consequences of this frustration: "Emily's inability to fulfill herself in marriage may account for the subject matter and number of poems she wrote."[26]

Consistent in these analyses is the assumption that Dickinson's art is a mapping of her personal frustration. This is, of course, evidence of a critical failure to hold the poet separate from the poetry, but that assumption also emerges from a genuine sense of frustration that is somehow *realized* through the critical reading of the poetry. If we consider the affective cultivation of a sense of frustration in the reader as a deliberate rhetorical practice, as evidence of Dickinson's aesthetic theory of sumptuous destitution in action, then that frustration is, of course, far from representative of the poet's state of mind. On the contrary, that frustration is the reader's (who has not had a frustrated reading experience with a Dickinson poem?). Therefore, the critical assertion that Dickinson was herself unfulfilled or frustrated may be a projection of the reader onto the poet, and the impetus of that projection may be traced to the reader's unsatisfactory reading experience of the poems. This frustrative overlapping suggests that there is either an inappropriate critical distance achieved between the critic and the poem initially, or an appropriate critical distance that duly collapses in the course of his reading of the poem. The comments of Blackmur, Tate, and Higgins suggest that the collapse of objectivity is inevitable when the critic's approach to the poem is predetermined by an attitude toward the woman poet, an attitude in part predetermined, in turn, by an attitude toward women as a whole. This might be expressed more succinctly by saying that one apparent problem for the male Dickinson critic is his potentially falling in love with the poet. In Robert Hillyer's observation of 1922 on the slow spreading of the Dickinson cult—"Year by year knowledge of the secret spreads, as friend whispers to friend and confides the inimitable poet to a new lover"[27]—we can see how falling in love with the poet, falling in love with the poetry, being a poetry lover, or being a lover can become somewhat blurred. It was to Archibald MacLeish's credit that he was willing to admit that *"most of us* are half in love with this dead girl" (emphasis added).[28]

Falling in love with Emily Dickinson produces many of the typical symptoms of the experience: the unsteadiness of equilibrium and of surefooted judgment; the losing of a sense of objective distance and consequent submerging of the self in the Other; and, most of all, the inadvertent betrayal of that self. Perhaps the most evident symptom of this process of critical falling in love is a studied protectiveness toward the poet. This protectiveness, often manifesting itself as a tender male gallantry, is an effect of the intimate Dickinson voice—the vehicle for an address that often suggests a direct, personal relationship with her reader. This feeling of protectiveness is as apparent in the most sophisticated poststructuralist critic as it is in a "common" reader who, it must be said, has always been more ready to acknowledge such feelings as an integral part of reading Dickinson. It is when that sense of a unique personal communication metamorphoses into a feeling, on the critic's part, of intuitively personal comprehension that it becomes a peculiar self-righteous elitism from which the "common" reader is immune. The sense of intuitive personal relation with the poet can produce a stunningly patronizing mode of address in the male critic. For example, when David Higgins discusses Dickinson's potential relationship with the "Master," he does so in these words: "Did Emily or did she not have sexual relations with her master? Almost certainly she did not . . . her accounts of the crucial event indicate that 'Master' only held her on his knee: intimacy enough for Emily."[29] Here Higgins provides us with a superb example of the unconscious irony implicit in the patronizing male critical approach to Dickinson; the tone of a critic's approach to his subject ("intimacy enough for Emily") can mimic the event described by his prose. We see here the patronizing description of a patronizing event. But Higgins has simply succumbed to the temptation that Dickinson invariably offers to all her male critics—to *become*, momentarily, "Master."[30]

That strange mélange of critical protectiveness and superiority is evident in many Dickinson critics, not all of them male. For example, George Whicher's observation of 1930 that "her poetry is not the formal mask of a personality, but a living face vibrant with expressiveness. . . . Though many looking into the well of her being have seen only the distorted image of their own desires, a free mind may discern beneath the surface her true form and substance," to a degree simply echoes Ella Gilbert Ives's 1907 comment that "in life she was arrogantly shy of a public that now shares her innermost confidence, and touches with rude or hallowed finger the flesh of her sensitive poetry; the soul of it, happily only the sympathetic can reach."[31] But the interaction of a critical sympathy and an elitist protectiveness in the male reader more often produces a strangely defensive appreciation of the poet's art. Allen Tate's comment of 1932 that the poetry is "a magnificent personal confession" but "in its self-revelation, its honesty, almost obscene," and Edmund Blunden's observation of 1930 that "passions like hers are not for immodest circulations" would seem, at first, to suggest that these male critics find something potentially immodest in the content of the poetry.[32] But perhaps it would be more precise to locate the "immodesty" these readers find in the *naive* reader's potential interaction with the poem; hence, the critical admonitions that Dickinson can be easily misread by an audience liable to find her "immodestly" circulating. It is the interaction between the Dickinson poem and its reader that needs regulation of some sort. This is not a surprising conclusion if we review the critical comments above and ask: What makes a personal confession become *obscene*? What kind of poetry can be read in an *immodest* manner? What does it mean to *touch the flesh* of a poetry that has a living face? What kind of poetry can mirror the *distorted image* of its reader's *desire*? The vocabulary of this criticism makes its own case for the regulation of such a suggestively stimulating sensuous art.[33]

Perhaps what makes Dickinson's verses so peculiarly uncomfortable for their male reader is best articulated by the *Boston Herald* reviewer of the 1890 first edition, who felt that "to turn over the pages . . . is to feel as if committing an intrusion, so direct and so forcible are many of its utterances. . . . There is a peculiarly penetrating quality about these scraps of verse [that] fill one with the delight of a new possession."[34] While it is the reader who is intrusive, it is the verses that are penetrating. That is nothing if not a strange penetration, for it is a penetration *of* the reader that "fills" him, in turn, with the delight of a new possession. To penetrate the verses is to be penetrated by them, while to *be* possessed by them is the prerequisite for possession of them. Reading the poems calls into question notions of appropriation and ownership—particularly, given the evidence of the critic's vocabulary, the sexual appropriation that is often the approximation of aesthetic ownership.

Interestingly, and presumably not coincidentally, a similarly peculiar critical vocabulary emerges from discussions of Dickinson's radical poetic irregularity. This lexicon invariably focuses on the problem of the "attractiveness" of Dickinson's form. Nineteenth-century critics, bemused by Dickinson's experimental poetics, inevitably concluded, given the century's poetic norm, that "her *modeling* is almost fatally defective" and that "neglect of form involves the sacrifice of an *element of positive attractiveness*" (emphasis added).[35] Later critics, even while praising the experimental complexity of her poetic, maintain their predecessors' vocabulary in describing its "form." That fatally defective, and therefore unattractive, sense of form becomes a *fatale* attractiveness to the extent that Yvor Winters could say in 1938 that "her popularity has been mainly due to her vices."[36] The assimilation of the unattractive form can be seen as far back as 1923 and Martin Armstrong's comment that "these imperfections come to seem things *appropriate and attractive, just as an imperfection of accent or awkwardness of gesture becomes an added charm in a charming personality*" (emphasis added).[37] This is the sentiment echoed a year later by Conrad Aiken in his observation that "Miss Dickinson's singular perversity, her lapses and tyrannies . . . become a *positive charm"* leading to "our complete surrender to her highly individual gift, and to the *singular, sharp beauty, present everywhere, of her personality"* (emphasis added).[38] Again, this is a succinct demonstration of the apparent inability of so many critics to keep the personality of the poetry separate from their reading of the personality of the poet, and that confusion is equally apparent whenever twentieth-century critics have recourse to descriptive metaphor when dealing with Dickinson's unique style: Aiken's 1930 comment that he was impressed by the "spinsterly angularity of the mode" and Geoffrey Hartman's 1980 observation that Dickinson criticism "has to confront an elliptical and chaste mode of expression. . . . The danger is not fatty degeneration but lean degeneration: a powerful, appealing anorexia" are evidence of an apparently timeless biographical reading of poetic form.[39] The critical shift from Dickinson's poetry being metaphorically recontextualized as the work of a twentieth-century anorexic girl as opposed to a nineteenth-century spinster is fascinating enough to warrant a separate study.

It would therefore certainly seem to be the case that no matter the circumstances of the historical reading, Dickinson's strange attractiveness to her critical analysts is inextricably connected to her attractiveness as a woman. In his perceptive 1891 review of the first edition of the poems, William Dean Howells made this provocatively thoughtful statement: "The strange poems . . . we think will form something like an intrinsic experience with the understanding reader of them."[40] A review of the criticism of Dickinson's poetry since Howells suggests that the intrinsic experience was one of seductive attractiveness, for which Aiken's comment "the colors tease, the thought entices, but the meaning escapes" is emblematic.[41] Inevitably, the reader's description of his interaction with the poem, an interaction involving that element of teasing attractiveness, evokes an intense physical proximity to the poem. Howells's own "intrinsic experience" of the love poems was that they were of "the same piercingly introspective cast as those differently named. The same force of imagination is in them; in them, as in the rest, *touch often becomes clutch"* (emphasis added). Maurice Thompson's reading experience is even more vividly metaphorically suggestive: "it gives one a *thrill of vexation to be trifled with* just on the horizon of what appears about to turn out to be a fine lyrical discovery. . . . A large part of the *fascination* of verse like this is generated by the *friction of disappointment on delight.* You are *charmed with the thought and fretted by the lapses* from intelligible expression" (emphasis added).[42] Similarly, Blackmur's negative comparison of Dickinson with Dante is also suggestively physical; in the latter's work "immortality is so much more enlivening than in Dickinson that a *different part of our being quivers* in response to it."[43] This, of course, raises the interesting question of which "part of our being" *does* quiver in response to Dickinson. Without being overly flippant, I would suggest that Dickinson's *is* a poetics of quivering being and that the analyses of these critics provide compelling evidence that extended contact with the poetry of Dickinson reproduces, in their texts, a metaphorical vocabulary of tactile, physical contact. Knowing the poetry is knowing the poet. I doubt if even Whitman generated the range of critical vocabulary that Dickinson has in this study: charmed, fascination, touch, thrill, half in love with, entices, tease, trifled with, lapses, defective modeling, anorexic, imperfections, unattractive, spinsterly, immodest, flesh, vulgar, obscene, vices, perversity, vampirage.

Perhaps it should therefore not be surprising that contemporary male critics often express a foreboding insight, normally in marginal asides, into the dangers of personal revelation, of the implication of self, in their reading process. We can see this in John Cody's pondering whether readers "may recognize in her poetry *some of their own anxieties and reservations*" (emphasis added), and in his observation, while discussing the misreadings Dickinson elicits, that sometimes "the *psychological atmosphere of the poem has repelled the critic* before he could come to grips with the message" (emphasis added).[44] Cody concedes that he is himself vulnerable to just such a response when he notes that "the convulsions of the spirit found in Emily Dickinson's poems are only the *culminating manifestation of processes incipient in all of us . . . most of us who read her poems recognize ourselves in them*" (emphasis added). As a practicing psychoanalyst, Cody is only too aware that an analysand can be a potential seducer. And it is hardly surprising that he identifies seduction as a specifically female wile. In one significant digression, an examination of Austin Dickinson's courtship of Sue Gilbert, Cody makes that point explicitly: "If it was a question of seduction, the seduction was Sue's." Since the female can be so easily characterized as the artful seductress, it is with some inevitability that Cody chooses to interpret Dickinson's rhetorical tactics in her dealings with Higginson as an example of her "*repeatedly seducing him* into submitting his self-important and inept literary advice" (emphasis added). Nor should it be at all surprising that Cody feels it necessary to reject out of hand any notion that the nature of his own study is "*seducing one's attention away* from a proper regard for literary values through an inquisitiveness about personalia" (emphasis added).[45] Throughout Cody's analytic text, his avoidance of a possible seduction by the subject of his analysis is palpably evident. This resistance to Dickinson's text (and thereby to Dickinson herself) is perhaps most evident in his tendency to portray her in the most unappealing physical terms imaginable. A typical narrative digression, from what Cody sees as a rape scenario within a poem, describes Dickinson as "a not very attractive, reclusive spinster whom her would-be rapist would scarcely have had occasion even to see, much less lust after." Elsewhere she is unfairly portrayed as "loveless, excluded, almost burned out as a poet, and reduced to the status of a queer, hypochondriacal, and depressed old maid."[46] This is not the place to indulge in a full-scale analysis of Cody's analysis of Dickinson—despite the fact that, as an analyst in an inevitably countertransferential situation, he leaves himself open to precisely that reading—but it is worth noticing that, just as it was for so many of the New Critics, an identifiable frustration seems to be the key to Cody's interpretation of Dickinson's life and work: his exposition of that personal frustration is heavily dependent on the assumption that her "insatiable love needs and their frustration saturate the poetry and the letters."[47]

Alternatively, David Porter's poststructuralist focus on the poet's language leads him to identify frustration as a quality of the poetry itself: "There is frustration in the poems, an obscure agitation that often does not break through into consciousness." Porter's study of the apparent autonomy and self-reflexivity of Dickinson's language concentrates on the linguistic strategies of poems that give the reader "the constant possibility of slipping off the ledge of the familiar. . . . Readers get taken to the edge and must look over." This unsettling sense of being on the brink of comprehension, of poems that "agitate without ever quite bringing issues to clear articulation," is central to Porter's definition of modernity. The "modern" is precisely this agitating teasing quality of withholding: "This . . . is a modern poem because it gives enough to engage but withholds all the rest."[48] For Porter, what makes Dickinson an exemplary modernist is the fact that she exemplifies modernism's strategy of semantic teasing. To some extent, therefore, Dickinson's linguistic strategy, the syntactic engagement that is simultaneously a withholding, is Porter's contemporary version of the frustration paradigm that we have seen developed by other of Dickinson's male critics. Repeating that earlier pattern, it is with some inevitability that Porter's specific focus on Dickinson's "frustrating" language becomes also a focus on her corporeal self. For while he asserts that Dickinson did not establish a "designed body of completed work" and that her idiom "cannot be a model for a body of work or a body of knowledge," he does believe that her language had an "autogenous energy that *worked deliberately to create its own corporeality* (emphasis added).[49] And it is to the language of the poetry as seductive body that Porter reacts, often ambiguously; if, at one point, "her devouring language grips and startles," at another it is found "trembling with nervousness and need."[50] Dickinson's is a poetic language both shy and aggressive, coy and direct, and it is only with difficulty that Porter can reconcile the apparently paradoxical processes of poems that simultaneously draw from and overpower the reader: "Her parables are propelled by a need that overpowers us. They embarrass us by drawing from us with their enactment of need." Thus, while it is Dickinson herself who "*courts*" allegories of visitation "with *indecent glee*" (emphasis added), it is her poems that evince "what one must call *brilliant impurity*" (emphasis added). If, frustratingly, "instead of proceeding by the reasonableness of syntax or the obligations of representation, her poems *dart and posture*" (emphasis added), it is only to be expected that "the list of her *deviations* would be the *recitation of the body of her poetry*" (emphasis added).[51]

This reading of Dickinson is allegorical to the extent that the critic describes one subject (the figure/body of Dickinson) under the guise of another subject of aptly suggestive resemblance (the poem). Commenting on the difficulties of reading a particular Dickinson poem, Porter observes that "cumulative weirdness of this sort impedes habitualization . . . *preventing us from sliding off poems with easy gratification*" (emphasis added), a spatial metaphor that clearly evokes the presence of the female poet who perpetually gives us "*figure* and not concept." What Porter's phenomenological critical vocabulary often identifies in Dickinson is a readerly frustration almost palpably physical: "In short, a reader emerges from *the most empathetic and pleasurable immersion in the body of poetry* quite unable to report its order of knowledge or perception" (emphasis added). The world created by this poetry holds "an *attention excited by the lexical frisson* that trips an instant of terror or blindness" (emphasis added). When the reading experience is described in these terms—"As readers before the pale traces of the literal sense, we end up *in the web of words*, and *like siren-struck sailors*" (emphasis added)—can it really be said to be the *poem* that is in some sense spider or siren? Or is it more probable that the explanation for such terminology is more likely found in the attitude of the critic toward the spider-woman, the siren herself, the woman "who destroys habitual encounters, and for this we cherish her," the one who is a "fetching country lass"?[52]

Yet, at the same time, Porter seems only too aware of the dangers of the subjective reading to which other Dickinson critics have proven so readily susceptible. Of an earlier critic he pointedly notes, "Winters discovered in this woman of surpassing linguistic power, as other critics have, what he wanted to find in the first place." More importantly, he also recognizes just what produces that subjective reading; that it is the effect on the individual reader of a language that is a "void of mystery that changes its appearance as the reader's various approaches create this or that origin." Porter's significant comment on those various approaches, and the battery of purely subjective inferences they bring to bear on a poem, is also a perceptive summation of the history of Dickinson criticism: "Dickinson's ambiguity, indefiniteness, and lack of reference create mystery that invites, indeed traps, readers into sexual *speculation of a predictable and even self-revelatory kind*" (emphasis added).[53] Porter's text is consequently the scene of a revealing power struggle. If Dickinson's central problem was that, "having no authority outside her own nerve ends [she] centrifugally dispersed her art and made it unmanageable," then Porter considers his own critical text an attempt to make that art *manageable*. To that end, his typical reading strategy unpacks the compressed Dickinson poem into a prose statement in order better to articulate a specific meaning, to clarify its semantic dimension. The poem is then recondensed into its initial form. His reading of poem 546 is representative of this process: "Finally, and this is what moves us most, the poem deceives itself. It claims a Master but has none. . . . And so the poem remains a matter of words, an instrument capable of submission or of capture or of control of the world only if put in the right hands, but by itself without a clear idea about doing any one of these things."[54] What "moves" Porter, in particular, has been his providing the right hands (his own) for that instrument. Porter's provocative reading of the poem as language speaking itself might therefore be considered his own elaborate attempt to "master" the poem.

This strategy of mastery, one that Porter applies problematically throughout his valuable *and* masterful study, requires the denial of the textual element that most often challenges critical authority. Porter's "decompression" of the poem's semantic dimension, his settling on one obvious "meaning," typically demands the elision of that syntactic complexity that can produce a plethora of alternate, often opposed, semantic reconstructions. Earlier we saw how the impacting of language became the locus of Dickinson's personal signature: it is precisely by means of her collapsed syntax that genotextual elements produce the trace inscription of body as text. Porter's critical argument, often requiring the temporary suppression of Dickinson's syntactic complexity, might be considered a simultaneous denial of the poet as potentially embodied presence. But Dickinson's presence as dispersed in her text's syntax, the locus of hybridization, cannot be completely suppressed. That presence duly returns resurrected as the metaphorical undertow within the critical text, as an unconscious of language that destabilizes Porter's argument and which, predictably, challenges his authority as critical "master." Porter's *The Modern Idiom* is consequently the scene of the most vivid extant power conflict between a male reader and Dickinson's poetic text. We will later see that this scrimmage for control is not dissimilar to that which occurs between Dickinson's text and other readers. Ultimately, however, those struggles follow a slightly different agonistic route.

The peculiarities of these twentieth-century critical responses to the poetry shed retrospective light on the responses of nineteenth-century readers whose affective response to Dickinson, in this context, appears a model of critical perspicacity. Summarizing Dickinson's reception in the 1890s, Willis J. Buckingham observes that the typical reader responds to her "as a friend and correspondent, bold, brilliant, attractive, and passionate, *a loved presence evoking uplifting feelings*" (emphasis added). For Buckingham, this points to "an often unrecognized feature of nineteenth-century literary activity: the way in which poetry reading, though taking place in solitude, joined itself to other social activities, especially communion between like-minded persons. . . . [P]oetry reading at its best creates *an intimacy between the reader and the poet, a sacramentalized society of two*" (emphasis added). This almost sacramental intimacy is sustained by the prevalent affective aesthetic of the cultural moment, in which admiration for technique is "an adjunct to inspired thought and feeling"; the process of reading is a "series of pleasing aftermaths; on the genius side, a kinetic push of forceful mental presence; on the sympathy side, a warmth or bonding response to personal presence . . . one cannot parse while reeling from a blow or opening to love"; and the successful poem (and in this particular historical context Dickinson's poems were most successful) ensures that "something within reels and stumbles."[55] However, while to some extent the readers of the 1890s inevitably imposed elements of their own affective aesthetic on Dickinson's poetry, their particular reading strategies did not completely create what the *Boston Transcript* reviewer identified as that "strange magic of meaning so ethereal that one must apprehend rather than comprehend it."[56] Rather, the late nineteenth century provided an opportune aesthetic moment for the reception of a poet who had been, in her interest in rhetorical affectiveness at least, a little ahead of her time. The prevalent reception aesthetic of the 1890s readers permitted them considerable insight into Dickinson's rhetorical techniques: these were readers equipped to recognize a poetry that is primarily an experience; a poetry that does not give rise to conceptual knowledge but to excitation, thralldom, captivation; a poetry that effects seduction by requiring the complicity, the willing surrender, of the experiencing subject; and a poetry that imposes on that subject, in appropriate rhythms, a singular syntax that manages and directs the flow of his or her libidinal energy. The readers of the 1890s were simply in a felicitous position to see what twentieth-century readers, steeped in various rigid hermeneutics, cannot see. The irony is that, so often concerned with the irrelevancies of interpretation, twentieth-century readers lose sight of the reader-implicating components of Dickinson's rhetoric in the process of continually succumbing to its uncanny effects.

Twentieth-century male readers of Dickinson's poetry provide a consummate demonstration of how the critical appropriation of the literary text may occur in a situation analogous to the psychoanalytic dialectic. In that dialectic, the analyst seeks to imitate lack itself in order to incite an analysand to work with desire. The successful analyst, miming the analysand's unsatisfied desire, therefore has no palpable reality in the analytic situation: he or she is the creation of the analysand, essentially an illusion of something not said in the analysand's *other*. In a similar fashion, the syntactic voids within Dickinson's poetic text (combined with the suggestively absent details of her incomplete life/text) incite readers to work through a hermeneutic desire that proves self-revelatory. The provocation of such subjective reading investments, the text's engagement of what can only be called a subjective objectivity, is evidence, I would suggest, of that poetic text's subtle analysis of its reader.

Psychoanalysis works because of the transference, because the patient transfers previous relations with others onto the analyst, reactivates the emotions, and can thus work them out in the analysis. Transference is therefore inevitably a recalling of obscure past events. As Peter Brooks has observed more generally of the location of analytic transference, "The transference . . . is a realm of the *as-if*, where affects from the past become invested in the present, notably in the dynamics of the analysand-analyst relation, and the neurosis under treatment becomes a transference neurosis, a present representation of the past. . . . *Within the transference, recall of the past most often takes place as its unconscious repetition, an acting out of past events as if they were present*" (emphasis added).[57] In many readings of Dickinson's poetry, the transferential situation established between poetic text and reader uncannily re-creates a dialogue between recognizable historical figures and resurrects, through signification, a specific past and its local scenarios of desire: the antebellum scene of seduction finds its unconscious repetition in the later critical scene of reading. The second coming of this particular antebellum power "neurosis" can problematize the supposedly "objective" critical rhetoric of a male reader to the extent that there may be a transferential repetition of the poetic text by the commentary that would seek to appropriate it critically. One obvious textual example of this curious phenomenon is William Shurr's *The Marriage of Emily Dickinson*. Shurr is a reader parenthetically concerned that if Dickinson's poetry is "a mere matrix, a form without content, which can give structure and meaning to the unformed experience of the reader," then it is potentially a "matrix for stimulating the subjectivities of each reader." It is therefore somewhat ironic that subjective stimulation should be precisely the narrative Shurr then "reads" in the fascicles; it is within those same poem packets that he finds evidence that the attraction between Dickinson and Rev. Charles Wadsworth "was mutually recognized and *sexual stimulation* was high" (emphasis added). So while Shurr comes to identify Dickinson's sexual stimulation of *that* privileged reader to an emotional pitch of response as the goal of the (supposedly) mailed fascicles, he fails to realize the implications of that identification for his own assumed perspective, for his own position as *another* male reader of those same fascicles. Consequently, when he states that "the narrative core of Emily Dickinson's fascicle poetry is the classic love triangle involving the married couple and the outsider," his obvious intention—that the reader visualize Dickinson at the apex of a triangle whose base positions are occupied by Reverend and Mrs. Wadsworth—is continually undermined by his own obtrusive textual positioning. The perspective he assumes as the critical observer of this relationship actually *re-creates* the love triangle: the new base of the triangle is the "marriage" between Dickinson and Wadsworth, with Shurr himself displacing the poet in coming to occupy the writer's apex.[58] The historical narrative is thus "recovered" by a critical narrative that duplicates it. The text has seduced Shurr into the repetition of a (father-daughter) seduction, and the past scene of seduction has returned in that of the transference—here and now does indeed repeat then and there. This mode of critical analysis is the repetition of the scene that led to the necessity of the analysis: it is not an interpretation but an act. Such a curious (and in this case obvious) unconscious critical repetition raises the more awkward question of whether there can ever be any interpretive metalanguage suitable for addressing Dickinson's poetic text.

Of course, the interpretive language male critics employ is often not so much the addressing of that text as its *undressing*. Metaphorically suggestive, that criticism produces a tropic discourse symptomatically revealing in its continual expression of a confusion of textual and physical *body*.[59] The resurrection of that body in critical language frequently prefaces a dismissal contingent on its failure to "satisfy" critical desires: the poem's "rejection" of the reader's interpretive "advances" is taken as a strangely personal affront. The failure of an interpretive reading strategy to appropriate the poem satisfactorily produces—as it frequently did in the New Critics—either a denial or the most qualified of acceptances of the poet's canonical merit. This rejection of the reader by the poet/poetry, which duly provokes a critical rejection of the poet/poetry by the reader, can be considered the useful figuration of rather more substantial transferential affects elsewhere evident in the male critical text. The most obvious of those affects is the defensive identification of unfulfilled desire as thematically central to Dickinson's poetry, when it is more obviously the reader's transferential repetition of a frustrated desire produced by, and implicit in, the inhibiting syntax of that poetry. As we have seen, male readers typically cope with a sense of interpretive frustration by projecting that sense of frustration onto the personality of the poet and asserting, from the evidence of the poetry, that Dickinson was either an infuriatingly *frustrating* individual or in some way personally *frustrated*. But if the cultivation of that frustration was an intrinsic component of the poet's practice of "sumptuous destitution," in which a complex syntax became the rhetorical vehicle for the simultaneous stimulation and deferral of her readers' interpretive desire, then that frustration becomes self-evidently the property of the reader.

It would therefore appear to be the case that we understand this poetic text only insofar as we understand the disturbances it sets up within its critical reader. In this case, it is not simply a matter of the text's transference onto its reader/analyst. That reader is also an analysand. This reader-implicating poetic is analogous to the psychoanalytic dialectic precisely insofar as it is a dialectic: the text's transference is experienced by the critical analyst only through his countertransference responses. Arthur Marotti has argued that "countertransference responses certainly occur in literary experience, especially in the critical interpreter who not only reacts immediately to literary works but also makes it his business to react to his reactions. Since his task is the rational one of discursive explanation, he must cope with the apparently disordered processes of his own unconscious in a more rigorous way than the ordinary reader who does not normally make the effort to translate his deepest thoughts and feelings into verbal form." Marotti emphasizes the "interpsychic dimension" of literature, which produces a "basic intellectual-emotional bond between author and reader, a transaction in which creative and aesthetic responses are not merely analogous but intermingle," and he suggests that "just as the analyst, in the psychotherapeutic situation, develops a working model of his patient, so too the reader of literature forms an emotional image of the human being at the other end of the literary communication."[60] Marotti's model of countertransferential reading certainly seems applicable to those many readings of "Dickinson" where interpretation is predetermined by the tendency to form an "emotional image" of the poet. I would, however, take issue with Marotti's confining of the dialectic to that of reader and (implied?) author. In the reading of Dickinson's poetry, we find the established dialectic to be between the reader and *a text as psyche* (which may be confused with the "real" poet) exhibiting conscious and unconscious processes. The countertransference responses elicited from the reader involve the transferring of his own unconscious emotions onto the text, and often this occurs as a negative countertransference, in which an unanalyzed part of the reader becomes implicated in the analysis. Consequently, the reading-affects of Dickinson's text prove to be as often akin to love and hate as to meaning. As we have seen in this chapter, male readers of Dickinson's poetry have found innumerable ways to express fascination, repulsion, protectiveness, titillation, anger, frustration, and lust, thereby providing a thorough demonstration of the vagaries of transference love, of how seduction in psychoanalysis often appears as both affection *and* hostility.

Freud defined the relationship between the analysand and analyst in the transference as one of conflict, as an ongoing struggle for the mastery of resistances and the lifting of repressions. As the reading of Dickinson's poetic text occurs in a situation analogous to the psychoanalytic dialectic, it is only to be expected that interpretation should prove to be a vivid drama of desire and power. But while the Dickinson dialectic of seduction challenges any assumed subject position of mastery—the textual intervention that is the act of reading being both the transferential desire to master the text and a desire to be mastered by it—it is also clear that the male reader's strong desire to master the text, a desire for mastery evident in the sporadic affects of a negative countertransference, often actively interferes with or supersedes the transference. The text, structured as it is to confuse seduced and seducing subjects, to attribute power to no single subject, resists interpretive mastery. In this context, the negative guise of transference is resistance. The typical male critical analyst's reading of Dickinson's text can still evidently be the personal mapping of an unconscious psychic route, but it would appear to be not so much the transference itself as the reader's avoidance of, or deflection from, the possible transferential situation that structures the male critical text. In this way, the poetic text's troping on desire serves primarily as a superb stimulation of its male analyst's defense mechanisms.[61] Happily, however, this is not always the case. The variation in critical reading response is what makes the critical case history such a seductively appealing object in itself. In the next chapter, I will examine what occurs when the poetic text succeeds in effecting the more complete analysis of its critical reader.

6

Reading Seductions (2)

I would even suggest [that] certain literary texts have an "analytic" and
deconstructive capacity greater than certain modes of psychoanalytic
discourse which *apply* to them their theoretical apparatus.

—Derrida, "Positions 2"

Like Eyes that looked on Wastes—
Incredulous of Ought
But Blank—and steady Wilderness—
Diversified by Night—

Just Infinites of Nought—
As far as it could see—
So looked the face I looked upon—
So looked itself—on Me—

—Dickinson, *Poem 458*

IN THE PREVIOUS chapter, I argued that the critical analyst of Dickinson's poetry may become implicated in some of the problematics of transference.
Often, the analyst (the critical reader) can be as surrendered to the process of
transference as the analysand (the poetic text) in a situation where both subject positions assume a dialectical fluidity. I also observed that what allows the
intersubjective play (and, in this context, the actual process of reading can be
considered a form of intersubjective play) of the unconscious of the analyst and
the unconscious of the analysand is the production of a transference that supersedes the desire to master, and that in the case of Dickinson's male readers
the overwhelming desire to master the text interpretively may produce countertransferential affects that skew the critical analysis. Of course, this poetic seduction theory intimates the probable prevalence of subterranean power dynamics
in *any* analytical reading of Dickinson's text. It is therefore important to examine whether the textual enticements of a reading transference are more overtly
marked by specific patterns of dominance and submission. Does the pattern of
dominance evidenced by so many male analyses of the poetic text represent

only one possible reading paradigm? While seduction offers the possibility of mastery, it also plays on a desire for submission, a desire to yield and to merge the separate self into the body of the seducer. Desire is always equally realizable as the eroticized submission *to* the Other. Hypothetically, the reading paradigm that combined both elements—mastery *and* submission—would create an even more revelatory transferential situation.

This reading paradigm is in fact far from hypothetical. There are a number of critical readings of Dickinson's poetry that are overtly "hysterical" in nature. In this context, the diagnosis of a reading as "hysterical" is not a critique. On the contrary, since one of the key effects of the psychoanalytic dialogue is the "hystericization" of the patient in the transference, such readings of the poet are often inspired.[1] The transferential dialectic established between "hysterical" readers and the Dickinson poetic text actually makes these critical interpreters extraordinarily "close" analysts of the poetry. Indeed, the particularly expressed closeness to the poet is one of the more obvious signs of the "hysterical" reader, because his or her transference onto Dickinson's poetic text is most evident in the confessional intrusions that gently occlude boundaries between subject and object positions, between memoir and criticism, between transference and interpretation. Typically, Dickinson's supposedly hysterical poetic text itself proliferates hysterical critical narrative.

Let me begin, however, with this qualification. Although the majority of my examples of "hysterical" readers are women, and although it is certainly implicit in this study that the reader's gender makes a considerable *difference*, it would be simply stereotypical for me to assert that while male readers attempt to dominate Dickinson's text (i.e., seduce it), female readers submit to its affects (i.e., are seduced by it). Throughout this study, I have emphasized the bifurcated nature of seduction—the fact that one reads as seducer and seducee simultaneously—and *many* of Dickinson's female readers have read no differently from their male counterparts. For example, Louise Chandler Moulton's nineteenth-century response precisely parallels that of her male colleagues when she finds in the poetry "a fascination, a power, a vision that enthralls you, and draws you back to it again and again. . . . It enthralls me, and will not let me go . . . with every page I turn and return I grow more and more in love. I am half tempted to wish that while Emily Dickinson lived she had given more of herself to the world."[2] These assertions of "love" and, significantly, of "half temptation" could have been produced by any number of Moulton's male contemporaries. Similarly, the twentieth-century feminist account of the genesis of Dickinson's poetics is as likely as any other to assume that the poetry "originates in frustration" or to assert that "the experience of having desires that were imperfectly gratified through her major relationships . . . is the central fact of Emily Dickinson's life."[3] Contemporary feminist readings that exaggerate Dickinson's frustration in order to emphasize her entrapment in patriarchal structures replicate the interpretive paradigm authorized by the New Criticism. Feminist critics are equally liable to uncover a textuality of hysteria. Martha Nell Smith finds "hysterical rhetoric" in Dickinson's correspondence and notes the "hysterical, urgent tone and the relentless present tense of [the] pleading" of poems and letters alike. Even Mary Loeffelholz, in her exemplary feminist study of the poet, will claim that one of Dickinson's speakers "displays her forbidden, transgressive knowledge of feminized Nature almost *in the manner of an hysterical symptom: she takes on, signifies in her own person the 'hiddenness,' and quasi-sexual resistance* of the natural scene she violated" (emphasis added).[4] In this way, the contemporary feminist reader who excludes the hypothesis of hysteria from the Dickinson life-narrative often rediscovers (or recovers) neurosis within the poetic narrative. Expelled from one area, hysteria will usually resurface in another location in the manner of a repressed symptom. So while gender is certainly a factor in both the production and the assumed form of the "hysterical" critical reading, it is not necessarily a determinant one.

The most convincing evidence that a male reader is capable of reading "hysterically" can be found in the critical texts of Karl Keller. His freewheeling interpretation of Dickinson's poetry could be called many things, but "frustrated" is certainly not one of them. Keller's reading of Dickinson, as exemplified by his 1979 study *The Only Kangaroo among the Beauty*, is highly provocative. The provocation is not so much in the main business of that study, an analysis of the contemporary American cultural influences on the poet, as it is in Keller's stylistic approach to his subject matter—irreverently postmodern, deconstructively playful, cheekily chic. Keller's most important critical dictum is this: "It is necessary to be outrageous about Emily Dickinson, for of all American poetry before 1900 her work, it seems to me, is the most outrageous." In the course of his argument, the outrageousness Keller finds in Dickinson's poetic text and the stylistic outrageousness of his own critical text meld as one. For Keller, Dickinson's "cardinal virtue . . . is the Temptation to Excess," and the ambiguous syntax of his sentence is presumably the point: not only is that temptation one to which Dickinson succumbs, it is the temptation she proffers to those who write about her.[5] It is also, evidently, a temptation to which Keller is more than willing to surrender.

From the outset, Keller is intensely sympathetic toward his subject's outrageous "temptation to excess." What he celebrates in Dickinson is the "playful boldness, therapeutic excess . . . the polymorphous perverse" that can provide for her reader "a little naughtiness, a little nastiness, a little playfulness, a little freakishness, a spectacle." The poet "searches for delinquency, desires it, works at it, for it gives her a maturity, a delight," and although "what she writes, while freak, is virtually unbelievable," it may still be appreciated as the "almost schizophrenic route" of an artist whose often assumed "elfin/gamin role is . . . the recognition of the relation of herself to world and universe as a person in the form of a deviant streak."[6] For Keller, Dickinson's outrageousness is more than the consciously willed stand of an outsider for whom shock is an assertion of difference. Hers is an exhibitionism represented as an almost palpably physical deviation from nature. That deviation is perhaps epitomized best by the function a circus "freak" (to borrow one of Keller's favorite descriptive adjectives for the poet) has when displayed for a viewer; the freak's aggressive physical assertion of difference serves as the mechanism for the observer's relieved (because suitably distanced and cathartic) cerebral acknowledgment of an otherwise ugly distinction. In a similar way, Dickinson's poetry, and the vivid assertion of difference contained therein, may prove to have a useful therapeutic or purgative value for its reader.

Although clearly susceptible to the temptation to be herself outrageous, Dickinson's more significant temptations are thus directed at that reader. In fact, Keller can progress quite naturally, in the course of a sentence, from the temptation *of* Dickinson to the temptation *by* Dickinson: "Tempted by heresy, she is never sterile in religious imagination: the woman in her is the presumed and the presuming. Refractory, rampant, playful, excessive, vital, tough, she animates faith, not yielding easily to masculine authority."[7] The movement of Keller's prose from Dickinson's temptation *by* heresy to her own temptation, as a "presuming" woman defying the attempt of masculine control, *of another* is symptomatic of a more pervasive rhetorical drift. More specifically, throughout Keller's critical text there is an implicit association of the poetical and critical motives as intermingled phenomena. The critical act is little more than the reproduction of an initial poetic affect, or its uncanny doubling: thus, Dickinson's poetic outrageousness demands an identically self-conscious outrageousness in her critical reader, a celebratory recognition by that reader of what is immanent in, and produced by, the text he is analyzing.

Keller's own outrageousness is exemplified by his constant insistence on the sexuality of Dickinson's poems. This he emphasizes by employing a slangy, trivializing vocabulary and modern analogies that have the force of a juxtaposition. For Keller, Dickinson is primarily a sensualist, and "the abundance/ease of sensation appears to have made her intolerant and impatient with the banal and therefore desirous of the extreme." The sensational extremity of his own text is the shock effect of continual flip (and hip) reference to the apparently burgeoning sexuality in (and of) the poetic text. Examples of this stylistic quirkiness are strewn throughout Keller's text: for the poet, "sex is a consuming companionship consummately to be desired consummated. In other words, it is a making out, a trying out"; the sex described within poems "forms no program but is made up of individual bold moments, flashes of desire, mainly masturbatory"; the poems themselves are little more than "expressions of sexual loneliness, desires recalled in the tranquillity of heat . . . masturbation fantasies" to be "treated according to the esthetics of the hardcore"; Dickinson herself is "the lovely, lost vamp," who, undergoing a "conflict between hormones and integrity . . . whored often enough to make one wonder which was primary with her"; she is a poet "as much of a poetic voyeur as Whitman" who "manages to make Freud trite." Keller's focus on Dickinson's poetic deviance eventually becomes, through the rhetorical extravagance of his presentation, a meditation on a sexual deviance of sorts; the poet's ultimate outrageousness is that of an individual who skirts the dangerous fringes of sexuality, outdoing Freud through imaginatively lived experience. Keller's discussion of Dickinson as "whore," "voyeur," and "masturbator" takes its most spectacular rhetorical flight in another of the calculated excesses that he employs to discuss his subject's "sheer love of excess": "As soon as one probes Emily Dickinson's flamboyance, one recognizes her determination to violate the family's and the community's strict standards. . . . One cannot imagine her as responsible—as a governess or schoolteacher, for example, or a nurse or professional. Not hard to imagine her, though, as a performer of some sort, or as a hooker."[8]

Crucial in understanding Keller's critical process is the keyword "tease," which he uses in a multiplicity of contexts in relation to the poet. For example, Dickinson's experience of a godless universe led her to find "the ambiguous universe a tease." As the experience of near revelation is an essential part of the romantic aesthetic heritage, she also "shared with Emerson . . . an esthetic of ideas: the thrill of being on the brink of a revelation." Consequently, the tease was her privileged mode of thought and her frequent recourse to the epigram a method of critical riddling that is "an esthetic expression where the means is more alive than the meaning made; thinking is a tease; possibility intellectualized satisfies." Moreover, this imaginative teasing is the expression of a distinct personality, because the way the poet sets out her *life* is a tease: "We must recognize that Emily Dickinson is a great tease. Her life, like her poetry, seduces without offering complete satisfaction. For all the expansiveness, there is always something lacking, insufficient, incomplete, tentative, not really finished at all." Finally, this personal teasing is also evident in a poetic persona overtly sexual in its flirtatious display; while Dickinson may on occasion assume "a small, shrewd manner, an attitude of teasing and taunting," she is more likely to strut with the bold assertiveness of a "crude seductress" or beguile with the invitation of a "daring virgin inviting seduction, foreplay and penetration." Thus, while in Keller's binary critical paradigm Whitman is the "caresser-absorber, the seduced: Emily Dickinson is the prig-tease, the seducer," the latter also appears to be capable of playing the roles of seducer and seducee with an equally seductive facility.

Dickinson's elaborate system of teasing is then *reproduced* by Keller, whose declared intent it is to "play with what I—teased—know about Emily Dickinson . . . *a tease of my own, to see what life a subject may yet yield*" (emphasis added). The purpose of this critical analysis is rather more than the mental "teasing out" of a subject for clarity's sake. Keller's critical reading embraces within its structure the rhetoric of the tease; not only is it thoroughly playful in its verbal outrageousness, but it plays with the reader, is itself something of a joke, a spoof, a tease. And implicit in that critical teasing is a sexual component that serves both as a reply to and echo of the teasing of the original poetic text and its outrageous creator. Keller observes of Dickinson that "my own teases here explore some possibilities for *enjoying her critically* by talking about her in a substantially different way" (emphasis added).[9] The critical "enjoying" of the poet is physical in detail. Not only is a teasing quality of the poems' rhetoric presumed to be the representation of a flirtatious, provocative presence behind that poetry, but it is that evoked presence that then determines the reader's approach to the poems. This slippage to the surmised physical presence of woman-as-tease from the original notion of the *poetry* being capable of the seduction of its reader is also facilitated through the smoothest of transitions. Dickinson is envisaged "trying out the tease, the playful desire, and foreplay" within the poems: the "restless movement" of those poems is duly considered *"more kinetic for the reader's senses* than almost any American verse before Pound and Berryman" (emphasis added). When that verse is described as "the polymorphous perverse, giving the reader, through the form, *sensuous delights suggesting the promiscuous*" (emphasis added), the poetic discourse has itself been accorded the contours of the physical body. The writer and the written conceived rhetorically as one ("Whitman laves, Emily Dickinson *jerks synesthetically*" [emphasis added]), Keller's words continually evoke the poet's intrusive physical presence within the critical text. Reprising the pattern evinced by previous male readers of her poetry, Keller's muted concern is with Dickinson's formal "attractiveness": "The tease in her goes well beyond mere *attractiveness.* . . . The affinities help one know her, without the pretence that one will know her whole. Her connections with some of the more *attractive features* of the world around her, along the whole range of American literary history, give us some fairly *bold features of her* to think about" (emphasis added). In retrospect, the readers of Keller's critical text come to consider those to be "bold features" of Dickinson indeed, not so much a graphical suggestion as a *graphic* display.

To some extent, Keller's willingness to accept the seductive offer of the poetry simply marks the self-reflexive postmodern turning on itself of a timeless critical technique of reading Dickinson. He is merely making explicit what has been implicit in so many previous male critical readings of the poet. In this, at least, his reading of Dickinson's poetry is shocking only in its honesty. While other male readers of that poetic text display a certain defensiveness, Keller's critical text is often confessionally powerful and most revealing in its duplication of the rhetorical strategies it analyzes. His interpretation proceeds in an arena where the critical and poetic texts have established a certain equilibrium: the personal sympathy of the writer becomes also a vivid rhetorical sympathy. Obviously, Keller's notion that "her love poems are often sex poems, and the verse is not therapy but brag: her explicit desires become acts. They are fictions fulfilled" is partially true insofar as the explicit desires fulfilled as fictions can also be those of the reader, realized in the guise of the literary-critical fictional genre. And Keller's assertion that "to put poetry to the service of prolonging one's sexual thrills, one's orgasms, is of greater interest to her" is surely validated when we consider that, in another of Keller's many syntactic doublings, the referent for "one" can be the reader quite as easily as the poet.[10]

It may well have been Keller's realization that the narrative form of *The Only Kangaroo* was a fundamentally inadequate means of dealing with the complexity of his own reader response to Dickinson that led him to the experimental format of his essay "Notes on Sleeping with Emily Dickinson" four years later. This essay is a series of short, confessional fragments (with no pretense of complete *coverage* now), some of the more startling of which are worthy of complete quotation:

> The poems on sleeping with someone are instructions, I believe, on how to "take" her. When she writes about wild nights, she is not only describing her ecstasy but also instructing us how to react to her, what to expect, what to get. She thus couples with the critic. She thus holds.
>
> This woman can tease a man. But though she goes far towards the really crazy, she never loses her inhibitions, for then there would be no imagination necessary, no lure. She pulls a man in.

Emily Dickinson's anticipation of a male readership (her critics, not her cult) nears anxiety. She performs; they analyze. When they perform the poetry, they near anxiety. She then becomes *their* critic.

Imagining her audience to be male gave Emily Dickinson opportunity to play the deviant. Perhaps she could have played that among women, too, but she would not have had to be as brisk, as nasty, as coy, as teasing, as sure. These postures were created by the men in her mind.

She created the space for someone to understand her, enclose her, love her—quite like all the white space around one of her poems. *She* created that white space, I think we have to believe. She lets one in lovingly.[11]

On this occasion, when Keller's postmodernism was also a matter of style, the fragmentation of form as well as content, he produced what is, in my estimation, a stunningly perceptive analysis of the poetics of seduction. Succumbing completely to the transferential affects of Dickinson's poetry, the critical reader cannot help but find himself in the acutest sympathy with her. Keller's final teasing of and by Dickinson—marked by so complete an identification that it culminates in the interpenetration of critical analyst and critical analysand in the analysis until the reading becomes one indistinguishable transferential blur—thus became more significantly revelatory precisely to the extent that it was increasingly "hysterical."

More recent feminist criticism has argued that Dickinson's poetic strategy emphasizes a metonymy that establishes a process of intimacy with the reader.[12] Since metaphor is the relation between possible equivalents and metonymy the relation between contiguous signifiers, it has become a more general commonplace of feminist criticism to associate metaphor with the hierarchical mediation of the visible that sustains male phallic desire, and to associate metonymic contiguity—contiguity suggesting touching, nearness, presence, contact, adjacency—with female sexuality. Margaret Homans, working with this linguistic model, has suggested that the "undecidability of referentiality" offered by Dickinson's metonymic strategy empowers her reader by emphasizing that reader's equal importance in a reading communication that can be a near analogue of sexual communion. Karen Oakes develops Homans's "metonymic" reading somewhat in order to argue that the implied gender of Dickinson's reader significantly affects the poet-reader relationship as it is manifested in a dialectical tension between self and other. For Oakes, Dickinson's poetic discourse can be characterized as feminine insofar as she "attracts, frustrates and endangers a participant, affective reader whom she imagines as feminine" and because she "transforms the traditionally feminine, passive, and inferior role" usually assigned to the reader by stressing an equal and active role. Thus, in opposition to what Oakes identifies as the masculine reading position of judgmental detachment, Dickinson's poetry collapses hermeneutic distance in order to actively endanger the "self-integration and autonomy" of its reader.[13]

Oakes's reading is interesting, but she also significantly elides a problem that Homans addresses in her examination of those difficult Dickinson poems whose subject matter is specifically the relationship between two women in a "reading" situation. If we choose to read the internal dialectic of such poems as Dickinson's poetic figuration of a "feminine," metonymic reading strategy, then we would also have to acknowledge that the endangering of "self-integration and autonomy" that such a reading effects was considered by the poet herself to have distinctly ambiguous results. In particular, poem 458 seems to delineate the particularly unfortunate consequences that can be the product of a too-contiguous "reading" of one woman by another:

> Like Eyes that looked on Wastes—
> Incredulous of Ought
> But Blank—and steady Wilderness—
> Diversified by Night—
>
> Just Infinites of Nought—
> As far as it could see—
> So looked the face I looked upon—
> So looked itself—on Me—
>
> I offered it no Help—
> Because the Cause was Mine—
> The Misery a Compact
> As hopeless—as divine—
>
> Neither—would be absolved—
> Neither would be a Queen
> Without the Other—Therefore—
> We perish—tho' We reign—

This is a puzzling poem, but the gender marking that defines both speaker and addressee as female (both are "Queens") is most certainly significant, particularly because, in the course of our reading, it is difficult to tell whether the "Eyes that looked on Wastes" refers to *how* the speaker looks or to the method of looking of those eyes *into* which the speaker looks. The poem both describes and syntactically effects a collapsing of object and subject, seer and seen, into contigual sameness. That contigual sameness is more precisely a complete mirroring itself neatly duplicated (or mirrored) by the verbal repetition of words and phrases—"So looked . . . So looked . . . Neither—would be . . .

Neither would be"—within the poem. Grammatical duplication becomes the figure of personal duplication. In this case, the mutual recognition of the two women, their awareness of equivalence and sameness, produces a necessary but ambiguous duplicatory stalemate: "The Misery a Compact / As Hopeless—as divine." This process of mirroring-leading-to-stalemate pattern is itself apparently duplicated within this later poem:

> 'Tis Seasons since the Dimpled War
> In which we each were Conqueror
> And each of us were slain
> And Centuries 'twill be and more
> Another Massacre before
> So modest and so vain—
> Without a Formula we fought
> Each was to each the Pink Redoubt—
>
>   (P. 1529)

The fact that speaker and addressee are participants in a "Dimpled War" suggests, of course, that they are women and, once again, specifically women who experience confrontation as the mutual recognition that leads to total equivalence and duplication. That established equilibrium of the two parties is to a degree the consequence of the mutually indistinguishable vocabulary ("Without a Formula") that leaves only specular self-definition ("Each was to each the Pink Redoubt") as a possible communicative medium. Homans's perceptive commentary on the specular stalemate of these puzzling Dickinson poems is useful and worth quoting at some length:

> Without different terms, without hierarchy, the two figures are too much the same . . . language fails to prevent what seems now to be the wholly undesirable collapse of one identity into the other. . . . Where metaphor preserves a relationship of distance and hierarchy between the two elements of a comparison, while seeming to bring them together, the poems about two women are characterized by a lack of distance so complete that there is only one identity and one set of terms for the two figures. This rhetoric of sameness may be considered a form of metonymy, in which each figure could be said to be the name of the other, as when the two faces that look at one another are identical and also stand for each other.[14]

Lacanian feminists have always viewed the female child's entering of the symbolic order, with the consequent elision of the pre-oedipal mother/daughter dyad, as a very problematic process.[15] Luce Irigaray, an obvious influence on Homans's interpretation, figures the developing relation between mother and daughter as one of specular entrapment: "I look at myself in you, you look at yourself in me."[16] In a relation without difference Irigaray finds only freezing identity. Similarly, while object-relations theory places the child-mother relationship at the center of psychoanalysis and positively reconceives the mother-infant dyad as the reciprocation of mutually enforcing egos, it reaches almost identical conclusions regarding the mother/daughter relation. Nancy Chodorow speculates that the initial lack of separation between mother and daughter results in the female self being less individuated. The dual unity that precedes the sense of separate self blurs the boundaries between that self and others. The female child, sharing the female body and its symbolic cultural location, is thus locked in an ambivalent struggle for a separate identity with a mirror image who is both self and other, and is fated to remain always trapped in a troubled symbiosis. In this way, the transactions of infancy shape the development of female individual autonomy insofar as the pre-oedipal bond produces a diffuse and fluid female identity of flexible and permeable ego boundaries: since female development is a process of identification with and differentiation from a mother permanently incorporated into the daughter's psyche, it predetermines her relations with others to be marked by interdependence.[17] Applying the more positive aspects of this model to literary texts, feminist critics locate female textual difference in "an adherence to values of fusion, fluidity, mutuality, continuity and lack of differentiation."[18]

But most obviously the conception of fluid female textuality has implications for the intertextual relationship. The woman writer's ambivalent autonomy presumably produces powerful responses to potential mergers with the precursor texts of literary foremothers. The intertextual relation, according to Kristeva, involves not merely a reference to another text but the "absorption and transformation" of that text.[19] The fluidity of intertextual relation—fluid because it accesses the semiotic—thus produces uncanny, disturbing effects in the textual repetition. The drive of the pre-oedipal to recapture the original unity with the mother's body opposes the symbolic register's requirement that the linguistic subject separate from her objects. When the urge to reproduce that primal unity enters the text, via the intertextual dyad, it disrupts the basis of linguistic structure, the singular position of speaking subject and the separate position of objects. Kristeva insists that this is a "productive dissolving" insofar as "the semiotic processes themselves, far from being set adrift . . . set up a new formal construct: a so-called new formal or ideological 'writer's universe,' the never finished, undefined production of a new space of significance."[20] Evidently, this "new space of significance" is a site of "productive dissolving" precisely insofar as the intertextual dyad activates unconscious textual processes and thus triggers semiotic affects.

Kristeva's speculative "semiotic" is irredeemably abstract, but her location of that "new space of significance" in the intertextual relation is validated by an object-relations theory that argues that just as the child's developing self-hood is a dyadic project, in the sense that initial self-perception is centered by the presence of the Other, so the creation of the artistic self can be centered by the re-creation of an intersubjective dimension, at least insofar as the presence of an other accesses impulses from the unconscious. As Ruth Perry observes, "The most propitious conditions for writing, for playing with versions of reality, might include the presence of another—someone who bears a complicated rela-tionship to that initial presence in which the self came into being."[21] D. W. Win-nicott posits the existence of a transitional zone of artistic creation, which cor-responds to the child's transitional stage of development between the merging with the mother and the perception of her as a separate entity.[22] Reclaiming the psychic ground of this "potential space" as an adult facilitates a parallel blur-ring of the line between self and other in a shifting field of merging and differ-entiation, and it is in this "ambiguous space where the distinction between self and other dissolves that we most easily recognize and accept creative impulses from the unconscious."[23] In the transitional space, the artist is permitted "to flounder," "to become unintegrated," "to let go of her orientation to reality," and it is in that "space," therefore, that unconscious process has space to work.[24] I think we can easily conceive of that "transitional space" of artistic creation as the area where texts blur, dissolve, and separate, and locate the "intersubjective dimension" in a dialogic intertextuality where texts are both sites of linguistic intersection and psyches exhibiting conscious and unconscious processes.

Winnicott's "transitional space" and Kristeva's "space of significance" can thus serve as a useful demarcation of the fluid intertextual space between women writers in a reading situation. These concepts are especially useful for my purposes here in their implication that the intertextual relation between two mutually aligned women writers is felicitous in its potential activation of un-conscious textual process, not least because Winnicott asserts that the interplay of the psychoanalytic dialectic also occurs in just such a re-created "potential space."[25] Therefore, the processes of transference and countertransference in the critical dialectic established between Dickinson's poetic text and its readers would, presumably, be especially evident, or most perfectly realized, in the boundary-blurring context provided by a female critical reader. In other words, it would be useful to shift Homans's emphasis by viewing Dickinson's dyadic poems as allegories of reading—in particular, as allegories of the metonymic reading strategy that the poet considers it probable she will elicit from a sym-pathetic female reader. The metonymic reading that produces such equivalence between subject and object, seer and seen, reader and read, can, obviously, be considered the representation of a transferential reading model. Is it the case that the peculiar equivalent of analytic transference described within these poems is more evident (or more successfully actualized) within the texts of Dickinson's female readers? Are those readers less likely to swerve rhetorically from Dickinson's offering of herself as embodied presence? In the pages that follow, I examine two completely dissimilar female readers of Dickinson— Camille Paglia and Adrienne Rich—in order to demonstrate how both, despite fundamental differences in personality, critical methodology, and intentionality, produce stunningly metonymic readings of Dickinson. These are readings that I see as precisely modeling the situation described in the poem "Like Eyes that looked on Wastes," critical analyses that are in themselves effective examples of analytic transference. What these readings demonstrate is that the transposition of the poetic text into the female critical text opens a hot line to the unconscious and triggers a series of intertextual ghost affects.

The sentence that concludes Camille Paglia's *Sexual Personae* is also the summation of her analysis of Emily Dickinson, the last literary figure she chooses to discuss: "Voyeurism, vampirism, necrophilia, lesbianism, sadomaso-chism, sexual surrealism: Amherst's Madame de Sade still waits for her readers to know her."[26] As *Sexual Personae* is the first of a projected two volumes, it is understandable that its author would choose to close with memorable impact, to leave the reader with the type of vivid image that can whet a future commercial appetite. That the sentence in question does make an impact is indisputable. But while the larger part of that impact comes through shock, more interesting is the lesser rhetorical disturbance that is its slight equivocation: if Dickinson's readers *still* wait to know her, does that reflect on the inadequacy of Paglia's preceding discussion of the poet? If, as she notes elsewhere, "one cannot dismiss any hallucination when reading Dickinson,"[27] does her own reading have itself some of the qualities of a critical hallucination? In order to address those questions, I want to focus only on Paglia's "reading" of Dickinson. Although the chapter devoted to Dickinson's poetry is part of the larger argument of *Sexual Personae*, it is more interestingly considered as a self-contained unit. There are significant differences between this chapter and those that precede it. Most strikingly, the Dickinson discussion is where the critical reader is herself most self-implicated. While Paglia habitually indulges a fondness for rhetoric throughout the book, her reading of Dickinson displays her both at her most stridently excessive and at the height of stylistic quirkiness. As I hope to demonstrate, the exaggerated rhetorical *effects* assumed by Paglia when writing specifically on Dickinson are themselves symptomatic of the wider *affects* of her own analytic process or, more precisely, of her own ongoing analysis *by* Dickinson's poetic text.

Paglia's thesis is that Dickinson is a "female Sade" and her poems "the prison dreams of a self-incarcerated, sadomasochistic imaginist." She argues that Dickinson's "displaced eroticism" produces an extreme sadomasochism; indeed, "the brutality of this belle of Amherst would stop a truck." While Dickinson's "love of gore" and "perverse self-pleasuring" can be sometimes masochistic—"The poet is a self-maiming pelican, tearing clots of flesh from her breast to feed her song"—it is more frequently the sadism of this "shark lured by spilled blood" that Paglia finds evident in the poetry. In the course of her discussion, she implies that Dickinson's poetry is sadistic in a number of ways. The fact that the poet "strew[s] puncture wounds liberally through her poetry" suggests that violence is intrinsic both to the thematic content of the poetry *and* in what Dickinson does to its form: the poetry is bloodied in the double sense of representing violence via the formal experience of it. Further, that poetry is also "assault and battery on the body," where the violence of form and content eventually imposes itself also on a reader. Therefore, when Paglia says of a Dickinson poem, "No matter what reading we choose, we are left with a spectacle of Sadean torture," that is equally her reading of the entire bloodied corpus.[28]

This is not a Dickinson with whom we are familiar. Indeed, it is perhaps not a Dickinson with whom we are familiar even after having read a chapter of "evidence" to the contrary. Interestingly, however, it is a Paglia whom we know well; not only does she celebrate the Marquis de Sade in an earlier chapter of her book, but he remains a perpetual, and never negative, reference point throughout. Paglia's attraction to Sadean innovation is her intense identification with that literary project. To some extent, her critical technique as applied to Dickinson is an exercise in adapted sadism. While one British reviewer said that the experience of reading *Sexual Personae* was "a bit like being mugged," a *New York Times* reviewer called Paglia's assessment of Dickinson, in particular, a "hatchet job" long "overdue."[29] But while a "hatchet job" is precisely what Paglia does to Dickinson, it should not have the negative connotations intended by the reviewer. For Paglia does not take her critical hatchet to Dickinson's literary reputation. On the contrary, she is one of Dickinson's fiercest defenders.

What Paglia's reading method does dismember is Dickinson as text. Never quoting from or analyzing a complete poem in detail, she instead takes individual lines from poems (often the first, startling lines) and rearranges them in new sequences within her own text. The dramatically abusive catalogs she creates serve as the evidence of her thesis. Paglia's own text is therefore founded on the initial fragmentation of the poetic text, decontextualization followed by recontextualization. This could be called a cut-and-paste technique if it were not such an intrinsically violent reading method: lines are ripped out from within the poetic text under analysis and stitched sequentially into the prose of

the critical text. Images of the sadistically cut up "body" that Paglia finds re-
curring within Dickinson's text are therefore to a degree the trace replication
and product of her own "sadistic" reading process, which necessarily fragments
the "body" of that text initially. The unacknowledged violence that Paglia imposes, as reader, on the textual body of Dickinson is defensively deflected into
a thesis of abuse by that textual body on its reader. Curiously, the fragments
of Dickinson's poetry then embraced within Paglia's own text are soon sur-
rounded by traces of another, personal stylistic fragmentation. While Paglia's
style is typically idiosyncratic, no other chapter of *Sexual Personae* is quite so
solidly packed with blank assertions, curt exclamations, and sentence fragments. Examples of this exaggerated stylistic quirkiness particularly proliferate in the Dickinson chapter: "Enough of brains. On to lungs."; "Another example of Dickinson sex and violence:"; "Back to our catalog of Sadean abuses of
the body:"; "Horrorshow again:"; "What a psychodrama!"; "No charity here.";
"Tasty morsels."; "Glug, glug."; "Wham! Chop!" Paglia's prose is particularly
choppy in the act of chopping.[30]

The mutual fragmentation of the two texts is only one example among
many of a more pervasive mirroring of critic and poet in the course of the analysis. Throughout *Sexual Personae*, Paglia implicates herself within her own critical narrative. This is presumably quite deliberate. Her bold assertion of a critical personality is a reaction to the pseudo-objectivity of so many critical texts.
What is interesting about Paglia's Dickinson chapter is the extent of this conscious personal interference. Every aspect of Paglia's life comes to pervade her
reading; she can say, as a result, that a poem's scenario "*reminds me* of a break-
fast-hour high-school driver-education film" or that a metaphor "*reminds me* of
my Vermont landlord" (emphasis added). Paglia's analogies often involve the
authority of her personal experience of others: "*One has known* people who do
this, fatiguingly," or "For example . . . *my formidable grandmother would* . . . " (emphasis added). Sometimes this takes the form of a kind of personalized professional confessionalism—it is not "a colleague notes" but instead "*Heidi Jon
Schmidt told me* this sounds like . . . " (emphasis added).[31] On other occasions,
the interference of the personal is almost stifled, only to appear in parentheses,
such as "(a real statue *in my baptismal church*)" (emphasis added).[32] The reader
quits Paglia's chapter on Dickinson having learned more about Paglia—about
her birth (the baptisimal statue), family (her formidable grandmother), school-
ing (the driver-education film she remembers), friends and colleagues (Heidi Jon
Schmidt et al.), living situation (used to rent in Vermont), and tastes (*not* for
garrulous people)—than about the ostensible subject of her critical narrative.

Paglia's intense personal investment in the text culminates in a complex imposition of not only her own *text* on Dickinson's text, but her own *self* on Dick-

inson. Indeed, the real subject of Paglia's Dickinson narrative is always ultimately herself, and the poet, increasingly, is the means of gaining possession of
that self. That this is a more violent use of the Other than we have observed
previously is explicable in terms of the author's sadomasochistic reading
method. The extent of violence necessary in the reading is the primary difference between Paglia's text and those of her male critical predecessors; because
this female critic's *identification* with Dickinson is more intense, the rhetorical
seduction concludes in a more aggressive supplanting of the original poet by
her analyst. The intensity of that original identification with the poet is most
evident in Paglia's unacknowledged (and unconscious?) affinities with the poet.
These are often stylistic. For example, Paglia asserts that "Dickinson's humor
is jarringly curt." Of course, this is perfectly true. But it is equally true of
Paglia's humor. It is Paglia the humorist who observes that Dickinson's enclos-
ing a "heart" poem in a gift fruit basket is evidence that "wrapping her heart
on her sleeve would be too conventional for our poet, *who slaps it on a fruit dish
and sends it down the street like a phone-order pizza*" (emphasis added). Similarly,
Paglia's discussion of that Dickinson poem beloved by psychoanalysts, "In Winter in my Room / I came upon a Worm / Pink, lank and warm," begins with the
valid observation that "any eely creature that manages to blow itself up from
'Pink, lank and warm' *to a long weiner doing the hula tends to seize the attention of
us moderns*" (emphasis added). Very witty, true, but surely also a sense of humor
for which the adjectives "curt" and "jarring" are not inappropriate. Of course,
Dickinson's "jarringly curt" sense of humor is perhaps best understood as part
of her more general "zeal for indelicacy." This is a zeal shared by the analyst
of that poet. Almost parodically, Paglia's assertion that Dickinson has this particular zeal immediately follows her own analysis of a poem whose controlling
metaphor "ends in a release of intention, *a urinary letting go, a sudden warm
drenching*" (emphasis added) and her memorable comment that the lines "Go
manacle your icicle / Against your Tropic Bride" (P. 1756) are "approaching por-
nographic invective," the equivalent of "Up your nose with a rubber hose."[33]
Evidently, Dickinson is not the only writer with a "zeal for indelicacy."

Similarly, Paglia's comment that "much of Dickinson's sadism comes from
her sardonic speech, a rustic bluntness about life and death" might equally refer
to a *reading* of Dickinson that itself cultivates a "rustic" bluntness. An example
is Paglia's speculation on how a reader might visualize Dickinson's image of
birdsong as pianos that "mangle": perhaps as "a victim tangled up in piano
wires and lashed by felt hammers, like a farmhand caught in a thresher"?
Paglia's own brand of rustic bluntness about life and death often involves a sur-
real comparison to familiar (rustic?) objects: a poem's famous analogy of the
grave to an inn is "like the commercial for Black Flag Roach motel, a little box

tiled with insecticide glue: 'Bugs check in, but they don't check out.' " Later we find a skull "trepanned, like a cookie jar."[34] The most interesting of the apparent mirrorings of critic and poet is Paglia's continual fixation on the style and purpose of Dickinson's metaphors, especially given the obvious fact that she herself is a writer exceptionally dependent on metaphor as the motor of her own prose style. Paglia observes, with no apparent irony, that the *poet* enjoys "disconcerting the reader with freakish conjunctions." Dickinson's metaphors are "on the epic scale and mean business," and are "brutal metaphors" that "record her search for a rhetoric equal to what God has wrought." Not only do these metaphors represent "an emptying out of female internality," they also "illustrate Dickinson's monumentality . . . a self-masculinizing style." Of course, metaphors, similes, and the strangest analogies memorably pervade Paglia's text, too. Sometimes the analogy is as relatively simple as a passing allusion to a classical figure in a plausibly similar situation; an example of this would be the comparison of a rhetorical blinding within a Dickinson poem to "Odysseus blinding Cyclops with a red-hot stake." But more frequently such a comparison would be taken further through subsequent analogy; for example, the narrator of another poem "is like Odysseus bound to the mast or *like a Kewpie doll stuck to a dashboard*" (emphasis added). The perpetual collision of high and low culture analogies is a feature of Paglia's text, obviously "freakish conjunctions" that "disconcert the reader." The dynamic of her discussion is its perpetual recourse to such metaphor in examples such as "thought is paralyzed, with the brain *dropped like a handkerchief*" or "the lids are tacked *like a carpet or nailed like a shutter or coffin lid*" (emphasis added), but more memorably in those spectacularly odd situations in which Dickinson "stretches and squeezes the artificial gap between superior and inferior, *as if working an accordion or chest expander*," or where the removal of an eye is "like a *finance company repossessing a refrigerator*" or where "to wanton with bones is to toss them about, *as if mixing a salad*" (emphasis added). Does Paglia really believe that "Dickinson's cynical surrealism is unparalleled among great woman writers" when the parallel example of her own cynical surrealism is so constantly intrusive? At times, this continual process of metaphorization can result in the suggestion of a jarring mix: "Dickinson's *feisty ear* is among history's more *exotic arms* of war" (emphasis added). This is one of the pitfalls of metaphor, and Paglia's persistent reliance on it, despite the dangers it presents, suggests that *her* metaphors "mean business" too. Indeed, there is ample evidence that they are Paglia's attempt at channeling out her own female "internality," an attempt at a self-masculinizing style of her own.[35]

Ultimately, of course, Dickinson's entire "masculinizing" project is really Paglia's own, and her assertion that "Brontë and Dickinson succeed as Romantics because they are women of masculine will who tend toward sadism" is the key to understanding the element of identification in that project. After all, throughout her text Paglia invokes Sade as authority, and a comparison to the divine Marquis is praise indeed; when she observes that "I cannot produce the name 'Judge Lord' without smiling. . . . The mere recitation of so imposing a conflation of hierarchisms must have provided the poet with exquisite shivers of Sadean subordination," the most obvious effect of that name, at least for the reader of Paglia's text, appears to be on the author herself (smiling through her own exquisite shivers?). Of course, that response must be expected in a thorough reader of a poet who is "the creator of Sadean poems *but also the creator of sadists, the readers whom she smears with her lamb's blood*" (emphasis added). Paglia is a reader whose own sadism is fired by her subject through identification. Indeed, while she marvels at "the rarity of the woman driven by artistic or intellectual obsession," by implication she herself is just such a woman, for what most impresses Paglia about Dickinson is the spectacle of a "small feminine body charged with a mighty masculine mind" and the fact that she was "a male genius and visionary sadist, a fictive sexual persona of towering force." This dovetails neatly with Paglia's view of the human condition; her earlier observation that "if civilization had been left in female hands, we would still be living in grass huts" is the kind of remark that tends to stay with a reader.[36] It might well be argued that since Paglia asserts that Dickinson's "homoerotic flirtations were integral to her masculine poetic identity," the critic, in turn, is having her own homoerotic flirtation with the poet through her text. But Paglia is *more* than Dickinson's lover: she is *herself* "Dickinson." One of her more provocative readings of Dickinson's poetry is the assertion that the "mirrorlike returns upon her of her own ocular aggression explain many of Dickinson's eccentricities." Of course, that is first and foremost an exceptionally perceptive analysis of Paglia's own critical reading of Dickinson; her own *stylistic* eccentricities are clearly a result of the mirrorlike return upon her of the ocular aggression *she* brings to Dickinson's text.

Paglia's aggression manifests itself as the appropriation of Dickinson as a means of writing about herself. Her dwelling on Dickinson's use of "sexual personae" is a personal interest, an individual fascination with the technique. The "sadist woman speaker" is "one of the west's unique sexual personae" and is assumed as such by Paglia. It is she who is the most vividly alive sexual persona in her book as a narrative voice. The voice of Paglia's assumed persona is, not surprisingly, every bit as aphoristic as Dickinson's. Typical of her lively postmodern colloquialism is her "Snack time rocks around the clock in sadean nature." The hip reductiveness of such a style is evident in her curt summary of Dickinson's "Stun myself with bolts of melody": "There's Emily Dickinson sitting in the yard, hitting herself on the head with lightning bolts."[37] Perhaps the most significant moment of Paglia's text is her attempt to represent Dickinson's voice by appropriating it, by regulating it into the grain and timbre of her own. So Dickinson's writing for information on the death of a friend becomes "She writes to a complete stranger . . . to dig up data on the last hours of a childhood friend. *Had she a current address, she says, she would be pumping the wife of the deceased instead*" (emphasis added). "Digging up data" and "pumping the wife" are two typically Paglian constructions. What is interesting is how effortlessly the two voices here meld—effortlessly because they have always been interchangeable. And bodies can merge as easily as voices. In her revealing analysis of poem 640, Paglia's comment on the line "Nor could I rise with You / Because Your Face / Would put out Jesus" is the observation that "there is inferred violence in this blotting out of one face by another." Such a comment can be regarded as the embedded "figure" of precisely the process occurring within Paglia's own text: it is there that the face of Dickinson is constantly blotted out by that of her analyst, and the "inferred violence" of that procedure (inferred violence being Paglia's sadean method) is the only real subject of the ongoing discussion. In this context, Paglia's discussion of Dickinson's message to Sue Dickinson—"Where my Hands are cut, Her fingers will be found inside"—is incredibly ironic: "*Flesh of my flesh: the women are Romantic twins, mentally and physically one.* But Susan has aggressively invaded and occupied the poet, like the vampire penetrating Christabel. . . . Surreally, it is Susan who cuts her and Susan who painfully probes the wounds she has made. And one cannot avoid the *hallucinatory sexuality* here, where female fingers have buried themselves through a slit in another woman's flesh. This is Dickinson at her sadomasochistic best" (emphasis added).[38] Rather, it is surely Paglia at *her* sadomasochistic best, her own hallucinatory identification with Susan Dickinson the more convenient figure of her own penetration of the poet, her own incision and penetration into Dickinson's skin/text. That critical aggression ensures that it is not Dickinson's poetry but Paglia's entire *Sexual Personae* that is the real "late Romantic prose-poem" and that it is Paglia's own work that is the "stunning chronicle of necrophilia and voyeurism," not Dickinson's.[39] However, it is also Paglia's comprehensive failure to separate herself from the subject of her analysis that makes her—even at her most extreme, out on her (severed) limb—such a brilliant "hysterical" reader of Dickinson.

It would therefore appear that while Paglia's acute sympathy with Dickinson is personal (a fact made even more apparent in interview asides such as "The example of Emily Dickinson was extremely inspiring to me—she also tried to get published but couldn't"), the manifestation of that sympathy assumes vividly rhetorical form. This may have unforeseen consequences for the reader of *Paglia*'s text. For example, Richard Poirier's observation that Paglia "has a talent for tending to language—though her *temperament drives her on oc-casion to excess*" (emphasis added) is remarkable in its echoing of male critical assessments of Dickinson. The ironies of rhetorical duplication proliferate in the most unexpected ways. Of course, the proliferation of violence implicit in Paglia's temperamental excess is only natural given her main critical influence: she has been aptly identified as "a politically incorrect Athena sprung full-blown from the head of [Harold] Bloom."[40] The fascination of Paglia's subjective adaptation of Bloom's "anxiety of influence" (in which her own critical text be-comes the site of a strong misreading of her critical *and* poetic precursors) into a more personal aesthetic is that it creates an analysis of literary history more "analytical" than the analyst herself apparently suspects. Curiously, however, the combat model of Dickinson analysis (i.e., self-analysis) that Paglia pioneers is not, at least at first sight, too dissimilar to the strangely reciprocal poetic "reading" of the poet performed by a reader who owes absolutely nothing to Bloom's neo-Freudian theories, Adrienne Rich.

> two women, eye to eye
> measuring each other's spirit, each other's
> limitless desire,
>   a whole new poetry beginning here[41]

Adrienne Rich's influential essay, "Vesuvius at Home: The Power of Emily Dickinson," is now considered "an exemplary essay" of feminist literary criti-cism and "an implicit commentary on the process of reading women's writ-ing."[42] It has even been anthologized as an exemplary practice of feminist read-ing worthy of imitation. Indeed, Rich's foregrounding of gender as the crucial determining factor behind the construction of Dickinson's poetry, her correc-tive critical positioning as a "witness" for the poet's defense, and her emphasis on the importance of placing Dickinson's text in the sociohistorical and cultural context in which it was originally written have in recent years become the stan-dard critical approach *and* subject positioning for many feminist critics. How-ever, it may well be that the significance of Rich's pioneering anticipation of con-temporary critical techniques has unduly deflected attention from her essay's occasional rhetorical peculiarity and thereby elided its underlying *poetical* com-plexity. In fact, the rhetorical nuances of Rich's essay provide evidence of a pow-erful countertransference, those transferential effects ultimately transforming the essay from a mere critical study into a fascinating prose poem, a poetically overdetermined epistle, a love letter if you will, to its author's most significant precursor. In order to do justice to this essay's concern with Dickinson's poetry, we would therefore be well advised to read it as though it were itself a key text in the Rich poetic canon.[43]

Central to Rich's critical reading of Dickinson's poetry is her expression of an extreme sympathy with her precursor's poetic imagination. Dickinson's poetic text is viewed by Rich not as the convenient object of critical analysis but rather as the vivid manifestation of the subjectivity of its absent author. To read Dickinson is to hear her voice, to make her presence felt—in Rich's metaphor, to "visit" with her. Personal imaginative speculation is therefore valid—envisaging the poet "listening from above-stairs . . . watching, you feel, watching ceaselessly" is eminently acceptable. What is unacceptable is any significant appropriation of, or imposition on, Dickinson by her reader. Thus, within her brief article, Rich quotes twenty-three poems *in full*. Ideally, Dickinson is allowed to speak for herself. Moreover, in the course of offering an interpretation of an individual poem, Rich denies any personal critical authority and acknowledges her own possible intellectual *and* temporal limitations: "I do not pretend to—I don't even wish to have—explained this poem, accounted for its every image; it will reverberate with new tones long after my own words about it have ceased to matter." Always, she puns, the poet is to be examined on *her own premises.*[44]

Rich's reading method might indeed have been a radical departure when applied to another author, but there is nothing particularly radical in its application to Dickinson. While the rhetorical energies of Rich's essay are directed toward evoking Dickinson as the substantial, palpable presence animating her works, an urging of the reader to encounter not just a text but a subjectified object, the heart and mind of the poet, the implication that the most effective reading of Dickinson is the equivalent of an intersubjective encounter does not depart greatly from the practice of other Dickinson critics. We have already seen how critical readings of Dickinson inevitably tend to become intersubjective encounters. What is radical in Rich's reading, therefore, is simply her straightforward acknowledgment of that fact, her critical foregrounding of the intersubjective encounter as crucial to a reading of the poetry. It is the self-reflexiveness of Rich's sympathy with her subject, and the consequent attempt to regulate that sympathy, to control its degree, to render it critically *useful*, that energizes the rhetoric of her own argument. Rich's rhetorical control of her empathy with her subject is, however, decidedly variable. While she does categorically emphasize the significant differences between Dickinson and herself—"The methods, the exclusions, of Emily Dickinson's existence could not have been my own; yet more and more, as a woman poet finding my own methods, I have come to understand her necessities, could have been a witness in her defence"—and therefore subtly qualifies the degree of empathy (if the poet-critic is a speaker in Dickinson's defense, then—witness and not defendant—she is *another* palpable presence in the critical courtroom), it often appears to be Rich herself who is in the dock. Making a case for the woman-identified Dickinson can easily, as in this passage, become a simultaneous self-defense: "We will understand Emily Dickinson better, read her poetry more perceptively, when the Freudian imputation of scandal and aberrance in women's love for women has been supplanted by a more informed, less misogynistic attitude toward women's experiences with each other."[45]

Rich's reading of Dickinson is therefore, evidently, often a reading of herself. In order to come to some understanding of Dickinson, Rich asserts, she must return in space and time: "I am travelling at the speed of time, in the direction of the house and buildings." Rich's time travel is, however, also a more personal spatiotemporal return, a revisiting of her own youth. This is especially evident in her recollective description of Amherst College: "New England college buildings spread around two village greens, a scene I remember as almost exactly the same in the dim past of my undergraduate years when I used to come there for college weekends." Apparently, Rich is engaged in two parallel and not dissimilar historical searches: the exploration of the source of Dickinson's poetic creativity is simultaneously an exploration of the source of her own.[46] This may explain why throughout the essay the poet-critic's empathy with her nineteenth-century precursor is so ubiquitous as a particular *rhetorical* intrusiveness. After all, Rich's assertions that "*I have a notion that genius knows itself*; that Dickinson chose her seclusion, knowing she was exceptional and knowing what she needed" and that "*Given her vocation*, she was neither eccentric nor quaint . . . she was determined to survive, to use her powers, to practice necessary economies" (emphasis added) can be considered authoritative statements, coming as they do from a reader who is herself a poet. This critical authority, elsewhere denied, is sometimes more subtly emphasized through the use of the collective pronoun—"It is always what is under pressure *in us*, especially under pressure of concealment—that explodes in poetry"—or perfectly emphasized by an aggressively parasitic parenthesis—"What was it like to be writing poetry you knew (*and I am sure she did know*) was of a class by itself" (emphasis added).[47]

The extent of Rich's poetic sympathy with Dickinson ultimately transforms her essay into both an exquisite analysis *and* a demonstration of the simultaneous necessity and danger of poetic possession. The first necessary possession Rich discusses is that *of* Dickinson by contemporary women poets: "I have been surprised at how narrowly her work, still, is known by women who are writing poetry, how much her legend has gotten in the way of her being re-possessed, as a source and a foremother."[48] The second possession is the inescapable consequence of that initial re-possession—the "possession" that is the occupying of a mind by an external force, by the power of a personal poetic "genius," in both

senses of the word. This is the poetic possession Dickinson herself so effortlessly delineated in her poem "I thought I was Enchanted," the narrative of her
own possession by the poetic genius of Elizabeth Barrett Browning. It soon becomes clear that Rich's essay is itself the narrative of a similar possession, but
that possession is not so much discussed within the essay's argument as it is
exemplified by the suggestiveness of its rhetorical nuance as a prose poem.
Rich's particular focus on Dickinson's poetry *of* possession is therefore crucially
important: "These . . . poems are about possession, and they seem to me a poet's
poems—that is, they are about the poet's relationship to her own power, which
is exteriorized in masculine form." This notion of possession by an internal
imaginative power exteriorized in human form resonates strongly behind
Rich's admission of the personal importance of Dickinson to her, of the fact that
"in the trail of that genius my mind has been moving, and with its language
and images my mind still has to reckon, as the mind of a woman poet in America today."[49] For Rich's own critical essay, as the tracking of an influential personal trajectory, is the allegory of her relationship with not only the precursor
"genius" who was the historical poet Emily Dickinson but also the living "genius" that Rich both possesses and is possessed by—the "Dickinson" who is the
convenient exteriorization and figuration of her own creative imagination. The
significance of Rich's essay is that it constitutes a major rewriting of the possession paradigm: the contemporary woman writer can now have a relationship
with her own power exteriorized in more overtly female form—as "Emily Dickinson."

Rich's project is therefore identical with that which she identifies for Dickinson: her mind is equally one "engaged in a lifetime's musing on essential
problems of language, identity, separation, the integrity of the self." Within
the contours of this particular essay, that mind is particularly engaged with
questions of how the self's integrity can be compromised by the possession of
and by a powerful precursor: if "the art of poetry is the art of transformation,"
then, Rich pointedly asks, "who, if you read through the seventeen hundred
and seventy five poems—who—woman or man—could have passed through
that imagination and not come out transmuted."[50] Obviously, the degree of that
transformation, that transmutation, must be frightening in its intensity, in its
potential for self-disintegration. It is therefore entirely appropriate that in the
face of such potential disintegration an author should assume an adequate defense, that a "lifetime's musing" should center on the "lifetime" of that author's
particular personal "muse."

Given the fact that Rich describes poetic creativity in psychoanalytic
terms—"Poetry is too much rooted in the unconscious; it presses too close

against the barriers of repression"—it is also entirely appropriate for readers of her essay to map the disintegration and reintegration of the integrity of her own self as it is manifested in the unconscious movement of her prose. Since Rich's discussion of the doubleness of possession is a metaphorical approximation of the mechanism of countertransference, that mapping of the essay's unconscious route would be primarily a charting of areas of intertextual rhetorical transference. The validity of such a reading is obvious: Rich's initial assertion is, after all, that "for years I have not been so much envisioning Emily Dickinson as trying to visit, to enter her mind, through her poems and letters, and through my own intimations of what it could have meant to be one of the two mid-19th-century American geniuses, and a woman, living in Amherst, Massachusetts." Rich's image of "entering the mind" of Dickinson is almost immediately repeated and rephrased: "She was, and is, a wonder to me when I try to imagine myself into that mind."[51] As I will now demonstrate, the rhetorical consequences of the countertransference that results when one poet seeks to imagine herself into the mind of another can be wonderfully powerful.

We have already seen how rhetorical sympathies can overlap with personal and biographical sympathies. For example, Rich's discussion of Dickinson's retreat into seclusion (the repeating of Martha Dickinson Bianchi's apocryphal story of her aunt's turning the key to an imaginary lock on her upstairs bedroom and saying "Here's freedom") is mirrored by the narrativization of her own response on arriving in the same room: her exclamation on reaching the Dickinson bedroom—"Upstairs at last"—is a personal expression of relief that might mirror Dickinson's response a century before. Considerably more interesting than this minor rhetorical doubling, however, is Rich's use of this strangely affecting metaphor to represent her own critical "approach" to the poet: "I am travelling at the speed of time, along the Massachusetts Turnpike. For months, for years, for most of my life, I have been *hovering like an insect against the screens* of an existence which inhabited Amherst" (emphasis added).[52] Aside from the interesting question of why Rich chooses to represent herself as an insect, the most immediate problem is why Dickinson's poems are here represented as the "screens of an existence." Perhaps the poems could be considered movie "screens," the projections of Dickinson's varied personae, her "representatives of the verse." However, since Rich is elsewhere in the essay perturbed by the fact that Dickinson has been "sentimentalized, fallen-in-love with like some gnomic Garbo," the most obvious image evoked by the "screen" is a quite different one: the poems are the screens placed on windows, the screens that tantalizingly deny access to the insect. This is the screen that is a necessary protection, a shield from unnecessary disturbance and discomfort, a prohibition to the outsider. This is not the first association of Dickinson with such a protective screening in the essay. During Rich's earliest reported visits to the Amherst homestead a similar form of screening was evident: "I recognize the high hedge of cedars *screening the house,* because twenty five years ago I walked there, even then drawn toward the spot, *trying to peer over*" (emphasis added).[53] We might also recall that in her *Springfield Republican* obituary for her sister-in-law, Susan Gilbert Dickinson remarked that the poet "*screened* herself from close acquaintance" (emphasis added). However, if the screen is a representation of the poem as an inhibiting device, as the prohibition of the easy reader access that is hermeneutic penetration, then the image is an entirely appropriate one. Dickinson's poems notoriously inhibit easy interpretive access. Critical vision becomes necessarily opaque when it passes through her syntactic meshing. However, the appropriateness of the metaphorical tenor does not necessarily explain the chosen vehicle. Why an insect screen? And why does Rich specifically figure herself as the *insect* on that screen? To comprehend the full significance of this image it is necessary that we read Rich's comment on the canonical centrality of the poem "My Life had stood a Loaded Gun" as being ever so slightly disingenuous. Rich says of this particular poem that it is the "one poem which is the *real 'onlie begetter' of my thoughts here about Dickinson: a poem I have mused over, repeated to myself, taken into myself over many years*" (emphasis added).[54] This assertion is misleading because there is clearly another poem, a poem that Rich does not discuss within the essay, that is rhetorically omnipresent in her reading *of* Dickinson and therefore an equally significant "begetter" of her thoughts. This is not a poem Rich has taken into herself but, itself having been powerfully "mused over" by her, is instead a poem that has, metaphorically, *taken in her self.* The absent and yet all-too-present poem is this one:

> I heard a Fly buzz—when I died—
> The Stillness in the Room
> Was like the Stillness in the Air—
> Between the Heaves of Storm—
>
> The Eyes around—had wrung them dry—
> And Breaths were gathering firm
> For that last Onset—when the King
> Be witnessed—in the Room—
>
> I willed my Keepsakes—Signed away
> What portion of me be
> Assignable—and then it was
> There interposed a Fly—

With Blue—uncertain stumbling Buzz—
Between the light—and me—
And then the Windows failed—and then
I could not see to see—
   (P. 465)

It is the image of the interposing insect from this poem that continually recurs in Rich's reading of the poems.[55] Her response to being in Dickinson's room is this: "Here I become, again, an insect, vibrating at the frames of windows, clinging to panes of glass, trying to connect. The scent here is very powerful."[56] Of course, "the scent here" refers not merely to Rich's olfactory response to the flowers in the Amherst homestead but also to the imminent denouement of her detective trailing of the escaping trajectory of her precursor. The scent is "very powerful" not only for Rich (for it is where, through her self-figuration as insect, she comes closest to Dickinson's poetry) but also for Rich's reader (the image of the insect is the key to her empathetic method of reading Dickinson). If elsewhere in this essay Rich admits to taking Dickinson's poetry into herself in the sense of incorporating, of collapsing the boundaries of inside and outside, then, by the same token, her self-figuration as insect is simultaneously the unconscious admission of her capacity for self-projection into that poetry: she is therefore finally both the possessor and the possessed, the owner and the owned, the reader and the read. In short, the complete identification or "possession" that is transference has been perfectly realized.

In this transferential context, the author's meditation on the significance of Dickinson's writing "a woman poet's narrative poem of a woman poet's life" is richly ironic. That description might equally refer to the content of an essay that is itself a narrative poem dealing with the coming to terms with a personal muse. Evidently, it is not just Dickinson of whom it can be said, "The women and men in her life she equally converted into metaphor," or Dickinson who was "stirred by the existences of women . . . who possessed strength of mind, articulateness, and energy." Rich's essay is itself a powerful conversion of a powerful woman into metaphor, a detail that renders her observation that "It is an extremely painful and dangerous way to live—split between a publicly acceptable persona, and a part of yourself that you perceive as the essential, the creative and powerful self, yet also as possibly unacceptable, perhaps even monstrous" a strangely personal one, the second-person pronoun the mark of the confessional.[57] For Rich, Dickinson is more than a significant precursor; she is her muse, her own essential creative and powerful self. Rich's essay is therefore ultimately not so much an appreciation of Dickinson as an attempt to rescue her from a particular criticism, to make her seem less "monstrous," to make her finally "acceptable." The favorable critical reception of Rich's essay evidences its success as a poem insofar as her observation that "the art of poetry is the art of transformation" was simultaneously realized by the transformative influence of the essay on later feminist interpretations of Dickinson's life and work. Finally, therefore, Rich comes to terms with her precursor through an appropriate poetic reciprocation: if she was fundamentally transformed by her reading of Dickinson, then she has been equally successful in transforming the ways in which the poet can be read. In Rich's significant rewriting of the poem "I heard a Fly buzz," what Dickinson hears, at the limit of death, is the insect murmur of her transformative poetic progeny.

In these final chapters, I have shown how Dickinson's poetic texts, by means of their reader-implicating rhetoric of seduction, and in the subsequent analytic context of their critical reception, function as psychic structures exhibiting conscious and unconscious processes. In the equivalent of the psychoanalytic dialectic, the positions of text and analyst may become transferentially fluid, and "Dickinson" becomes the representation, or rather fictional creation, of her readers' unfulfilled desire. Further, the situation established by this poetics of seduction—the fact that Dickinson's rhetorical strategies effect a collapsing of the distance between the reader and the poem—results in an unconscious problematizing of the supposedly "objective" rhetoric of the critical "analysts" of her poetic text to the extent that the proliferation of transferential and countertransferential effects between reader and text in a metonymic "scene of seduction" may cause a critical rhetoric to become itself symptomatically "hysterical."

That the extent of interpretive mastery over the text sought by readers is gender variable accounts for the different degree of transferential effects apparent in the texts of the poet's male and female critics. The swerving of male readers from the transference is traceable to the poems' capacity to upset an assumed position of reader authority; the rhetorical dismantling of internal and external systems of metaphoric hierarchy and the establishment of reading "scenes" of metonymic equivalence frustrate the desire for mastery in a situation where the confusion of text and writer—the blurring neatly facilitated by Dickinson's strategy of textual hybridization, the flaunting in language of her corporeal self—has already led to a collapsing together of interpretive and sexual mastery on the part of the male reader. As a result, there is often more at stake in a male critical reading than the control that is interpretation. The tendency of the male reader to locate the poet in the position of analysand in an analytic dialectic also leads to unforeseen problems: the reader's ready assumption of the seducer's role and his consequent education in the vagaries of transference love produce a series of negative countertransferences that lead to a shortcircuiting of critical objectivity by unconscious resistances. Of course, it is all too possible to generalize unduly about "male" reading strategies. Aside from the fact that many "feminist" readings of the poet prove to be no different from their male counterparts in their frustrated reading of "frustration," Karl Keller's particular eschewing of critical mastery and willing seduction of *and* by the poetic text is an obvious "hysterical" exception to any male reading paradigm that could be established.

But it appears to be the case that Dickinson's poetic text more usually effects a different modality of transferential repetition for the female reader and that the relationship solicited by the text is founded on a different conception of desire. While for the male critical reader the poetic text resists the mastery of a penetrative hermeneutic desire, that text apparently accommodates a more obviously appropriate substitutive desire for its female critical reader. In this case, the dismantling of interpretive hierarchy and the establishment of a metonymic equivalence between text and reader has different consequences because the desire finds some substantive outlet in a countertransferential identification. In transference, identifications construct powerful imagoes, or love objects, whose function is to direct the scripting of transference love. Indeed, when Freud first theorized the operation of an identificatory mechanism in relation to seduction's production of hysterical symptoms, the word "mimicry" defined the hysteric's exhibitionary effects. But while the poetic text often elicits from Dickinson's male critical readers a type of *complementary* identification (one in which the analyst finds himself in the emotional position of some projected part of the analysand's self), women readers sometimes experience a type of *concordant* identification (one involving more empathetic responses to the analysand's thoughts and feelings). For the woman reader, Dickinson's text functions as a signifier that offers the possibility of its replacement—as opposed to duplication or effacement—by her own text. Thus, Dickinson's *significant* precursor text offers itself as a matrix of possibility for a later female reader.

Indeed, the value of some critical texts can be precisely in relation to the extent of their encoding of an apparently unconscious transferential mirroring. For example, Paula Bennett's recent study of Dickinson's life and poetry, which includes a lengthy "analysis of image patterns whose sexual significance may have been hidden from the poet on a conscious level," appears, at first glance, to be hardly the most revelatory of critical approaches. Bennett finds in the poems a "network of specifically female genital images . . . [which] suggest that both Dickinson's sexuality *and* her imagination were homoerotic and autoerotic, that is, they were preferentially centered on female sexuality." At one point, she argues that "whether or not" Dickinson actually intended a poem "to be 'about' the clitoris, the clitoris is the one physical item in a woman's possession that pulls together the poem's disparate and conflicting parts." That genital image also serves to pull together a number of situated readings. Thus, one poem is described as "an invitation to cunnilingus" and another as representing Susan Dickinson as " 'the House / behind' the hill (*the mons Veneris?*)" (emphasis added). Given this small focus, it is not surprising that Bennett (in a curious echoing of Karl Keller) should find Dickinson to be "the agent of her own desire and the creator of her own discourse, allowing her to reach an orgasm that was an act of poetry and an act of love together."[58] The primitive Freudianism that underscores Bennett's symbol safari is easily dismissed. And aspersions could certainly be cast at the creative construction of her critical narrative. The logic of this assertion, for example—"Not only does [Dickinson] focus on female sexual power, but the 'lover' who is invited to share this power is rarely specified as a human male. More often, he is a male bee and, hence, being small and round, ambiguously a covert female symbol"—is nothing if not creatively circuitous. But while Bennett's critical methodology is often clumsy, she also evidences a powerful unconscious understanding of how the poetry operates, or, more precisely, of how the poetry is working on and through her as reader: "The simultaneous *reflection* and *elicitation* of effect is, finally, what Dickinson's poetry is about. . . . We are forced, in short, to *become one with the poem.* Through the combined effect of *projection* and *identification,* we make it our *mirror*" (emphasis added). Bennett even identifies one poem as "explicitly a *projection* of the poet's inner life, a massive *transference* to the landscape of her inner state of being" (emphasis added). This vocabulary—reflection, elicitation, projection, identification, mirror, transference—perfectly locates Dickinson's aesthetic domain. The fact that Bennett has not worked through (in psychoanalytic terms) the full implications of her critical intuition, and therefore continually projects countertransferentially on the poetic text, actually ensures that hers is one of the more fascinating, because thoroughly self-exposed, of recent "hysterical" critical texts. Despite its diagnostic pretensions, Bennett's text should be considered itself a curious symptomatic effect and deserving of critical attention for precisely that reason.[59]

Even more interesting than Bennett's curious confessionalism is the *interested* dialectic of poetic possession foregrounded by L=A=N=G=U=A=G=E poet Susan Howe's insistently intimate reading of "*my* Emily Dickinson." Howe's vision of Dickinson "forcing, abbreviating, pushing, padding, subtracting, riddling, interrogating, re-writing . . . pull[ing] text from text" and her assertion that "out of Brontë's Self, out of her Myth, the younger woman chose to pull her purity of purpose" has, of course, a parallel application to Howe's own intertextual critical reading (and reinvention) of the precursor. In this case, the mirroring of the poetic text becomes also stylistic to the extent that Howe's critical prose acquires its own Dickinsonian (even garbled) syntax: "Naked sensibility at the extremest periphery. Narrative expanding contracting dissolving. Nearer to know less before afterward schism in sum"; "This is a frontier poem. Forester of New-England wayward pilgrim"; "Pitch of vowels, cadence of consonants, sound fused with sense—asceticism"; "Myself was as another, now 'I' dare to go farther"; "Adopted parataxis and rupture to tell the feverish haste, the loss, to warn of storm approaching—Brute force, mechanism. Cassandra was a woman."[60] Aside from the more generally pervasive "poetic" fragmentation of Howe's prose narrative, the slippery first-person pronoun of a passage such as this—"Identity and memory are crucial for anyone writing poetry. For women the field is still dauntingly empty. How do I, choosing messages from the code of others in order to participate in the universal theme of Language, pull SHE from all the myriad symbols and sightings of HE. Emily Dickinson constantly asked this question in her poems"[61]—serves as an effective demonstration of how Dickinson's dislocation of the linear temporality of the reading process finds its stylistic echo in the critical prose of her analytic reader in a context of at least *somewhat* problematic intentionality.

Like fellow poet Rich, and unlike manic projectors Bennett and Paglia, Howe clearly attempts to channel the poetic affects her critical analysis evokes into the most deliberate of formal strategies: the quirkiness of her critical prose is the visible manifestation of a *sublime* confrontation with the precursor and, one may assume, the intended intimation of her own distinctive "purity of purpose." Again, as was the case with Rich, the transferential route established also produces, as a dissipative side-*affect,* an *influential* (i.e., transformative) critical evocation of "Dickinson" for future readers, a critical narrative (of fascinating fascicles) to be reckoned with. Of course, Howe's concern with the primacy of the fascicle manuscripts, and her demand that other critical readers return to written origins and recover the meaning inscribed not in the language of the poems but in the actual context of poetic composition, is evidence of a very personal (and late-twentieth-century-specific) quest for a new poetic formalism adequate to annihilate content altogether. In essence, Howe's critical study is a self-serving poetic exercise, a route of desire bypassing a formal deadlock, and "Dickinson," in context, is a mere catalyst in the experimental search for a new poetic language. But Howe's obvious personal investment in the critical reimagining of her predecessor need not disqualify her interpretation. On the contrary, the depth of that subjective imposition in fact often validates the analytic insight: Howe's critical revision is revelatory precisely to the degree that the conscious control she exercises over the affects of Dickinson's poetic text proves more variable than anticipated. To the extent that, within the analytic dialect established by Howe's text, we are witness to the continual reciprocation of her effort to remake the precursor over in her own image, Howe's "Dickinson" is often also the figuration of Dickinson's "Howe." The fact that *My Emily Dickinson* is ultimately a collaborative venture of sorts, in which its surmised author functions as a useful vehicle of textual dissemination, as a local channeler of the poetic dybbuk, as a means *how(e)*, may eventually confer on this particular textual anamorphosis the status of the most *authoritative* of recent critical analyses of the poet.

There are two reciprocal transferential processes at work in all these critical texts. The first is the projection of the critic's self onto Dickinson, an identification with the poet that corresponds to the mirroring processes of the imaginary. Since the first concept of a unified self is developed through identification with an other, individuals "forever after anticipate their own images in the images of others, a phenomenon Lacan refers to as a sign of 'throwness.'"[62] If we initially establish the unity of our ego "in a fictional direction," it is probable that we continue to do so by "scanning the text . . . for the equivalent of a mirror image on which to 'throw' the turbulent movements of one's consciousness in order to get back a unified self-image."[63] To some extent the syntactic peculiarity of Dickinson's poetic text always facilitates this type of projection. But that projection is particularly realizable in the relation established between poetic text and the critical text of a woman writer because the opening of an intertextual "transitional space" more successfully activates the unconscious process that closes an analytic circuit. This success is evident in the second transferential process: the *reciprocation* of that analytic projection by the Other. Most obviously, we are likely to find some uncanny paralleling—sometimes thematic, sometimes stylistic—of the poetic text under analysis within the actual prose of its critical reader.

The countertransferential model of reading established between poetic text and reader is therefore also problematic for a sympathetic female critic. The problem is not the frustration of the drive to interpretive mastery. On the contrary, it is how a poetic framework that inverts critical hierarchy and establishes metonymic equivalence comes to effect a mastery of its own. Rich and Howe choose to write about Dickinson in order to possess her rhetorically, to confront the apparently superior power of the Other and so energize the egotistical sublime. As a result, these poets are also rhetorically possessed by their subject: surrendering their own readings to the transferential affects of their precursor's rhetoric, they ultimately find (and lose) themselves in the interstices of her poetic "sorcery." Theirs is a *double* possession. But while such a double possession challenges the supposed objectivity of criticism, it also proves an effective reading strategy when it transcends the aggressive supplanting of the precursor that is Bloomian misreading or misprision, when it surpasses the "anxiety of influence." The danger of projective identification, the empathetic and emphatic recognition of some aspect of the self in the Other, is that the boundary between "inspired" interpretation and megalomania is often breached. Paglia's derivative, combative model of reading is thus surpassed, both in sensitivity *and* effectiveness, by the textual intimacy of Rich's "possessive" one. Of course, the intimacy between precursor and ephebic writer traced in the latter's essay is anticipated by, and to a degree modeled on, Dickinson's own poetic "enchantment" by the text and person of Elizabeth Barrett Browning.[64]

But while Rich's appropriative reading is also the most *appropriate*, the powerfully subjective use made of the poetic text by Paglia and Keller, Bennett and Howe, is surely one Dickinson would have approved of in principle. Integral to her own poetics was the principle that precursor text and precursor poet serve an essentially catalytic function, that they are a primary stimulus to the new textuality or "sorcery" that is the further writing of "poetry." The "hysterical" reading of her poetic text so neatly demonstrated by these later readers, regardless of their subjective limitations, is the critical model that the poet herself would have found most appropriate. Emily Dickinson did not evaluate her own "readings" in terms of interpretive competence, but in the degree of their personal affective resonance. Knowing this, we must assume that the final triumph of the rhetorical strategy traced by this study—the posthumously successful "seduction" of the readers of Dickinson's poetic text—would have an *especially* affective resonance for the poet who, with considerably less irony than readers have suspected, declared herself "the belle of Amherst."

Coda

The Flower and the Bee

BEHIND THE Exxon station on Pleasant Street (just across from the twenty-four-hour Kinko's) is the old Amherst graveyard. In summer, I'd wander through the grave markers and read the inscriptions on the slabs, so many chipped alabaster chambers. Pioneer valley summer evenings are often humid, sometimes cruelly stifling. Usually, what tempted me downtown in the first place was the Barts ice-cream parlor. But after a few minutes of air-conditioned comfort beside the neon-plastic electric cow I'd have to get out of there. Melting cone in hand, I'd traipse over to the Dickinson family burial plot and sit down on the grass by the black railing that surrounds the four gravestones. It was very quiet there, excepting the murmur of crickets. I'd still be sitting there, on the verge, watching late detoured bees, long after I'd chewed the last of my wafer. Such was my routine for three summers until eventually, inevitably, I entered into the seductions of Emily Dickinson. Always strangely drawn to her, I was so easily diverted from my intended path.

In the late summer of 1990 someone began placing wildflowers on the poet's grave every Sunday afternoon. You rarely saw anyone there, except for the occasional obvious tourist, camera ready. And on those infrequent occasions when I found my place taken by an interloper, I'd stalk off, huffy and resentful, but also too respectful to intrude on the communion, however inadequate I suspected it might be from my own more intimate perspective. This was a sacred site, a place for religious meditation, and I could always lick my strawberry ice elsewhere for a moment. But I never saw the woman (it was a woman, I'm sure of it) who brought the wildflowers and laid them down so neatly on the grave, of a Sunday afternoon (after church?), although I always hoped to accost her. It was reassuring to know that someone else returned obsessively to that spot, that there was another, in the vicinity, as fascinated as myself, continually called back. By then, I was myself doubly fascinated: by the poet and by the art of fascination itself. Watching the tardy bees hum over the fresh flowers on the Dickinson plot, the fascinations would ever so slowly blur together—the yellow scent of daisies, the bees' abashless play, the absence of a woman—the intermingling there.

Notes

Introduction: The Bee and the Flower

1. Dickinson's poems (abbreviated "P.") are identified according to the numbering in *The Poems of Emily Dickinson;* her letters (abbreviated "L.") are identified according to the numbering in *The Letters of Emily Dickinson.*

2. Deborah Cadman identifies some thirty poems (including nos. 2, 19, 28, 31, 106, 138, 151, 206, 211, 213, 214, 230, 386, 481, 513, 557, 620, 647, 869, 994, 1042, 1224, 1337, 1339, 1526, 1627) concerned with the interaction of bee and flower in her "Material Things and Expressive Signs."

3. Dickinson expresses this same sentiment in an 1851 letter to Emily Fowler: "My flowers come in *my* stead, today, dear Emily. I hope you will love to see them, and whatever word of love, or welcome kindly, you would extend to *me,* 'do so even to *them.'* They are small, but *so* full of meaning, if they only mean the *half* of what I bid them" (L. 61). The notion of flowers having a metonymic connection to their sender was of course an integral part of the antebellum female custom of gift exchange.

4. Barthes, "The Pleasure of the Text," 405.

5. Higginson, "Letter to a Young Contributor," 410.

6. Barthes, "The Pleasure of the Text," 406.

7. Riffaterre, *Text Production,* 89.

8. This poem is often assumed to represent Dickinson's personal reading response to Elizabeth Barrett Browning's *Sonnets from the Portuguese.*

9. Rich, "Vesuvius at Home," 195.

10. J. Miller, *Seductions,* 2.

11. Baudrillard, *Seduction,* 77.

12. Ibid., 85.

13. Wolff, *Emily Dickinson,* 9, 163–64.

14. Cummings, *Telling Tales,* 3.

Chapter 1: The Milieu Of Seduction

1. Dobson, *Dickinson and the Strategies of Reticence;* St. Armand, *Dickinson and Her Culture;* and Reynolds, *Beneath the American Renaissance,* are all susceptible to varying degrees of historical determinism. All three critical texts are nonetheless invaluable contributions to Dickinson scholarship in general and to my own study in particular.

2. Erkkila, "Dickinson and Class," 23, 2, 1, 21, 13, 15.

3. The problematic term "new historicism" was coined by Stephen Greenblatt, who has since expressed a preference for the term "cultural poetics." The exemplary practice of "cultural poetics" has been in Renaissance studies, and its ultimate exponent is Greenblatt himself. See his *Renaissance Self-Fashioning* (Chicago: University of Chicago Press, 1980) and *Shakespearean Negotiations: The Circulation of Social Energy in Renaissance England* (Berkeley and Los Angeles: University of California Press, 1988). See also the various critical practices of the essays collected in *The New Historicism,* ed. H. Aram Veeser (London: Routledge, Chapman and Hall, 1989).

4. I am indebted to Honore David for suggesting the possible relevance of the Strong House lamp to poem 883.

5. It is surely just as valid to suggest that Dickinson's white dress was her never-worn graduation gown as it is to compare it with the fictional garments worn by Collins's *Woman in White*, Barrett Browning's *Aurora Leigh*, Dickens's Miss Havisham, Hawthorne's "Snow Maiden," or the redeemed spirits of Revelation, or to associate it with a nun's habit, an unwritten page, or Melville's white whale. See Gilbert and Gubar, *Madwoman in the Attic*, 613–21.

6. This article has an interesting copyreading error. In its introductory summation of the case, the *Hampshire and Franklin Express* states that the seducer's name is Michael Kane. However, in the editorial quoted from the *New York Tribune* it is stated three times that the seducer's name is Hare (the *Tribune* is unsure of the seducer's first name but certainly not his surname). The surname Kane unfortunately destroys the allegorical, animal fable symmetry of the Fox/Hare case. The *Express*'s confusion of two similar (four-letter) Irish surnames exemplifies the newspaper's tendency to negatively stereotype the new and growing Irish community. However, I also like to think that the biblical resonance of the surname (Cain), with its connotation of unrepentant sinner, may have had something to do with the slip.

7. *Paradise Lost*, 9.455–66.

8. Ibid., 9.996–99.

9. In particular, see Gilbert and Gubar's extensive discussion of Victorian novels by women in *Madwoman in the Attic*.

10. On the issue of women readers' responses to the Miltonic tradition, see Sandra M. Gilbert's "Patriarchal Poetry and Women Readers: Reflections on Milton's Bogey," *PMLA* 93, no. 3 (May 1978): 368–82.

11. Felman's characterization of seduction in *The Literary Speech Act*, 28.

12. In particular, see the temptation of Athens in the fourth book of *Paradise Regained*, where Milton himself participates in Christ's rejection of (pagan) literary traditions, explicitly of the rhetoric of classical orators.

13. A misreading most apparent in William Blake's "The reason Milton wrote in fetters when he wrote of Angels & God, and at liberty when of Devils & Hell, is because he was a true Poet and of the Devil's party without knowing it" (*The Marriage of Heaven and Hell*, plates 5–6).

14. Capps, *Dickinson's Reading*, 71.

15. One of the most significant of those recurrences is Dickinson's hermetic declaration that "in all the circumference of Expression, those guileless words of Adam and Eve were never surpassed, 'I was afraid and hid myself' " (L. 946).

16. Edith Wharton, writing in her unpublished autobiography, uses the myth of Persephone to explain her first fascination with writing in very similar terms. She recalls that words were "almost tangible presences.... And like the Erlkonig's daughters, they sang to me so bewitchingly that they almost lured me from the wholesome noonday air of childhood into some strange supernatural region, where the normal pleasures of my age seemed as insipid as the fruits of the earth to Persephone after she had eaten of the pomegranate seed" (quoted in Candace Waid, *Edith Wharton's Letters from the Underworld: Fictions of Women and Writing* [Chapel Hill: University of North Carolina Press, 1991], 198–99).

17. Homans, *Woman Writers and Poetic Identity*, 171.

18. See letter 342b.

19. Diehl, *Dickinson and the Romantic Imagination*, 20, 13.

20. Ibid., 82.

21. Davidson, *Revolution and the Word*, 91.

22. Ibid., 106.

23. The same subversive ambiguities are evident in other major "female" genres of the period, notably the Gothic novel, which, apparently obsessed with male omnipotence and violence and female vulnerability and violation, was, by centering on female vulnerability rather than male mastery, a realistic portrayal of the dynamics of women's enclosed mental lives in

the nineteenth century. These novels of powerlessness infused a certain power, through reader identification, into the socially constricted space within which women moved. Novels such as the Brontës' *Jane Eyre* and *Wuthering Heights*, both of which Dickinson delighted in, served as a release into a fictional space of charismatic, exaggerated feeling and offered women power in resistance, the possibilities of passive aggressiveness. The appeal of the Gothic novel to generations of women readers is evidence of their realization of its metonymic representation, in fictional form, of society's gender-based inequalities.

24. Reynolds, *Beneath the American Renaissance*, 363.

25. Lawrence, *Studies in Classic American Literature*, 88.

26. Davidson, *Revolution and the Word*, 110.

27. Halttunnen, *Confidence Men and Painted Ladies*, 2.

28. Ibid., 122.

29. St. Armand, *Dickinson and Her Culture*, 11.

30. Ibid., 73.

31. Reynolds, *Beneath the American Renaissance*, 54–55.

32. My interpretation of the significance of the moral reform movement is heavily indebted to the argument of Carroll Smith-Rosenberg's "Beauty, the Beast, and the Militant Woman: A Case Study in Sex Roles and Social Stress in Jacksonian America," reprinted in her *Disorderly Conduct*, 109–28. My own argument is particularly indebted to her suggestion that "nineteenth-century women channelled their frustration with women's restricted roles combined with a sense of superior righteousness legitimized by the Cult of True Womanhood into the reform movements of the first half of the nineteenth century and in the controversial moral-reform crusade such motivations seem particularly apparent" (110). See also Smith-Rosenberg, "Writing History," and Berg, *The Remembered Gate*.

33. Smith-Rosenberg, *Disorderly Conduct*, 120.

34. *Hampshire Gazette*, Dec. 26, 1848, Jan. 2, 1849. See also the *Hampshire and Franklin Express*, Sept. 8, 1848, which concludes yet another tale of seduction with this pointed rejoinder: "When we last heard of the scoundrel he was living in Boston, Mass, where he may have the pleasure of reading this story for his villainy. And if he feels any uncertainty at his own identity, let him go to the town of Orono, Maine, or to the recorder of the United States Court, and enquire for the name of Mr Woods, who figured conspicuously some ten or twelve years ago, as a thief, mail robber, convict, seducer and ingrate." Such public exposure was clearly not exceptional.

35. Quoted in Berg, *The Remembered Gate*, 212.

36. D'Emilio and Freedman, *Intimate Matters*, 70–71. The preventive rhetoric of moral reform emphasized the extent of the new fall: "If virtue be lost . . . oh, what a poor, forlorn, withered, wretched creature you become! Abandoned by your seducer, rejected from your place, disowned by your friends" (*Advocate of Moral Reform* 1 [1835]: 6).

37. Such displacements were also apparent in other contemporary reform movements with an active female participation, particularly those concerned with temperance; there, predominantly female "criticisms of drinking were laced through with imagery of the bestial, violent quality of male sexuality, but blaming alcohol also allowed a displacement of focus, an avoidance of criticizing men and marriage directly" (Gordon and Dubois, "Seeking Ecstasy on the Battlefield," 11).

38. Quoted in Berg, *The Remembered Gate*, 182; Smith-Rosenberg, *Disorderly Conduct*, 117.

39. Griffith reads the poem as a general expression of Dickinson's fear of the masculine (*The Long Shadow*, 171–73, 180); Cleanth Brooks, R. W. B. Lewis, and Robert Penn Warren see "Him" as God (*American Literature: The Makers and the Making* [New York: St. Martin's Press, 1973], 1238); and Kher makes the case that the "Soul" and "He" are willing reader and powerful poet, respectively (*The Landscape of Absence*, 18, 107).

40. See, for example, Charles Anderson, "From a Window in Amherst: Emily Dickinson Looks at the American Scene," *New England Quarterly* 31 (June 1958): 157; William R. Sherwood,

Circumference and Circumstance: Stages in the Mind and Art of Emily Dickinson (New York: Columbia University Press, 1968), 108–9; and Sewall, *Life of Emily Dickinson*, 2:451, 703.

41. At the same time, of course, it is one of Dickinson's most effective representations of a seducer in action. In that context, see the workshop discussion of this poem as power play between Robin Riley Fast, Suzanne Juhasz, and Ellen Rigler-Henderson in Juhasz and Miller, *Emily Dickinson*, 53–84.

42. *Hampshire Gazette*, Sept. 9, 1845.

43. Headline in ibid., Jan. 9, 1849.

44. Ibid., Nov. 25, 1845.

45. Ibid., Jan. 6, 1846.

46. Ibid., May 1, Nov. 27, 1849.

47. Ibid., Aug. 28, 1849.

48. Leyda, *Years and Hours*, 2:168.

49. *Amherst Record*, Feb. 9, 1871; *Hampshire Gazette*, Feb. 14, 1871; *Springfield Republican*, Feb. 8, 1871.

50. *Amherst Record*, Feb. 9, 1871.

51. *Hampshire Gazette*, Apr. 30, 1872; *Amherst Record*, Feb. 9, 1871; *Springfield Republican*, Feb. 8, 1871.

52. *Hampshire Gazette*, Apr. 30, 1872; *Amherst Record*, Feb. 9, 1871.

53. *Springfield Republican*, Feb. 8, 1871.

54. *Amherst Record*, Feb. 9, 1871.

55. The enthusiastic reporting of such narratives ensured that the local newspapers participated to a degree in the same salaciousness they editorialized against. To list three separate stories under the heading "Moral Depravity" (*Hampshire Gazette*, Oct. 13, 1846) is formally to attract and encourage in the reader a tendency that is simultaneously, if obliquely, condemned in the newspaper's treatment of the subject matter.

56. The Dickinson family subscribed to the *Springfield Republican* and the *Hampshire and Franklin Express* (which later became the *Amherst Record*). The *Hampshire Gazette* would have been available locally, and there is some evidence that Dickinson had access to it. For example, the poem "The Life Clock," which is the probable model for her own "A Clock stopped" (P. 287), first appeared in the *Gazette*.

57. Kelley, *Private Woman, Public Stage*, xi.

58. Smith-Rosenberg, *Disorderly Conduct*, 160.

59. See N. Walker, "Wit, Sentimentality and the Image of Women."

60. Sewall, *Life of Emily Dickinson*, 2:670.

61. "Scenelessness" is the useful term coined by Robert Weisbuch in *Dickinson's Poetry*, 15–39.

62. C. Walker, *The Nightingale's Burden*, 38.

63. Jameson, *The Political Unconscious*, 81.

64. Smith-Rosenberg, "Writing History," 41. The format of the *Advocate* differed from that of contemporary male journals precisely insofar as the usual sermons, articles, and editorials were displaced by letters to and from the membership of the moral reform movement.

Chapter 2: Seduction and the Male Reader

1. Bowles's letter quoted by Leyda, *Years and Hours*, 2:235.

2. Higgins, *Portrait of Emily Dickinson*, 163; Sewall, *Life of Emily Dickinson*, 2:781; C. Miller, *A Poet's Grammar*, 5. The connection was emphasized by Mark Van Doren in his introduction to the Mabel Loomis Todd edition of the letters when he declared, "The power of her letters is like the power of her poetry—the two are from the same source" (*Letters of Emily Dickinson* [New York: World Publishing Company, 1951], v).

3. Porter, *Modern Idiom*, 81.

4. Juhasz, "Reading Dickinson's Letters," 171.

5. Stonum, *The Dickinson Sublime*, 54, 84, 23.

6. See Homans's important essays "Vision of Language" and "Syllables of Velvet," 579–90.

7. Variations of the same rhetorical strategy occur in Dickinson's important correspondence to the editor of the *Springfield Republican*, Samuel Bowles; in her teenage correspondence to her brother, Austin Dickinson; and in her later love letters to Judge Otis Lord. This is not to say that Dickinson's letters to a female audience did not similarly function as rhetorical devices. Indeed, Dickinson's female relationships that were at least partially defined by rivalry and intellectual combat—for example, the correspondences with Helen Hunt Jackson and Sue Gilbert Dickinson—do contain traces of the same rhetorical power struggles. The battle for rhetorical control is, however, more blatantly obvious when she confronts a male correspondent.

8. That flirtatiousness is celebrated most spectacularly in Keller's confessional essay, "Notes on Sleeping with Emily Dickinson."

9. Riviere's classic 1929 essay "Womanliness as Masquerade," 35, 37.

10. In this context, it is interesting that Edward Dickinson was described by his political colleagues in these terms: "Sneers or censures can never drive, nor can flatteries or bribes seduce him from the straight forward path" (Leyda, *Years and Hours*, 1:256).

11. Juhasz, "Reading Dickinson's Letters," 171.

12. Dickinson's technique of syntactic doubling is analyzed in great detail by C. Miller in *A Poet's Grammar*, 37–44.

13. The usual critical assumption is that Dickinson is referring to Benjamin Newton, but any identification of the "dying tutor" remains conjectural.

14. Higginson would later admit his own confusion as regards the meaning of this phrase: "There is something startling in its opening image; and in the yet stranger phrase that follows, where she apparently uses 'mob' in the sense of chaos or bewilderment" (quoted in Buckingham, *Dickinson's Reception*, 187).

15. Deixis (from the Greek *deiktikos:* capable of proof, directly pointing out) is a grammatical pointing, the means by which a writer establishes her location, her specific spatiotemporal situation. Deixis is the necessary compensation in writing for the writer's physical absence. Obviously, it is unnecessary in a proximate speech situation.

16. Margaret Fuller, in frequent expressions of self-doubt in her journals and letters, also often chooses the word "palsy" to describe her failure to find an adequate written form for her thoughts.

17. Sewall, *Life of Emily Dickinson*, 2:617.

18. Annie Leclerc, in another context, has a wonderfully evocative rhetorical take on the general significance of the word "Master" to any feminist critique: "Master, Master: there is the master word of all our submissions to the greatness of man. . . . Will we ever be able to break our ideas free of that tyrannical law of the master? . . . So the master is one who commands. Fine. But as you only command those who obey, it was first necessary to win obedience of those who might seek to act and speak for themselves. It was necessary to conquer them, to take away their acts and words. It was necessary to possess them" (quoted in Marks and de Courtivron, *New French Feminisms*, 81). Dickinson's choosing to address her correspondent as "Master" in three letters particularly concerned with notions of rhetorical mastery might well be another of her casual exercises in irony.

19. T. S. Eliot is another poet with the audacity to rhyme "go" and "Michelangelo" in his "Love Song of J. Alfred Prufrock." Further evidence that Dickinson's letter approaches modernism in its stylistic audacity?

20. Robert Weisbuch memorably observes that "language is an inherited system, an imposed Master, but Dickinson can jostle it to master the Master" (*Dickinson's Poetry*, 63).

21. Cristanne Miller examines at length Dickinson's technique of nonrecoverable elisions within the poetry in her detailed study of the poet's language (*A Poet's Grammar*, 24–30).

22. Certainly this is also related to a poetics that asserts, "By intuition, Mightiest Things / Assert themselves—and not by terms" (P. 420).

23. Stonum, *The Dickinson Sublime*, 90.

24. Charles Anderson was surely correct in his observation that Dickinson's letters "were rarely concerned with straightforward autobiography" (*Dickinson's Poetry*, 327), as was David Higgins in his assessment that "the trouble with Emily Dickinson's letters is that . . . only at rare moments are there glimpses of the poet" (*Portrait of Emily Dickinson*, 27).

25. Halttunnen, *Confidence Men and Painted Ladies*, 144.

26. See Smith-Rosenberg's classic study "The Female World of Love and Ritual," reprinted as chapter 2 of her *Disorderly Conduct*.

27. Halttunnen, *Confidence Men and Painted Ladies*, 160–61.

28. Ibid., 159.

29. Ibid., 121.

30. Cameron, *Lyric Time*, 12.

31. Juhasz, "Reading Dickinson's Letters," 190.

32. Ibid., 175.

33. Kristeva's theory of poetic language is developed in *Desire in Language* and *Revolution in Poetic Language*.

34. Stonum, *The Dickinson Sublime*, 97.

Chapter 3: The Poetics of Seduction

1. Dobson, "Dickinson and the Archetype," 80.

2. Griffith, *The Long Shadow*, 166.

3. Ibid., 171.

4. Ibid., 164.

5. Numerous Dickinson poems establish just such systems of hierarchy. See, for example, nos. 2, 31, 32, 61, 70, 85, 96, 103, 106, 114, 124, 151, 152, 162, 186, 190, 211, 223, 232, 235, 236, 246, 247, 251, 256, 271, 273, 275, 279, 284, 299, 315, 336, 339, 400, 429, 454, 462, 480, 506, 520, 603, 616, 630, 638, 667, 732, 738, 754, 921, 1053, 1059, 1290, 1339.

6. Rich makes the case in "Vesuvius at Home" that the male figure is Dickinson's figuration of her poetic imagination; Diehl adapts the "anxiety of influence" theories of Harold Bloom in *Dickinson and the Romantic Imagination* to reinterpret the figure as a composite precursor-muse; Gelpi develops the idea that the figure is a Jungian animus in "Emily Dickinson and the Deerslayer."

7. Dobson, "Dickinson and the Archetype," 90.

8. Among the more well known poems that feature an unspecified male figure are nos. 47, 186, 190, 236, 242, 273, 279, 284, 315, 339, 463, 493, 506, 580, 603, 638, 738, 865. The most famous (and most often discussed) example is probably poem 754 ("My Life had stood—a Loaded Gun").

9. Other poems that evoke images of seduction to good effect are such canonical standards as poems 506 ("He touched me, so I live to know"), 520 ("I started Early—Took my Dog"), and 603 ("He found my Being—set it up").

10. Quoted in Smith-Rosenberg, "Writing History," 44.

11. Smith-Rosenberg, "Writing History," 45.

12. Loeffelholz, *Boundaries of Feminist Theory*, 21.

13. The inversion of an internally established power dynamic within a poem is evident, to varying degrees, in nos. 4, 70, 85, 106, 124, 152, 162, 190, 211, 232, 256, 271, 273, 284, 429, 454, 616, 667, 732, 754, 909.

14. In Juhasz, *Feminist Critics*, this poem is cited by Sandra Gilbert (26), Karl Keller (73), Barbara Mossberg (94), Adalaide Morris (104–5), Margaret Homans (118–19) and Cristanne Miller (143).

15. Homans, "Vision of Language," 119.

16. Homans reinterprets this poem as being more firmly a precursor of *ecriture feminine* in her later essay "Syllables of Velvet."

17. C. Miller, "How 'Low Feet' Stagger," 137. This chapter is heavily indebted to Miller's pioneering work on Dickinson's "grammar."

18. Suzanne Juhasz notes that the poems often tease the direct objects of their address and their readers simultaneously. She observes that for the reader, "Dickinson teases by playing on and with another's desire, attracting or luring but not delivering—i.e., flirting. The sexual implications of this kind of tease cannot be overlooked. Images of striptease come to mind; visions of the poem as 'come-on.' " Simultaneously, "the poem becomes the space between the arousal of desire and its fulfillment. Teasing creates gaps—lacunae between images and words. . . . In these gaps we, the audience, insert ourselves, so that any satisfaction we experience comes as much from what we have put there as from what she has suggested" (Juhasz, Miller, and Smith, *Comic Power in Emily Dickinson*, 29).

19. Dickinson's rejected alternate for "Sound" was "reach," which, if chosen, would have made far more contextual sense. Dickinson's choice of "Sound," an example of her habitual preference for the abstract over the concrete image, is a significant comment on her method of word selection. See Porter's *Modern Idiom* for a thorough and significant discussion of Dickinson's final selection (or failure to select) from variant possibilities.

20. Of course, on this occasion the poet is also looking for a rhyme.

21. Poems 742 and 328 are specifically discussed in detail by C. Miller in *A Poet's Grammar* as examples of the poet's technique of syntactic doubling.

22. Fish, *Is There a Text in This Class?*, 13; Bleich, *Subjective Criticism*, 97–98; Holland, "Transactive Criticism," 198; Holland, "Unity, Identity, Text, Self," 814.

23. Alcorn, "Authority of the Signifier," 142–43.

24. Lacan, *Ecrits*, 87.

Chapter 4: The Word Made Flesh

1. H. R. Blackwell, "Literary Notices," in Buckingham, *Dickinson's Reception*, 461.

2. When she was only fifteen, in a visit to the Chinese Museum in Boston, Dickinson was struck by the appearance of two reformed opium eaters and moved to admit that "there is something peculiarly interesting to me in their self-denial" (L. 13).

3. Sandra Gilbert, "The Wayward Nun Beneath the Hill: Emily Dickinson and the Mysteries of Womanhood," in Juhasz, *Feminist Critics*, 24.

4. Ibid., 32.

5. Gilbert and Gubar, *Madwoman in the Attic*, 583. We must, of course, be circumspect when dealing with a *poetic* self-presentation conveyed in language as ambiguous as Dickinson's. The "Yarn of Pearl" (P. 605) spun by the artist/spider is also a suitable narrative of entrapment, a yarn of peril spun for a careless reader/insect.

6. Higginson, "Letter to a Young Contributor," 405–7.

7. Wilson, *Figures of Speech*, 248.

8. Higginson, "Letter to a Young Contributor," 403.

9. Ibid., 404, 402, 405.

10. Scarry, *The Body in Pain*, 307.

11. Dickinson's comment quoted by Joseph Lyman in Sewall, *The Lyman Letters*, 71.

12. Higginson, "Letter to a Young Contributor," 403.

13. Leyda, *Years and Hours*, 2:482.

14. Gilman's letter quoted by Cheryl Walker in *The Nightingale's Burden*, 34.

15. This letter quoted by Ann Douglas in *The Feminization of American Culture*, 166.

16. It would appear that at least one male writer shared this perception: Nathaniel Hawthorne, in a letter to his wife, Sophia, observes, "My dearest, I cannot enough thank God, that,

with a higher and deeper intellect than any other woman, thou has never—forgive me the bare idea!—never prostituted thyself to the public, as that woman [the author Grace Greenwood] has, and as a thousand others do" (*The Centenary Edition of the Works of Nathaniel Hawthorne*, ed. William Charvat et al. [Columbus: Ohio State University Press, 1962], 17:456–57).

17. See Dandurand, "New Dickinson Civil War Publications," 17–28, and the final chapter of Dobson's *Dickinson and the Strategies of Reticence*.

18. Of course, Paul also notes in this letter to the Corinthians: "Know ye not that your body is the temple of the Holy Ghost which is in you, which ye have of God, and ye are not your own?" (1 Cor. 6:18–19). Dickinson's gloss on that text is poem 578:

The Body grows without—
The more convenient way—
That if the Spirit—like to hide
Its Temple stands, alway,

Ajar—secure—inviting—
It never did betray
The Soul that asked its shelter
In solemn honesty

19. Johnson's exact note on the poem is, "This poem is incorporated in a letter written to Perez Dickinson Cowan" (*Poems of Emily Dickinson*, 3:1031).

20. Benfey, *Emily Dickinson*, 96.

21. What makes this poem's statement an unquestionably aesthetic one is the fact that everything about it is extremely questionable. The various possible reconstructions of its syntax by the reader make it an interpretive nightmare. However, that genotextual complexity, given the poem's obvious concern with embodiment, may well be the point: the poem, by means of the slow temporal processing it demands of its reader, demonstrates the event that it can only with difficulty discuss. For a recent analysis of the interpretive problems posed by this poem, see the discussion between Joanne Feit Diehl, Cristanne Miller, and Maurya Simon in Juhasz and Miller, *Emily Dickinson*, 177–209.

22. Derrida, *Speech and Phenomena*, 142. For an expanded view of Derrida's work on language and temporality see *Of Grammatology*.

23. Cameron, *Lyric Time*, 172.

24. Rich, *Of Woman Born*, 62.

25. Chawaf and Cixous quoted in Marks and de Courtivron, *New French Feminisms*, 177, 257.

26. Margaret Homans adapts the theories of Luce Irigaray in her two Dickinson essays, "Vision of Language" and "Syllables of Velvet"; Cristanne Miller speculates on the parallels between Dickinson's practice and the theories of Irigaray, Cixous, and Kristeva in the concluding chapters of *A Poet's Grammar*.

27. Anonymous reviewer, "Talk about New Books," in Buckingham, *Dickinson's Reception*, 73.

28. The implications of a critical revisionary materialism are discussed by Elaine Scarry in her introduction to *Literature and the Body*. She explores the possibility that an artist can effect a personal revisionary materialism in her essay on John Donne, "But Yet the Body Is His Booke" (ibid., 70–103).

29. Scarry, *Literature and the Body*, xv.

30. Cameron, *The Corporeal Self*, 3, 6.

31. Ibid., 11.

32. Ibid., 1–2.

33. Michie, *The Flesh Made Word*, 35.

34. Ibid., 35.

35. Ibid., 87.

36. Ibid., 28–29.

37. Kaplan, introduction to *Elizabeth Barrett Browning*, 15–16.

38. This letter is quoted in Blanche Glassman Hersh, *The Slavery of Sex: Feminist-Abolitionists in America* (Urbana: University of Illinois Press, 1983), 86.

39. Sanchez-Eppler, "Bodily Bonds," 36–40.

40. This aesthetic of sensibility was shared by at least one of her own favored critical readers. Sue Dickinson's response to the first stanza of "Safe in their Alabaster Chambers" was "I always go to the fire and get warm after thinking of it" (*Poems of Emily Dickinson*, 1:153). The poet who once declared "my own Words so chill and burn me, that the Temperature of other Minds is too new an Awe" (L. 798) must have been delighted.

41. This is also true of those modern-day romance novels referred to in the trade as either "bodice rippers," so named for the tearing hands of the lusting hero, or "bodice busters," so named for the mirroring, by a sympathetically aroused female reader, of the heaving breasts and arching spinal column of the heroine.

42. Gary Lee Stonum argues in *The Dickinson Sublime* that Dickinson's poetics is one of reader response centered on the romantic sublime. While I would certainly agree that Dickinson's aesthetic is reader oriented, I think that aesthetic is probably better understood relative to the central premises of sentimental fiction. While I often disagree with Stonum on specific details, such as the nature of the historical evolution of Dickinson's poetic, my own study is greatly indebted to *The Dickinson Sublime*. Stonum was the first Dickinson critic to elaborate a plausible thesis from the poet's obvious concern with affective response. My own study is, in a number of ways, the elaboration of the critical interpretation of Dickinson that Stonum legitimized.

43. The various forms the poems assume in the fascicle booklets is perhaps also *bodily* suggestive. Martha Nell Smith's comment that a poem has "different corporealizations" as a fascicle manuscript (*Rowing in Eden*, 6) may shed some unintended light on the recent critical turn toward reinterpreting the poems in their original written state. The critical study of the fascicles has of this moment replicated only two of the paradigms established by previous criticism: on one hand, the hidden life-narrative of the poems has become the hidden life-narrative of the fascicle structure (see Smith, *Rowing in Eden*; Farr, *Passion of Emily Dickinson*; and Shurr *Marriage of Emily Dickinson*); on the other hand, and rather more productively, the study of Dickinson's radical poetics of *process* has been extended beyond the poetry's grammatical tensions to the "unfinished" appearance of the original manuscripts, with their multiplicity of variants and alternative lineations (see Smith, *Rowing in Eden*; Howe, *My Emily Dickinson*; and Cameron, *Choosing Not Choosing*). Given this repetition, one might plausibly argue that the same basic poetic corporealization of "Dickinson" reasserts itself, regardless of the new critical context in which her poetry is read.

44. Cixous, *Newly Born Woman*, 95.

Chapter 5: Reading Seductions (1)

1. In particular, the linkage of specific linguistic "seduction" and psychoanalytic discourse is now frequent in literary criticism. See, for example, Felman's *The Literary Speech Act* and Gallop's *The Daughter's Seduction*. The link has been most fully developed by the assumption of contemporary narrative theorists that the relationship of narrator to listener is analogous to that of reader of text and that both are instances of psychoanalytic transference. See, for example, Chambers, *Story and Situation*, and Brooks, *Reading for the Plot*.

2. See, for example, Masson's *Assault on Truth*.

3. For a brief discussion of the applicability of psychoanalysis to Dickinson see Tanner, "Dickinson and the Psychoanalyst."

4. Cody, *After Great Pain*, 6.

5. Porter, *Modern Idiom*, 38–39.

6. Ibid., 79, 112, 163, 207.

7. Freud, *Complete Works*, 2:7, 1:256

8. Porter, *Modern Idiom*, 38.

9. Published anonymously in Dickinson's lifetime as part of Robert Bros. "No Name Series," readers considered this poem to be the work of Emerson. This provides further evidence that Dickinson could have successfully published poems in her lifetime if such had been her explicit desire.

10. Wilbur, "Sumptuous Destitution," 132–33. Suzanne Juhasz discusses the problematics of Dickinsonian desire is some detail in *The Undiscovered Continent* and later productively elaborates the relationship between desire and "performance" in "The Big Tease" (chapter 2 of Juhasz, Miller, and Smith, *Comic Power in Emily Dickinson*). Of course, civilization, as understood by Freud, is built on the repression of desire and the deferment of gratification. The pleasure principle of necessity knuckles under to the reality principle, in which case Dickinson is the quintessential bard of the latter: she never abandons the intention of ultimately obtaining pleasure but demands and carries into effect the postponement of satisfaction, the abandonment of a number of possibilities of gaining satisfaction, and the temporary toleration of unpleasure as necessary steps toward that goal. Therefore, Dickinson's poems, it might be argued, delineate an ideal for living.

11. In particular see chapter 1, "Renewing the Practice of Reading, or Freud's Unprecedented Lesson," in Felman, *Lacan and the Adventure of Insight*. Throughout this chapter the influence of Felman is ubiquitous—intentionally so, I believe.

12. Jacques Lacan, "Intervention in Transference," in Bernheimer and Kahane, *In Dora's Case*, 93.

13. Felman, *Lacan and the Adventure of Insight*, 23.

14. Ibid., 21–22.

15. Shurr, *Marriage of Emily Dickinson*, 189; Wolff, *Emily Dickinson*, 275; Juhasz, "Reading Dickinson's Letters," 171; Keller, *The Only Kangaroo*, 25–26.

16. Lacan, *Fundamental Concepts*, 232. On the subject of the textual unconscious see also Culler, "Textual Self-Consciousness."

17. My thesis that it is Dickinson's text that is an analytic case in the history of literary criticism and that Dickinson might be said to have a literary case history is, of course, modeled on Felman's magnificent treatment of Edgar Allan Poe (*Lacan and the Adventure of Insight*, 27–51).

18. See Rich's "Vesuvius at Home" and Juhasz's polemical editor's introduction to *Feminist Critics*.

19. Martha Noel Evans, "Hysteria and the Seduction of Theory," in Hunter, *Seduction and Theory*, 78. Evans uses the far more suggestive and highly precise French term *allumeuse* to describe the teasing persona. It does not translate well.

20. Freud, *Complete Works*, 12:169–70.

21. A. C. Ward, "A Major American Poet," in Blake and Wells, *Recognition of Emily Dickinson*, 146.

22. I am here specifically thinking of critical response to the poetry since the late 1960s and the fact that Dickinson has been so easily appropriated by phenomenological (Mudge, Juhasz), deconstructive (Porter, Miller, Homans), psychoanalytic (Cody, Gabowsky), feminist (Wolff, Gilbert) and new historicist (Erkkila, Reynolds) approaches. Dickinson's historical fashionability has, of course, been more sporadic, the poet attracting particular interest in different eras—for example, 1890, 1914, 1924, 1930, 1955.

23. These are the critical positions assumed by Cody, Wolff, Porter, and Rich, respectively.

24. Blackmur, "Dickinson's Notation," 80, 86, 83.

25. Allen Tate, "Emily Dickinson," in Sewall, *Dickinson: A Collection of Critical Essays*, 19.

26. John Crowe Ransom, "Emily Dickinson: A Poet Restored," in ibid., 97; Higgins, *Portrait of Emily Dickinson*, 86.

27. Robert Hillyer, "Emily Dickinson," in Blake and Wells, *Recognition of Emily Dickinson*, 98.

28. Archibald MacLeish, "The Private World: Poems of Emily Dickinson," in Sewall, *Dickinson: A Collection of Critical Essays*, 160.

29. Higgins, *Portrait of Emily Dickinson*, 105.

30. In a fascinating confessional essay that details the curiously affective gendered critical response toward another canonical female poet, George Nitchie observes, "I don't believe that I ever fell in love with Marianne Moore, but there's no question about my occupying that border country between affection and condescension, and that I suppose might as well be love." Nitchie is left pondering the resonances within many male critical readings of Moore of a "somewhat more sophisticated variety of the impulse to curl my mustaches and say gallant and foolish things" ("Condescension and Affection," 35, 37).

31. George Whicher, "A Centennial Appraisal," in Blake and Wells, *Recognition of Emily Dickinson*, 139; Ella Gilbert Ives, "Emily Dickinson: Her Poetry, Prose and Personality," in ibid., 71.

32. Tate, "Emily Dickinson," 27; Edmund Blunden, "An Unguessed Poetry," in Blake and Wells, *Recognition of Emily Dickinson*, 134. Dickinson's comment on such a phenomenon might well have been her pithy observation that "shame is so intrinsic in a strong affection we must all experience Adam's reticence" (L. 318).

33. Higginson is, surprisingly, an exception to this rule. He observed of Dickinson that "She interested me more in her—so to speak—unregenerate condition" ("Emily Dickinson's Letters," in Buckingham, *Dickinson's Reception*, 188).

34. Anonymous reviewer, "Scraps of Verse from the Pen of Emily Dickinson," in ibid., 67.

35. Maurice Thompson, "Miss Dickinson's Poems," in ibid., 96; anonymous *Scribner's* magazine reviewer, "The Point of View," in ibid., 120.

36. Yvor Winters, "Emily Dickinson and the Limits of Judgment," in Sewall, *Dickinson: A Collection of Critical Essays*, 28.

37. Martin Armstrong, "The Poetry of Emily Dickinson," in Blake and Wells, *Recognition of Emily Dickinson*, 108.

38. Conrad Aiken, "Emily Dickinson," in Sewall, *Dickinson: A Collection of Critical Essays*, 18.

39. Ibid., 15; Hartman, *Criticism in the Wilderness*, 130.

40. William Dean Howells, "Editor's Study," in Buckingham, *Dickinson's Reception*, 74.

41. Aiken, "Emily Dickinson," 14.

42. Howells, "Editor's Study," 77; Thompson, "Miss Dickinson's Poems," 96–98.

43. Blackmur, "Dickinson's Notation," 83.

44. Cody, *After Great Pain*, 396, 4, 354.

45. Ibid., 231, 433, 4.

46. Ibid., 288, 438.

47. Ibid., 39.

48. Porter, *Modern Idiom*, 293, 21, 118, 74.

49. Ibid., 82, 292, 135.

50. Ibid., 133, 79. It is worthwhile to compare Porter's twentieth-century response to Dickinson's language with that of one of her nineteenth-century reviewers, John White Chadwick, who comments on "phrases so packed with strangeness, force, suggestion, poems so tremulous with tenderness or so bent under the burden of their mystery, that they shock us with almost intolerable delight or awe" ("Poems by Emily Dickinson," in Buckingham, *Dickinson's Reception*, 63). This response to Dickinson's corporeal language is clearly an ahistorical one.

51. Porter, *Modern Idiom*, 171, 17, 106, 114, 56.

52. Ibid., 48, 74, 3, 292, 67, 129, 146.

53. Ibid., 280, 187, 125. See also Porter's interesting discussion of this phenomenon in his first book on the poet, where he observes that that reader, "lacking precise contextual direction provided by the poem itself, brings to it his casual inferences, and, in effect, is compelled to

give symbols a reading rooted in his own experience . . . the verbal equivalent of sfumato, the technique in expressionistic painting whereby information . . . on a canvas is given only piece-meal and thereby necessarily stimulates the imaginative projection of the viewer, who, out of his own experience, supplies the missing contours and, ultimately, the context" (*Dickinson's Early Poetry,* 99).

54. Porter, *Modern Idiom,* 248, 217.

55. Buckingham, "Poetry Readers," 165, 166, 168, 175.

56. Anonymous reviewer, in Buckingham, *Dickinson's Reception,* 61.

57. Brooks, "Psychoanalytic Literary Criticism," 341–42.

58. Shurr, *Marriage of Emily Dickinson,* 48–49, 195, 30.

59. It could also be argued that these male analyses tend to be subtly paradigmatic ex-amples of what Mary Ellmann called "phallic criticism," where a male reader not only con-fuses the female writer's intellectual and sexual faculties, but also uses her gender to impose an erogenic form on her work. Ellmann argues that Western culture is permeated by "thought by sexual analogy." Consequently, "with a kind of inverted fidelity, the discussion of women's books by men will arrive punctually at the point of preoccupation, which is the fact of femi-ninity. Books by women are treated as though they themselves were women, and criticism em-barks, at its happiest, upon an intellectual measuring of busts and hips" (*Thinking about Women,* 29). Susan Gubar also notes the frequency with which contemporary critics write about the act of reading in sexual terms ("The Blank Page").

60. Marotti, "Countertransference," 474–76.

61. Norman Holland's examination of how readers use literature to reenact personal style, creating from its materials characteristic wish-fulfilling fantasies, defensive or adaptive structures, and transformations of text into meaning, may be useful for tracking the psychic route of these mechanisms. Holland theorizes that in their unconscious engagement with a text, readers transform their fears and desires into significance and coherence, and he assigns the acronym DEFT to the typical reading process: "We match inner defenses and expectations to outer realities in order to project fantasies onto them and then transform those fantasies into significance. DEFT—Defense, expectation, fantasy, transformation" (in Flynn and Schweickart, *Gender and Reading,* 217). Perhaps in this way it could be demonstrated that Dickinson's male readers are more deft than they might at first appear.

Chapter 6: Reading Seductions (2)

1. Charles Bernheimer observes that hysteria is "implicated in psychoanalysis in the sense that the science enfolds the disease within it and is constituted simultaneously with this pathological interiority. Yet psychoanalysis contests this originary implication, insisting on its scientific authority and asserting mastery over hysteria as the illness of the other, typically of the feminine other" (*In Dora's Case,* 1). In other words, psychoanalysis is not simply the study of hysteria but is itself constituted as a hystericization of discourse. Dianne Hunter observes that feminism too is *transformed hysteria* insofar as hysteria (in its nineteenth-century "femi-nine" context) is a feminism lacking a social network in the outer world. Indeed, the adjective "hysterical," still used to discredit feminist expression today, foregrounds the fact that both are conceptualized as "out of control" conditions in a noncooperative alignment with standard patriarchal conventions. See Hunter's introduction to *Seduction and Theory.*

2. Louise Chandler Moulton, "A Very Remarkable Book," in Buckingham, *Dickinson's Re-ception,* 34–37.

3. Pollack, *Anxiety of Gender,* 9, 27.

4. Smith, *Rowing in Eden,* 118, 112; Loeffelholz, *Boundaries of Feminist Theory,* 23.

5. Keller, *The Only Kangaroo,* 250, 247.

6. Ibid., 230, 275, 31, 246, 30–31.

7. Ibid., 35.

8. Ibid., 248, 268, 278, 273, 26, 275, 268, 247.

9. Ibid., 7, 179, 2, 31, 25–26, 274, 3–4.

10. Ibid., 274, 3, 270, 273.

11. Keller, "Notes on Sleeping with Emily Dickinson," 67–70.

12. In particular, see Homans, "Vision of Language," and Oakes, "Welcome and Beware."

13. Oakes, "Welcome and Beware," 193, 201.

14. Homans, "Vision of Language," 124.

15. In Lacanian theory, integrated selfhood occurs in the "mirror" stage and the "imaginary" register of apperception. Lacan emphasizes the misrecognition implicit in the "imaginary" exchange of gazes, the *mesconnaissance* that is the act of mirroring. The mother's gaze does not mirror the infant as he or she actually is in the present but directs the infant toward an image of him- or herself. That image—stable, bounded, coherent, complete—is, however, an ego ideal and not a representation of the subject's actual bodily identity or experience. The image establishes the subject's ego as a necessary *fiction* of wholeness: it is internal difference that directs the subject's quest after coherence. The mirror stage occurs in relation to the "Law of the Father," and the mirroring dyad of mother and child already anticipates, in its further triangulation, the child's entry into a symbolic order where linguistically constituted subjectivity is superimposed on any original corporeal rapport with the mother. The Lacan "adapted" by the French feminism of Kristeva and Irigaray and the object relations of Winnicott is an optimistic, even utopian, gloss on the bleak original.

16. Irigaray, *This Sex Which Is Not One*, 61.

17. See Chodorow, *Reproduction of Mothering*.

18. Hirsch, "Spiritual Bildung," 27. This essay is especially indebted to the adaptations of object-relations theory in Wyatt's *Reconstructing Desire*.

19. Kristeva, *Desire in Language*, 66.

20. Ibid., 135.

21. Perry, introduction to *Mothering the Mind*, 7–8.

22. See Winnicott, *Playing and Reality*.

23. Wyatt, *Reconstructing Desire*, 103.

24. Winnicott, *Maturational Processes*, 34. Winnicott posits the first form of intersubjective mediation, the "transitional object," which is neither internal nor external but found in an ambiguous "space" that embraces both orders, as a prototype for a later communication activity that retains boundary blurring and forming aspects.

25. Winnicott observes that "playing facilitates growth and also health; playing leads into group relationships; playing can be a form of communication in psychotherapy; and, lastly, *psychoanalysis has been developed as a highly specialized form of playing in the service of communication with oneself and others*" (*Playing and Reality*, 41, emphasis added). Thus, Winnicott does not only specifically locate the paradigm of play and art in the "potential space" between infant and mother before subject/object boundaries are clearly drawn: he also finds psychoanalysis, which "takes place in the overlap of the two areas of playing, that of the patient and that of the therapist," analogous to the situation of interplay between mother and infant.

26. Paglia, *Sexual Personae*, 673.

27. Ibid., 626.

28. Ibid., 624, 629, 624, 634, 628, 633, 666, 627, 637, 626.

29. Stanfill, "Woman Warrior," 24.

30. Paglia, *Sexual Personae*, 626, 629, 631, 650, 660, 634, 636, 649, 630.

31. Ibid., 624, 643, 661, 660, 635.

32. Ibid., 630.

33. Ibid., 634, 630, 644, 635.

34. Ibid., 633, 650, 633, 625.

35. Ibid., 642, 637, 651, 640, 647, 632, 627, 625, 632, 661, 631, 629, 651, 630.

36. Ibid., 657, 670, 653, 535, 673, 38.

37. Ibid., 672, 666, 651, 649, 635.

38. Ibid., 663, 631, 671.

39. Ibid., 665.

40. Stanfill, "Woman Warrior," 27, 30, 24.

41. Adrienne Rich, *The Dream of a Common Language: Poems, 1974–1977* (New York: Norton, 1978), 76.

42. Schweickart, "Reading Ourselves," 45. While Schweickart's reading of the dialogism of Rich's essay provides an insightful mapping of its rhetorical strategies, her assertion that "metaphors of mastery and submission, of violation and control . . . are entirely absent" (53) is, I think, mistaken.

43. Rich also has three poetic addresses to Dickinson, which chart the evolution of the relationship with her eminent precursor: first in "Snapshots of a Daughter-in-Law" (*Snapshots of a Daughter-in-Law: Poems, 1954–1962* [New York: Norton, 1963]); again in "I Am in Danger—Sir—" (*Necessities of Life* [New York: Norton, 1966]); and a "third and final address" in *A Wild Patience Has Taken Me This Far: Poems, 1978–81* (New York: Norton, 1981). The most thorough study of Rich's *poetic* reading of her precursor is Erkkila's provocative "Dickinson and Rich."

44. Rich, "Vesuvius at Home," 178, 188, 178.

45. Ibid., 175, 179.

46. Ibid., 175, 176.

47. Ibid., 176, 178, 185.

48. Ibid., 182.

49. Ibid., 181, 179.

50. Ibid., 182, 180, 179.

51. Ibid., 188, 176.

52. Ibid., 176, 175.

53. Ibid., 176.

54. Ibid., 187.

55. Jean E. Kennard's interesting reading of Rich's essay as an example of the "polar reading" that exemplifies a lesbian reading strategy is somewhat undercut by her later assertion that the insect is a "Woolfian image." See Kennard's essay "Ourself behind Ourself."

56. Rich, "Vesuvius at Home," 177.

57. Ibid., 177, 178, 189.

58. Bennett, *Emily Dickinson*, 154–55, 175, 168, 171, 182.

59. Ibid., 166, 133, 118.

60. Howe, *My Emily Dickinson*, 14, 29, 131, 23, 35, 61, 116.

61. Ibid., 18.

62. Ragland-Sullivan, *Jacques Lacan*, 25.

63. Lacan, *Ecrits*, 2; Wyatt, *Reconstructing Desire*, 94.

64. Leigh Gilmore's thoughtful interpretation of intertextual ramifications of the poem "I think I was Enchanted" is valuable in this context: "The spectacle in Dickinson's poem is mutual: beholding the Lady enables the Girl to engender herself as poet and to accomplish the transition from Girl to Lady where neither must be negated" ("The Gaze of the Other Woman," 92).

Selected Bibliography

Alcorn, Marshall. "Rhetoric, Projection, and the Authority of the Signifier." *College English* 49 (February 1987): 137–59.

Anderson, Charles R. *Emily Dickinson's Poetry: Stairway of Surprise.* New York: Holt, Rinehart and Wilson, 1960.

Barthes, Roland. "The Pleasure of the Text." In *A Barthes Reader*, edited by Susan Sontag, 404–14. New York: Hill and Wang, 1982.

Baudrillard, Jean. *Seduction.* New York: St. Martin's Press, 1990.

Benfey, Christopher. *Emily Dickinson and the Problem of Others.* Amherst, Mass.: University of Massachusetts Press, 1985.

Bennett, Paula. *Emily Dickinson: Woman Poet.* Iowa City: University of Iowa Press, 1991.

Berg, Barbara J. *The Remembered Gate: Origins of American Feminism—The Woman and the City, 1800–1860.* London: Oxford University Press, 1978.

Bernheimer, Charles, and Claire Kahane, eds. *In Dora's Case: Freud-Hysteria-Feminism.* New York: Columbia University Press, 1985.

Blackmur, R. P. "Emily Dickinson's Notation." In *Dickinson: A Collection of Critical Essays*, edited by Richard B. Sewall, 78–88. Englewood Cliffs, N.J.: Prentice-Hall, 1963.

Blake, Caesar R., and Carlton F. Wells, eds. *The Recognition of Emily Dickinson: Selected Criticism since 1890.* Ann Arbor: University of Michigan Press; Toronto: Ambassador Books, 1964.

Bleich, David. *Subjective Criticism.* Baltimore: Johns Hopkins University Press, 1978.

Brooks, Peter. "The Idea of a Psychoanalytic Literary Criticism." *Critical Inquiry* 13 (Winter 1987): 334–49.

———. *Reading for the Plot: Design and Intention in Narrative.* New York: Vintage, 1985.

Buckingham, Willis J. "Poetry Readers and Reading in the 1890's: Emily Dickinson's First Reception." In *Readers in History: Nineteenth-Century American Literature and the Contexts of Response*, edited by James Machor, 164–79. Baltimore: Johns Hopkins University Press, 1993.

———, ed. *Emily Dickinson's Reception in the 1890's: A Documentary History.* Pittsburgh: University of Pittsburgh Press, 1989.

Cadman, Deborah. "Material Things and Expressive Signs: The Language of Emily Dickinson in Her Social and Physical Context." Ph.D. diss., University of Massachusetts, 1992.

Cameron, Sharon. *Choosing Not Choosing: Dickinson's Fascicles.* Chicago: University of Chicago Press, 1992.

———. *The Corporeal Self: Allegories of the Body in Melville and Hawthorne.* Baltimore: Johns Hopkins University Press, 1981.

———. *Lyric Time: Dickinson and the Limits of Genre*. Baltimore and London: Johns Hopkins University Press, 1979.

Capps, Jack Lee. *Emily Dickinson's Reading, 1836–1886*. Cambridge, Mass.: Harvard University Press; London: Oxford University Press, 1966.

Chambers, Ross. *Story and Situation: Narrative Seduction and the Power of Fiction*. Minneapolis: University of Minnesota Press, 1984.

Chodorow, Nancy. *The Reproduction of Mothering: Psychoanalysis and the Sociology of Gender*. Berkeley: University of California Press, 1978.

Cixous, Helene and Catherine Clement. *Newly Born Woman*. Minneapolis: University of Minnesota Press, 1986.

Cody, John. *After Great Pain: The Inner Life of Emily Dickinson*. Cambridge, Mass.: Belknap Press of Harvard University Press, 1971.

Cott, Nancy F. *The Bonds of Womanhood: "Woman's Sphere" in New England, 1780–1835*. New Haven: Yale University Press, 1977.

Culler, Jonathan. "Textual Self-Consciousness and the Textual Unconscious." *Style* 18 (Summer 1984): 369–76.

Cummings, Katherine. *Telling Tales: The Hysteric's Seduction in Fiction and Theory*. Stanford, Calif.: Stanford University Press, 1991.

Dandurand, Karen. "New Dickinson Civil War Publications." *American Literature* 56 (March 1984): 17–28.

Davidson, Cathy. *Revolution and the Word: The Rise of the Novel in America*. New York: Oxford University Press, 1986.

D'Emilio, John, and Estelle B. Freedman. *Intimate Matters: A History of Sexuality in America*. New York: Harper and Row, 1988.

Derrida, Jacques. *Of Grammatology*. Translated by Gayatri Spivak. Baltimore and London: Johns Hopkins University Press, 1976.

———. *Speech and Phenomena and Other Essays on Husserl's Theory of Signs*. Translated by David B. Allison. Evanston, Ill.: Northwestern University Press, 1973.

Dickinson, Emily. *The Letters of Emily Dickinson*. Edited by Thomas H. Johnson and Theodora Ward. 3 vols. Cambridge, Mass.: Harvard University Press, 1958.

———. *The Poems of Emily Dickinson*. Edited by Thomas H. Johnson. 3 vols. Cambridge, Mass.: Harvard University Press, 1951, 1955.

Diehl, Joanne Feit. *Dickinson and the Romantic Imagination*. Princeton, N.J.: Princeton University Press, 1981.

Dobson, Joanne. *Dickinson and the Strategies of Reticence: The Woman Writer in 19th-Century America*. Bloomington: Indiana University Press, 1989.

———. " 'Oh, Susie, it is dangerous': Emily Dickinson and the Archetype." In *Feminist Critics Read Emily Dickinson*, edited by Suzanne Juhasz, 80–97. Bloomington: Indiana University Press, 1983.

Douglas, Ann. *The Feminization of American Culture*. New York: Avon Books, 1977.

Ellmann, Mary. *Thinking about Women*. New York: Harcourt, Brace and World, 1968.

Erkkila, Betsy. "Dickinson and Rich: Toward a Theory of Female Poetic Influence." *American Literature* 56 (Winter 1984): 541–59.

———. "Emily Dickinson and Class." *American Literary History* 4 (Spring 1992): 1–27.

Farr, Judith. *The Passion of Emily Dickinson*. Cambridge, Mass.: Harvard University Press, 1992.

Felman, Shoshana. *Jacques Lacan and the Adventure of Insight*. Cambridge, Mass.: Harvard University Press, 1987.

————. *The Literary Speech Act: Don Juan with J. L. Austin, or Seduction in Two Languages*. Ithaca, N.Y.: Cornell University Press, 1983.

Ferlazzo, Paul J., ed. *Critical Essays on Emily Dickinson*. Boston: G. K. Hall and Co., 1984.

Fish, Stanley. *Is There a Text in This Class? The Authority of Interpretive Communities*. Cambridge, Mass.: Harvard University Press, 1980.

Flynn, Elizabeth A., and Patrocinio P. Schweickart, eds. *Gender and Reading: Essays on Readers, Texts, and Contexts*. Baltimore and London: Johns Hopkins University Press, 1986.

Freud, Sigmund. *The Standard Edition of the Complete Psychological Works of Sigmund Freud*. Edited by James Strachey et al. 24 vols. London: Hogarth Press, 1953–74.

Gallop, Jane. *The Daughter's Seduction: Feminism and Psychoanalysis*. Ithaca: Cornell University Press, 1982.

————. *Reading Lacan*. Ithaca: Cornell University Press, 1985.

Gelpi, Arthur. "Emily Dickinson and the Deerslayer: The Dilemma of the Woman Poet in America." In *Shakespeare's Sisters: Feminist Essays on Woman Poets*, edited by Sandra M. Gilbert and Susan Gubar, 122–34. Bloomington: Indiana University Press, 1979.

Gilbert, Sandra M. "Patriarchal Poetry and Women Readers: Reflections on Milton's Bogey." *PMLA* 93, no. 3 (May 1978): 368–82.

Gilbert, Sandra M., and Susan Gubar. *The Madwoman in the Attic: The Woman Writer and the Nineteenth Century Literary Imagination*. New Haven: Yale University Press, 1979.

Gilmore, Leigh. "The Gaze of the Other Woman: Beholding and Begetting in Dickinson, Moore, and Rich." In *Engendering the Word: Feminist Essays in Psychosexual Poetics*, edited by Temma F. Berg, 81–105. Urbana and Chicago: University of Illinois Press, 1989.

Gordon, Linda, and Ellen Carol Dubois. "Seeking Ecstasy on the Battlefield: Danger and Pleasure in Nineteenth Century Feminist Sexual Thought." *Feminist Studies* 9, no. 1 (Spring 1983): 7–25.

Griffith, Clark W. *The Long Shadow: Emily Dickinson's Tragic Poetry*. Princeton, N.J.: Princeton University Press, 1964.

Gubar, Susan. " 'The Blank Page' and Female Creativity." *Critical Inquiry* 8 (Winter 1981): 243–63.

Halttunnen, Karen. *Confidence Men and Painted Ladies: A Study of Middle-Class Culture in America, 1830–70*. New Haven and London: Yale University Press, 1982.

Hartman, Geoffrey. *Criticism in the Wilderness: The Study of Literature Today*. New Haven and London: Yale University Press, 1980.

Higgins, David. *Portrait of Emily Dickinson: The Poet and Her Prose*. New Brunswick, N.J.: Rutgers University Press, 1967.

Higginson, Thomas Wentworth. "Letter to a Young Contributor." *Atlantic Monthly* (April 1862): 401–11.

Hirsch, Marianne. "Spiritual Bildung: The Beautiful Soul as Paradigm." In *The Voyage In: Fictions of Female Development*, edited by Elizabeth Abel, Marianne Hirsch, and Elizabeth Langland, 23–48. Hanover and London: University Press of New England, 1983.

Holland, Norman. "A Transactive Account of Transactive Criticism." *Poetics* 7 (1978): 177–98.

———. "Unity, Identity, Text, Self." *PMLA* 90 (1975): 813–22.
Homans, Margaret. " 'Oh Vision of Language!': Dickinson's Poems of Love and Death."
      In *Feminist Critics Read Emily Dickinson,* edited by Suzanne Juhasz, 114–33. Bloom-
      ington: Indiana University Press, 1983.
———. " 'Syllables of Velvet': Dickinson, Rossetti, and the Rhetorics of Sexuality."
      Feminist Studies 11 (1985): 569–93.
———. *Woman Writers and Poetic Identity: Dorothy Wordsworth, Emily Brontë and Emily
      Dickinson.* Princeton, N.J.: Princeton University Press, 1980.
Howe, Susan. *My Emily Dickinson.* Berkeley: North Atlantic Books, 1985.
Hunter, Dianne, ed. *Seduction and Theory: Readings of Gender, Representation, and Rheto-
      ric.* Urbana and Chicago: University of Illinois Press, 1989.
Irigaray, Luce. *This Sex Which Is Not One.* Ithaca: Cornell University Press, 1985.
Jameson, Fredric. *The Political Unconscious: Narrative as a Socially Symbolic Act.* Ithaca,
      N.Y.: Cornell University Press, 1981.
Juhasz, Suzanne. "Reading Emily Dickinson's Letters." *ESQ* 30, no. 3 (3rd Quarter
      1984): 170–92.
———. *The Undiscovered Continent: Emily Dickinson and the Space of the Mind.* Bloom-
      ington: Indiana University Press, 1983.
———, ed. *Feminist Critics Read Emily Dickinson.* Bloomington: Indiana University
      Press, 1983.
Juhasz, Suzanne, and Cristanne Miller, eds. *Emily Dickinson: A Celebration for Readers.*
      New York: Gordon and Breach, 1989.
Juhasz, Suzanne, Cristanne Miller, and Martha Nell Smith. *Comic Power in Emily
      Dickinson.* Austin: University of Texas Press, 1993.
Kaplan, Cora. Introduction. In *Elizabeth Barrett Browning: Aurora Leigh and Other Po-
      ems,* 3–17. London: The Women's Press, 1978.
Keller, Karl. "Notes on Sleeping with Emily Dickinson." In *Feminist Critics Read
      Emily Dickinson,* edited by Suzanne Juhasz, 67–79. Bloomington: Indiana Uni-
      versity Press, 1983.
———. *The Only Kangaroo among the Beauty: Emily Dickinson and America.* Baltimore
      and London: Johns Hopkins University Press, 1979.
Kelley, Mary. *Private Woman, Public Stage: Literary Domesticity in 19th Century America.*
      New York: Oxford University Press, 1984.
Kennard, Jean E. " 'Ourself behind Ourself': A Theory for Lesbian Readers." In *Gen-
      der and Reading: Essays on Readers, Texts, and Contexts,* edited by Elizabeth A.
      Flynn and Patrocinio P. Schweickart, 63–80. Baltimore and London: Johns Hop-
      kins University Press, 1986.
Kher, Inder Nath. *The Landscape of Absence: Emily Dickinson's Poetry.* New Haven,
      Conn.: Yale University Press, 1974.
Kristeva, Julia. *Desire in Language: A Semiotic Approach to Literature and Art.* New York:
      Columbia University Press, 1980.
———. *Revolution in Poetic Language.* New York: Columbia University Press, 1984.
Lacan, Jacques. *Ecrits.* New York: Norton, 1977.
———. *The Four Fundamental Concepts of Psycho-Analysis.* Translated by Alan Sheri-
      dan. New York: Norton, 1981.
Lawrence, D. H. *Studies in Classic American Literature.* New York: Viking Press, 1964.
Leyda, Jay. *The Years and Hours of Emily Dickinson.* 2 vols. New Haven: Yale University

Press; London: Oxford University Press; Toronto: Burns and MacEachern, 1960.

Loeffelholz, Mary. *Dickinson and the Boundaries of Feminist Theory.* Urbana and Chicago: University of Illinois Press, 1991.

Lubbers, Klaus. *Emily Dickinson: The Critical Revolution.* Ann Arbor: University of Michigan Press, 1968.

Marks, Elaine, and Isabelle de Courtivron, eds. *New French Feminisms: An Anthology.* New York: Schocken Books, 1981.

Marotti, Arthur F. "Countertransference, the Communication Process, and the Dimensions of Psychoanalytic Criticism." *Critical Inquiry* 4 (Spring 1978): 471–89.

Masson, Jeffrey Moussaieff. *The Assault on Truth: Freud's Suppression of the Seduction Theory.* New York: Farrar, Strauss and Giroux, 1984.

Michie, Helena. *The Flesh Made Word: Female Figures and Women's Bodies.* New York and Oxford: Oxford University Press, 1987.

Miller, Cristanne. *Emily Dickinson: A Poet's Grammar.* Cambridge, Mass: Harvard University Press, 1987.

———. "How 'Low Feet' Stagger: Disruptions of Language in Dickinson's Poetry." In *Feminist Critics Read Emily Dickinson,* edited by Suzanne Juhasz, 134–55. Bloomington: Indiana University Press, 1983.

Miller, Jane. *Seductions: Studies in Reading and Culture.* Cambridge, Mass.: Harvard University Press, 1991.

Nitchie, George. "Condescension and Affection: Some Observations on Marianne Moore." *Poesis* 6 (3rd Quarter 1985): 34–39.

Oakes, Karen. "Welcome and Beware: The Reader and Emily Dickinson's Figurative Language." *ESQ* 34 (3rd Quarter, 1988): 181–206.

Paglia, Camille. *Sexual Personae: Art and Decadence from Nefertiti to Emily Dickinson.* New Haven, Conn.: Yale University Press, 1990.

Perry, Ruth. Introduction. In *Mothering the Mind: Twelve Studies of Writers and Their Silent Partners,* edited by Ruth Perry and Martine Brownley, 3–24. New York and London: Holmes and Meier, 1984.

Pollack, Vivian R. *Dickinson: The Anxiety of Gender.* Ithaca, N.Y.: Cornell University Press, 1984.

Porter, David T. *The Art of Emily Dickinson's Early Poetry.* Cambridge, Mass.: Harvard University Press, 1966.

———. *Dickinson: The Modern Idiom.* Cambridge, Mass.: Harvard University Press, 1981.

Ragland-Sullivan, Ellie. *Jacques Lacan and the Philosophy of Psychoanalysis.* Urbana and Chicago: University of Illinois Press, 1986.

Reynolds, David S. *Beneath the American Renaissance: The Subversive Imagination in the Age of Emerson and Melville.* New York: Knopf, 1988.

Rich, Adrienne. "Vesuvius at Home: The Power of Emily Dickinson." In *Critical Essays on Emily Dickinson,* edited by Paul J. Ferlazzo, 175–95. Boston: G. K. Hall and Co., 1984.

———. *Of Woman Born: Motherhood as Experience and Institution.* New York: Norton, 1976.

Riffaterre, Michael. *Text Production.* Translated by Teresa Lyons. New York: Columbia University Press, 1983.

Riviere, Joan. "Womanliness as Masquerade." In *Formations of Fantasy*, edited by Victor Burgin et al., 35–44. London and New York: Methuen, 1986.

St. Armand, Barton Levi. *Emily Dickinson and Her Culture: The Soul's Society*. London: Cambridge University Press, 1984.

Sanchez-Eppler, Karen. "Bodily Bonds: The Intersecting Rhetorics of Feminism and Abolition." *Representations* 24 (Fall 1988): 28–59.

Scarry, Elaine. *The Body in Pain: The Making and Unmaking of the World*. New York: Oxford University Press, 1985.

——, ed. *Literature and the Body: Essays on Populations and Persons*. Baltimore: Johns Hopkins University Press, 1988.

Schweickart, Patrocinio P. "Reading Ourselves: Toward a Feminist Theory of Reading." In *Gender and Reading: Essays on Readers, Texts, and Contexts*, edited by Elizabeth A. Flynn and Patrocinio P. Schweickart, 31–62. Baltimore and London: Johns Hopkins University Press, 1986.

Sewall, Richard B. *The Life of Emily Dickinson*. 2 vols. New York: Farrar, Strauss and Giroux, 1974.

——, ed. *Emily Dickinson: A Collection of Critical Essays*. Englewood Cliffs, N.J.: Prentice-Hall, 1963.

——. *The Lyman Letters: New Light on Emily Dickinson and Her Family*. Amherst: University of Massachusetts Press, 1965.

Shurr, William H. *The Marriage of Emily Dickinson: A Study of the Fascicles*. Lexington: University Press of Kentucky, 1983.

Smith, Martha Nell. *Rowing in Eden: Rereading Emily Dickinson*. Austin: University of Texas Press, 1993.

Smith-Rosenberg, Carroll. *Disorderly Conduct: Visions of Gender in Victorian America*. New York: Knopf, 1985.

——. "Writing History: Language, Class, and Gender." In *Feminist Studies/Critical Studies*, edited by Teresa de Lauretis, 31–55. Bloomington: Indiana State University Press, 1986.

Stanfill, Francesca. "Woman Warrior: Sexual Philosopher Camille Paglia Jousts with the Politically Correct." *New York Magazine*, March 4, 1991, pp. 24–30.

Stonum, Gary Lee. *The Dickinson Sublime*. Madison: University of Wisconsin Press, 1990.

Tanner, Stephen L. "Emily Dickinson and the Psychoanalyst." *University of Dayton Review* 19, no. 1 (Winter 1987–88): 103–9.

Walker, Cheryl. *The Nightingale's Burden: Women Poets and American Culture before 1900*. Bloomington: Indiana University Press, 1982.

Walker, Nancy. "Wit, Sentimentality and the Image of Women in the 19th Century." *American Studies* 22 (1981): 5–21.

Weisbuch, Robert. *Emily Dickinson's Poetry*. Chicago: University of Chicago Press, 1975.

Welter, Barbara. *Dimity Convictions: The American Woman in the Nineteenth Century*. Athens: Ohio University Press, 1976.

Wilbur, Richard. "Sumptuous Destitution." In *Emily Dickinson: A Collection of Critical Essays*, edited by Richard B. Sewall, 127–36. Englewood Cliffs, N.J.: Prentice-Hall, 1963.

Wilson, R. Jackson. *Figures of Speech: American Writers and the Literary Marketplace, from Benjamin Franklin to Emily Dickinson*. New York: Knopf, 1986.

Winnicott, D. W. *The Maturational Processes and the Facilitating Environment.* New York: International Universities Press, 1965.
———. *Playing and Reality.* London: Tavistock, 1971.
Wolff, Cynthia Griffin. *Emily Dickinson.* New York: Knopf, 1986.
Wyatt, Susan. *Reconstructing Desire: The Role of the Unconscious in Women's Reading and Writing.* Chapel Hill: University of North Carolina Press, 1990.

Index

A Bee his burnished Carriage (#1339), 3
A Bird came down the Walk (#328), 101–2
Aiken, Conrad, 152–53
Alcorn, Marshall, 107
Alcott, Louisa May, 35
All that I do (#1496), 141
Amherst Record, 47–48
"And with what body do they come?" (#1492), 118–24
Anderson, Charles, 202 (n. 24)
Anthony, Susan B., 131–32
Armstrong, Martin, 152
As if the Sea should part (#695), 96
A Visitor in Marl (#391), 84
A Word made Flesh is seldom (#1651), 125–26

Barthes, Roland, 5, 7
Baudrillard, Jean, 14–15
Because I could not stop for Death (#712), 83
Because the Bee may blameless hum (#869), 4
Behind Me—dips Eternity (#721), 94–95
Benfey, Christopher, 124
Bennett, Paula, 190–92, 194
Bernheimer, Charles, 208 (n. 1)
Bianchi, Martha Dickinson, 75, 186
Blackmur, R. P., 149, 153
Blackwell, H. R., 109
Blake, Lillie Devereux, 35
Bleich, David, 106
Bloom, Harold, 32, 182
Blunden, Edmund, 151
Bowles, Samuel, 56, 110, 201 (n. 7)
Brown, William Hill, 33
Browning, Elizabeth Barrett, 129, 131, 133, 185, 194
Buckingham, Willis J., 157–58

Cadman, Deborah, 197 (n. 2)
Cameron, Sharon, 76, 127, 129, 205 (n. 43)
Capps, Jack, 28
Cary, Alice, 35
Chawaf, Chantal, 128
Chodorow, Nancy, 173
Cixous, Helene, 108, 128

Cody, John, 136–37, 145, 154–55
Come slowly—Eden (#211), 4
Countertransference, 17, 160–64, 174–75, 186, 189–94. *See also* Hysteria; Transference
Cowan, Perez, 118, 124
Cummings, Katherine, 16–17

Dandurand, Karen, 114
Davidson, Cathy, 33–35
Death is the supple Suitor (#1445), 83
Delight is as the flight (#257), 141
D'Emilio, John, 39–40
Derrida, Jacques, 126–27, 163
Dickinson, Austin, 2, 57–58, 75, 77, 154, 201 (n. 7)
Dickinson, Emily: and aesthetics of frustration, 6–7, 142–43, 150; and embodiment, 15–16, 110–33, 148–49; and psychoanalysis, 16–18, 134–38, 143–48, 158–65, 189–94; identification with Eve, 28–31; and moral-reform, 42–44; and letter writing, 56–63, 71–80; and performance, 58, 62, 75–76, 109–110; and reader's desire, 106, 142–48, 160–62; and prostitution, 113–15; attitude toward publication, 113–15
Dickinson, Lavinia, 74
Dickinson, Susan Gilbert, 78, 154, 181, 187, 201 (n. 7), 205 (n. 40)
Did the Harebell loose her girdle (#213), 4
Diehl, Joanne Feit, 32, 82
Dobson, Joanne, 81–83, 114
Dubois, Ellen Carol, 199 (n. 37)

Ecriture feminine, 13, 59–60, 71–72, 128–29
Ellmann, Mary, 208 (n. 59)
Erkkila, Betsy, 19–20, 210 (n. 43)
Escaping backward to perceive (#867), 85–86
Essential Oils—are wrung (#675), 8
Evans, Martha Noel, 147
Expectation—is Contentment (#807), 142

Farr, Judith, 205 (n. 43)
Felman, Shoshana, 143–44, 205 (n. 1), 206 (n. 11)

Fern, Fanny, 113
Fish, Stanley, 106
Flowers—Well—if anybody (#137), 1
Foster, Hannah Webster, 35
Four Trees—upon a solitary Acre (#742), 102–5
Freedman, Estelle, 39–40
Freud, Sigmund, 128, 134–38, 143–48, 161

Gelpi, Arthur, 82, 202 (n. 6)
Gilbert, Sandra, 110, 198 (n. 5)
Gilman, Caroline, 113
Gilmore, Leigh, 210 (n. 64)
Going to Him! Happy Letter! (#494), 61
Go not too near a House of Rose (#1434), 142
Good to hide, and hear 'em hunt! (#842), 8
Gordon, Linda, 199 (n. 37)
Great Caesar! Condescend (#102), 82
Greeley, Horace, 38
Greenblatt, Stephen, 197 (n. 3)
Griffith, Clark, 81–83
Gubar, Susan, 110, 198 (n. 5), 208 (n. 59)

Halttunnen, Karen, 36–37, 73–76
Hampshire and Franklin Express, 22–24, 198 (n. 6), 200 (n. 56)
Hampshire Gazette, 38, 45–50, 200 (n. 56)
Hartman, Geoffrey, 153
Hawthorne, Nathaniel, 113, 129, 203 (n. 16)
"Heaven"—is what I cannot reach! (#239), 141
He fumbles at your Soul (#315), 43
He was my host—he was my guest (#1721), 89
Higgins, David, 59, 150–51, 202 (n. 24)
Higginson, Thomas Wentworth, 5, 31, 57, 63–68, 70–71, 77–78, 110–13, 137, 201 (n. 14), 207 (n. 33)
Hillyer, Robert, 150
Hitchcock, Edward, 2
Holland, Elizabeth, 50, 56, 72, 134
Holland, Norman, 107, 208 (n. 61)
Homans, Margaret, 31, 60, 73, 88, 170–74, 204 (n. 26)
How Human Nature dotes (#1417), 6
Howe, Susan, 191–94, 205 (n. 43)
Howells, William Dean, 153
Humphries, Jane, 29
Hunter, Dianne, 208 (n. 1)
Hysteria, 16–17, 107, 133–38, 146–47, 164–65, 208 (n. 1). *See also* Countertransference

I am afraid to own a Body (#1090), 112, 118–19
I breathed enough to take the trick (#272), 108

I felt a Cleaving in my Mind (#937), 92–93
I felt my life with both my hands (#351), 116–18
I heard a Fly buzz—when I died (#465), 187–88
I hide myself within my flower (#903), 5
I make His Crescent fill or lack (#909), 89–90
Impossibility, like Wine (#838), 141
In Ebon Box, when years have flown (#169), 64
I never lost as much but twice (#49), 85
In lands I never saw—they say (#124), 82, 90–91
In many and reportless places (#1382), 141
I read my sentence—steadily (#412), 80
Irigaray, Luce, 172–73
I rose—because He sank (#616), 89
I started Early—Took my Dog (#520), 86
I tend my flowers for thee (#339), 82, 105–6
I think I was enchanted (#593), 8–10
It was a quiet way (#1053), 83
Ives, Ella Gilbert, 151
I would not paint—a picture (#505), 140

Jackson, Helen Hunt, 57, 201 (n. 7)
Jameson, Fredric, 54
Johnson, Thomas, 124
Juhasz, Suzanne, 59, 62–64, 77, 145, 203 (n. 18), 206 (n. 10)

Kaplan, Cora, 131
Keller, Karl, 62, 145, 165–70, 191, 194
Kelley, Mary, 51–52
Kennard, Jean E., 210 (n. 55)
Kristeva, Julia, 71–72, 77–78, 128, 173–74

Lacan, Jacques, 78, 107, 117, 128, 138, 143–45, 209 (n. 15)
Lawrence, D. H., 35
Leclerc, Annie, 200 (n. 18)
Like Eyes that looked on Wastes (#458), 163, 171–72
Like Trains of Cars on Tracks of Plush (#1224), 3
Lind, Jenny, 45, 108–9, 133, 138, 146
Loeffelholz, Mary, 87, 165
Lord, Otis, 113, 201 (n. 7)

Macleish, Archibald, 150
Marotti, Arthur, 161
Melville, Herman, 129
Michie, Helena, 129–31
Miller, Cristanne, 59, 89, 201 (n. 12), 203 (n. 21), 204 (n. 21)
Miller, Jane, 12
Milton, John, 25–28

Moral reform, 13, 36–44, 84–85; *Advocate of Moral Reform*, 38, 55, 199 (n. 36), 200 (n. 64)
Moulton, Louise Chandler, 164

New Criticism, 148–49
New Historicism, 21, 197 (n. 3)
New York Tribune, 23–24, 38, 44
Nitchie, George, 207 (n. 30)
Norcross, Louise and Frances, 109

Oakes, Karen, 170–71
Object-relations, 173–74

Paglia, Camille, 175–82, 192, 194
Paradise is of the option (#1069), 100–101
Peril as a Possession (#1678), 142
Perry, Ruth, 174
Poirier, Richard, 181
Porter, David, 59, 137, 145, 155–57, 203 (n. 19), 207 (n. 53)
Power is a familiar growth (#1238), 96
Presentiment—is that long Shadow on the lawn (#764), 98–99
Publication—is the Auction (#709), 113–15

Ransom, John Crowe, 150
Reynolds, David, 35, 37
Rich, Adrienne, 10, 82, 127, 175, 182–89, 192–94
Richardson, Samuel, 33, 42
Riffaterre, Michael, 7
Risk is the Hair that holds the Tun (#1239), 81
Riviere, Joan, 62
Root, Abiah, 30
Rowson, Susanna, 35

St. Armand, Barton Levi, 37, 197 (n. 1)
Sanchez-Eppler, Karen, 132
Satisfaction—is the Agent (#1036), 141
Scarry, Elaine, 128, 204 (n. 28)
Schweickart, Patrocinio, 210 (n. 42)
Seduction: ambiguous nature of, 11–18; local newspaper accounts of, 23–25, 44–50; and *Paradise Lost*, 25–29; and romanticism, 31–32; and American novel, 32–36; and moral reform, 36–44, 84–85; rhetoric of, 59–63, 77–79, 87–92; and seducer image, 81–87; and psychoanalysis, 134–36, 145–48. *See also* Transference
Sewall, Richard B., 52, 59, 68
She rose to His Requirement—dropt (#732), 89

Shurr, William, 47, 145, 159–60, 205 (n. 43)
Sigourney, Lydia, 113
Silence is all we dread (#1251), 45
Smith, Martha Nell, 165, 205 (n. 43)
Smith-Rosenberg, Carroll, 52, 85, 199 (n. 32)
So bashful when I spied her! (#91), 86–87
Spring comes on the World (#1042), 2
Springfield Republican, 47–50, 187, 200 (n. 56)
Stone, Lucy, 131–32
Stonum, Gary Lee, 60, 73, 79, 205 (n. 42)
Success is counted sweetest (#67), 141
Sweet Skepticism of the Heart (#1413), 6

Tate, Allan, 149–51
The Daisy follows soft the Sun (#106), 87–88
The difference between Despair (#305), 93
The Flower must not blame the Bee (#206), 4
The Himmaleh was known to stoop (#481), 82, 88–89
Their Height in Heaven comforts not (#696), 1
The Moon is distant from the Sea (#429), 97–98
The Poets light but Lamps (#883), 10, 21–22
There is another sky (#2), 2
There's a certain Slant of light (#258), 127
The Show is not the Show (#1206), 139
The Spirit lasts—but in what mode (#1576), 116
The Way I read a Letter's—this (#636), 64, 79
They have a little Odor—that to me (#785), 1–2
They shut me up in Prose (#613), 79
This is my letter to the World (#441), 79
This was a Poet—It is That (#448), 5
Thompson, Maurice, 153
To disappear enhances (#1209), 141
To pile like Thunder to its close (#1247), 7
To see the Summer sky (#1472), 143
Transference, 16–19, 136, 144–46, 158–64, 174–75, 189–94. *See also* Countertransference; Hysteria

Uncertain lease—develops lustre (#857), 142
Undue Significance a starving man attaches (#439), 141

Van Doren, Mark, 200 (n. 2)

Wadsworth, Charles, 46, 145, 159–60
Walker, Cheryl, 53
Ward, A. C., 14
Weisbuch, Robert, 201 (n. 20)
What if I say I shall not wait! (#277), 116
What Soft—Cherubic Creatures (#401), 42–43

Whicher, George, 47, 151
Which is the best—the Moon or the Crescent?
   (#1315), 141
Whitman, Walt, 129, 131, 154
Who never lost, are unprepared (#73), 141
Who never wanted—maddest Joy (#1430), 141
Wilbur, Richard, 142–43
Williams, Henry, 138
Williams, Raymond, 51

Wilson, R. Jackson, 111
Winnicott, D. W., 174, 209 (nn. 25–26)
Winters, Yvor, 152
Wolff, Cynthia Griffin, 15, 95, 145
Wonder—is not precisely Knowing (#1331), 6

You said that I "Was Great"—one Day (#738),
   139–40